STAR WARS®
DARK TIMES

VOLUME TWO

PARALLELS

THE RISE OF THE EMPIRE

From 1,000 to 0 years before the Battle of Yavin

After the seeming final defeat of the Sith, the Republic enters a state of complacency.
In the waning years of the Republic, the Senate rife with corruption, the ambitious
Senator Palpatine causes himself to be elected Supreme Chancellor.
This is the era of the prequel trilogy.

The events in this story take place approximately nineteen years before
the Battle of Yavin.

STAR WARS®
DARK TIMES

VOLUME TWO WITHDRAWN

PARALLELS

Script
MICK HARRISON

Art
DAVE ROSS
LUI ANTONIO

Colors
ALEX WALD

Lettering
MICHAEL HEISLER

Front Cover Art
DOUGLAS WHEATLEY

Back Cover Art
ZACH HOWARD and
BRAD ANDERSON

DARK HORSE BOOKS®

Publisher
MIKE RICHARDSON

Collection Designer
TONY ONG

Art Director
LIA RIBACCHI

Editor
RANDY STRADLEY

Assistant Editors
**FREDDYE LINS and
DAVE MARSHALL**

special thanks to Elaine Mederer, Jann Moorhead, David Anderman, Leland Chee, Sue Rostoni, and Carol Roeder at Lucas Licensing

STAR WARS: DARK TIMES—Volume Two: Parallels

This volume collects issues six through ten of the Dark Horse comic-book series *Star Wars: Dark Times.*

Published by
Dark Horse Books
A division of Dark Horse Comics, Inc.
10956 SE Main Street
Milwaukie, OR 97222

darkhorse.com
starwars.com

To find a comics shop in your area, call the Comic Shop Locator Service
toll-free at 1-888-266-4226

First printing: August 2008
ISBN 978-1-59307-945-1

1 3 5 7 9 10 8 6 4 2
Printed in China

"FOR OVER A THOUSAND GENERATIONS THE JEDI KNIGHTS WERE THE GUARDIANS OF PEACE AND JUSTICE IN THE OLD REPUBLIC. BEFORE THE DARK TIMES, BEFORE THE EMPIRE."
—BEN KENOBI

At the point where our story opens, the dark times are still to come—a looming danger shrouded by the ever-changing possibilities of the future. It is a time of war, but a string of victories has lulled the Jedi into a false sense of hope. The end of the Clone Wars is in sight, peace is within the Republic's grasp. No one knows of the trap that has been laid, of the destruction which will rain on those caught in it, nor of the indelible scars with which the survivors will be branded ...

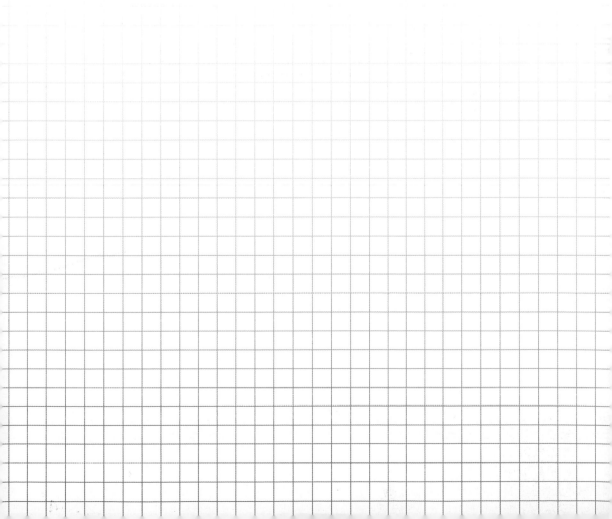

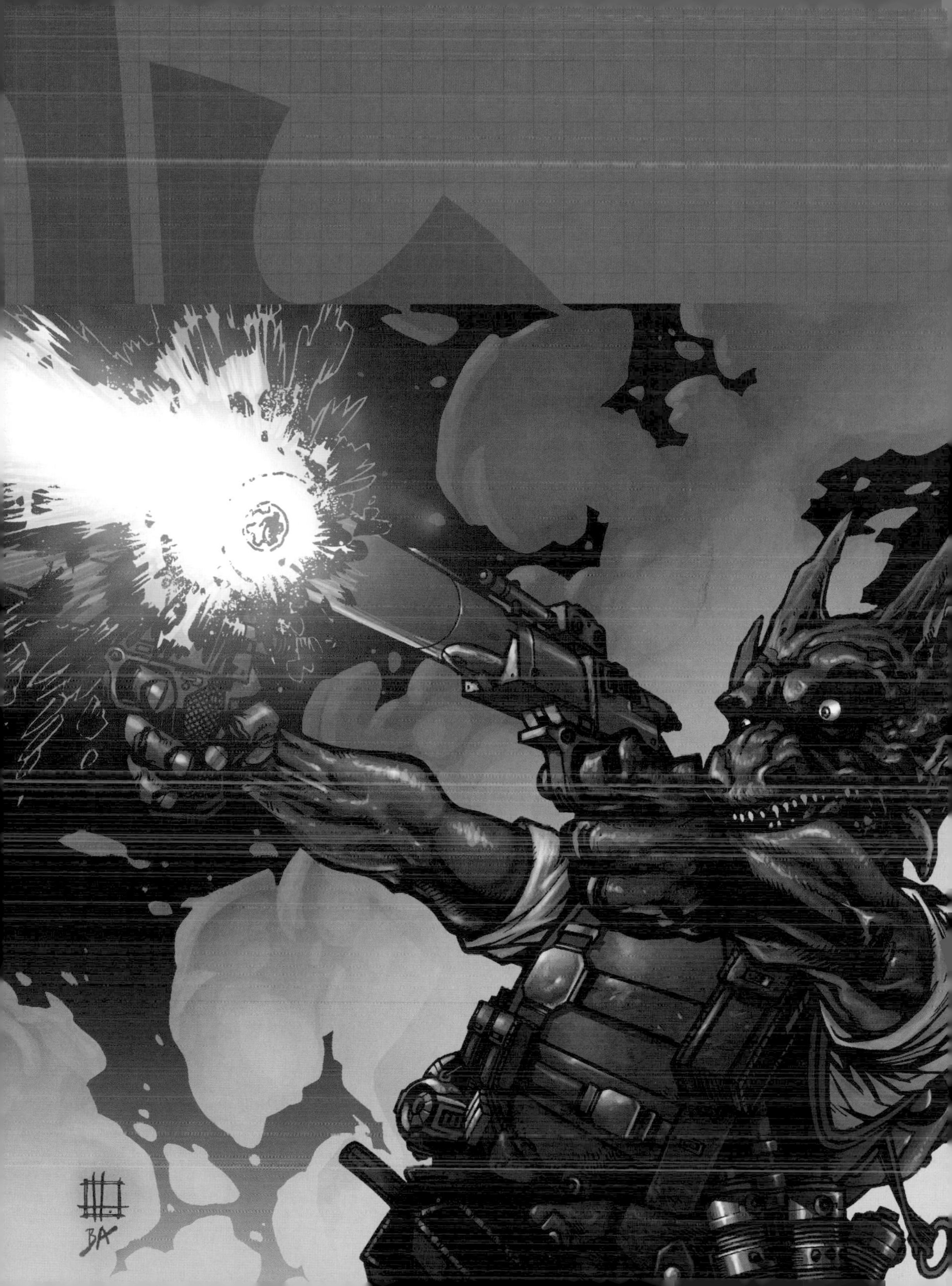

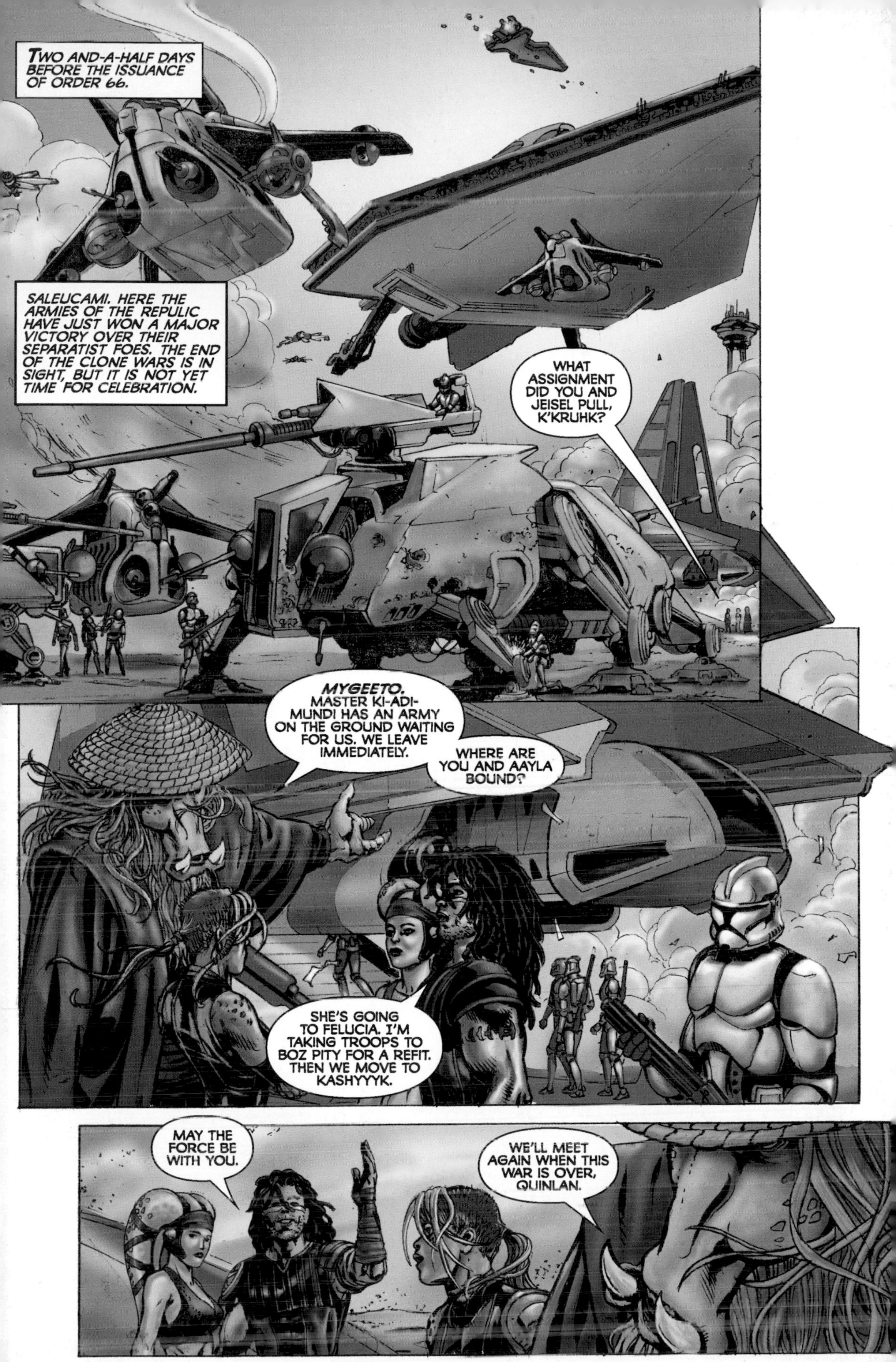
TWO AND-A-HALF DAYS BEFORE THE ISSUANCE OF ORDER 66.
SALEUCAMI. HERE THE ARMIES OF THE REPULIC HAVE JUST WON A MAJOR VICTORY OVER THEIR SEPARATIST FOES. THE END OF THE CLONE WARS IS IN SIGHT, BUT IT IS NOT YET TIME FOR CELEBRATION.
WHAT ASSIGNMENT DID YOU AND JEISEL PULL, K'KRUHK?
MYGEETO. MASTER KI-ADI-MUNDI HAS AN ARMY ON THE GROUND WAITING FOR US. WE LEAVE IMMEDIATELY.
WHERE ARE YOU AND AAYLA BOUND?
SHE'S GOING TO FELUCIA. I'M TAKING TROOPS TO BOZ PITY FOR A REFIT. THEN WE MOVE TO KASHYYYK.
MAY THE FORCE BE WITH YOU.
WE'LL MEET AGAIN WHEN THIS WAR IS OVER, QUINLAN.

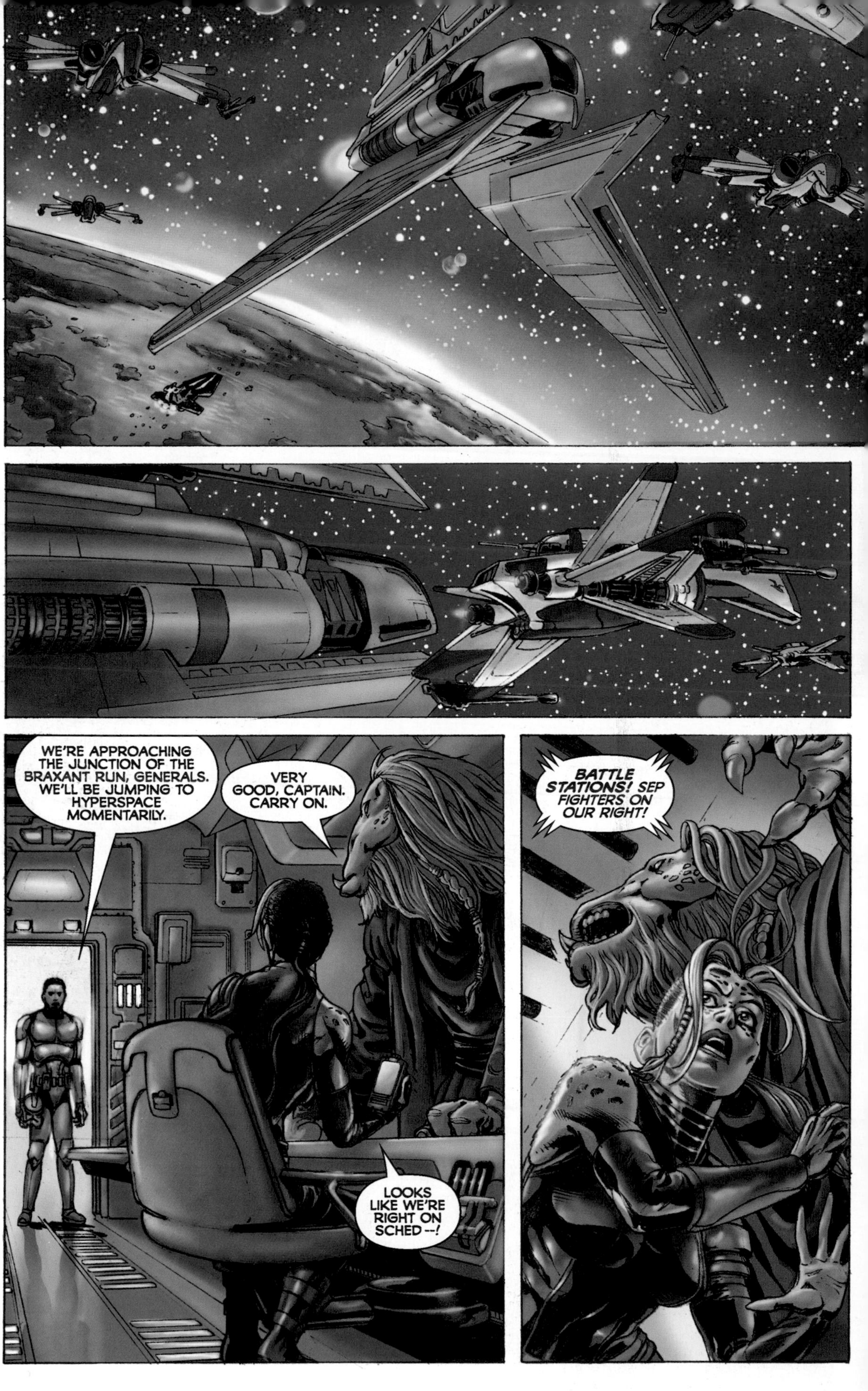
WE'RE APPROACHING THE JUNCTION OF THE BRAXANT RUN, GENERALS. WE'LL BE JUMPING TO HYPERSPACE MOMENTARILY.
VERY GOOD, CAPTAIN. CARRY ON.
LOOKS LIKE WE'RE RIGHT ON SCHED --!
BATTLE STATIONS! SEP FIGHTERS ON OUR RIGHT!

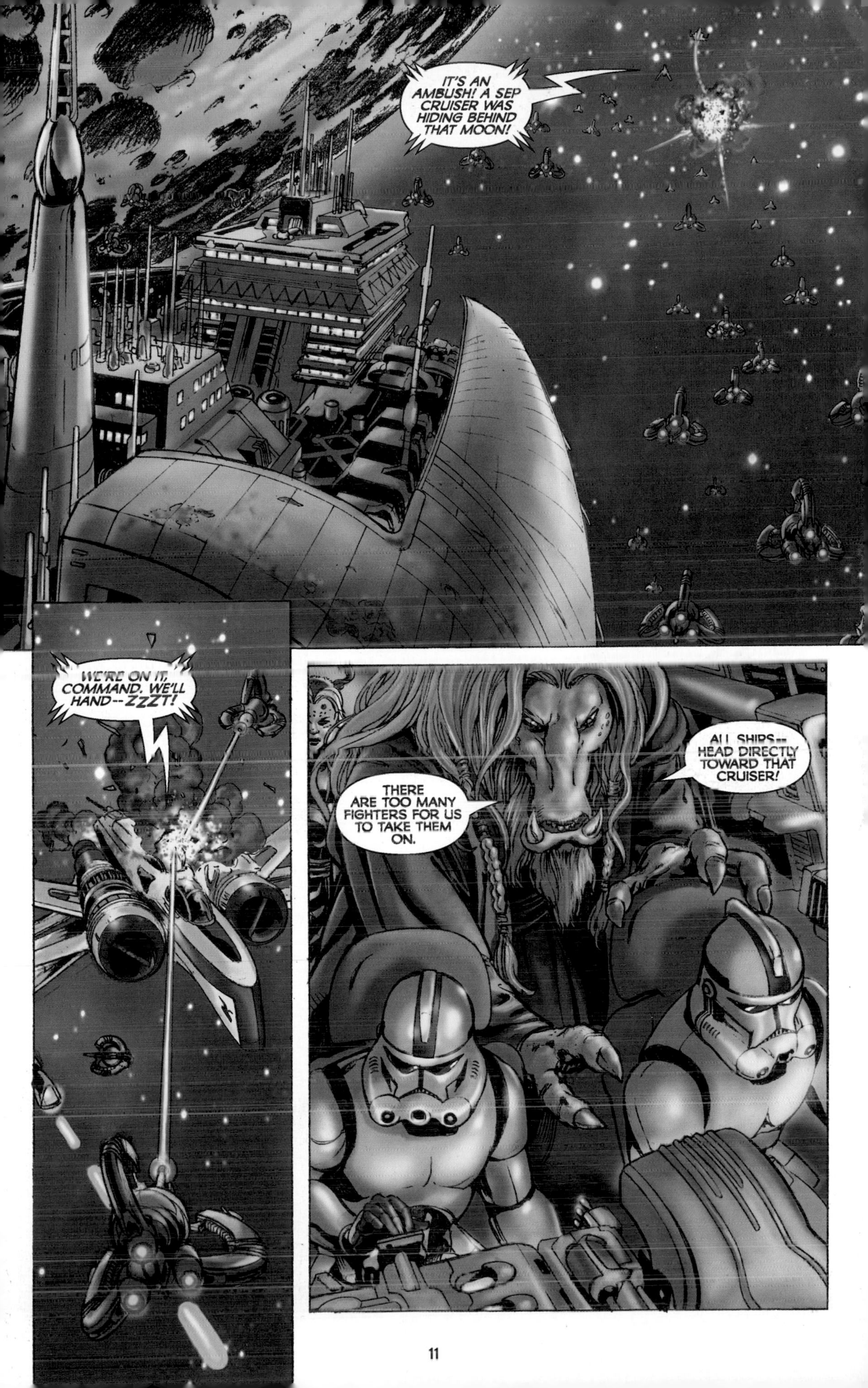
IT'S AN AMBUSH! A SEP CRUISER WAS HIDING BEHIND THAT MOON!
WE'RE ON IT, COMMAND. WE'LL HAND--ZZZT!
ALL SHIPS-- HEAD DIRECTLY TOWARD THAT CRUISER!
THERE ARE TOO MANY FIGHTERS FOR US TO TAKE THEM ON.

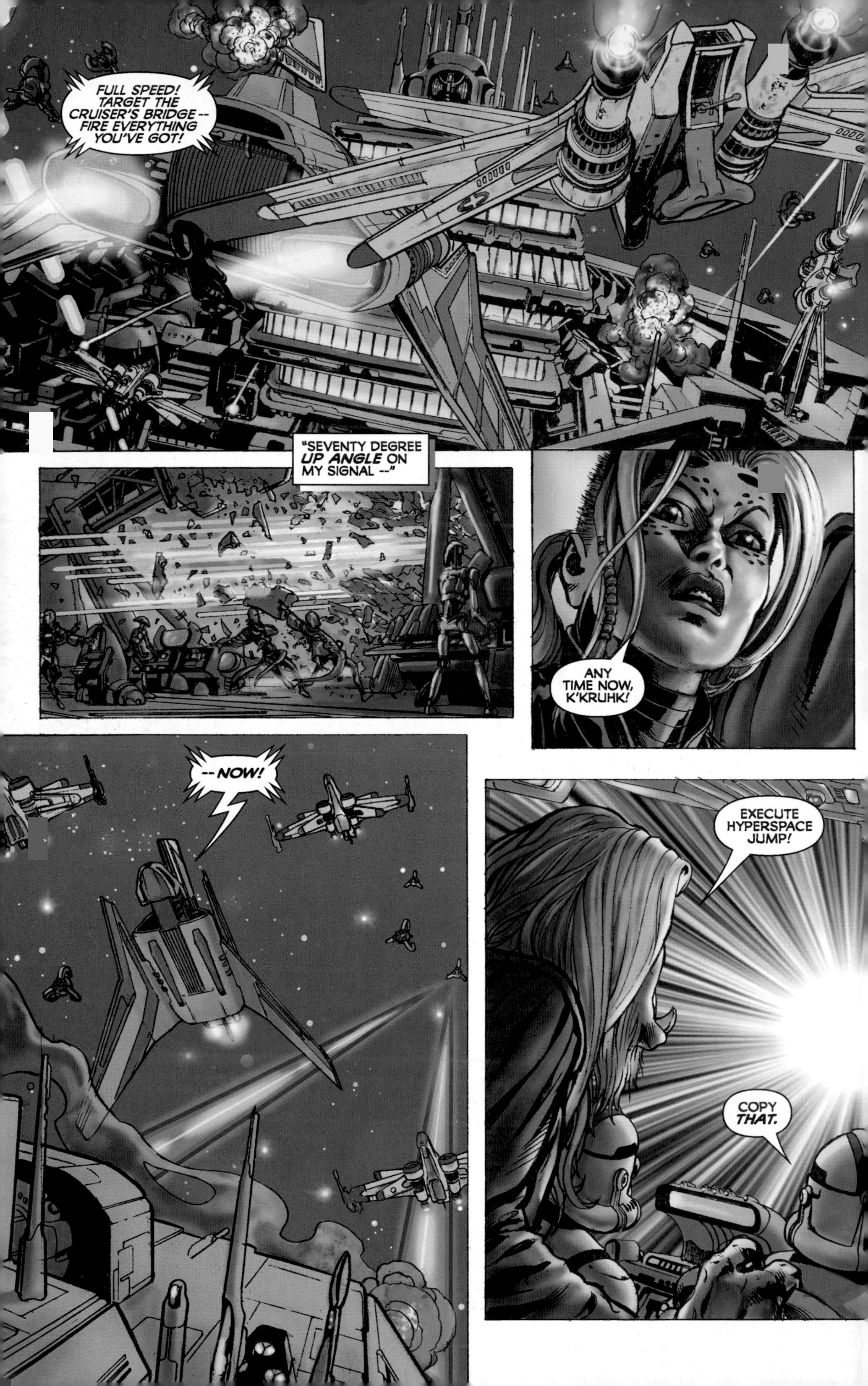
FULL SPEED! TARGET THE CRUISER'S BRIDGE -- FIRE EVERYTHING YOU'VE GOT!
"SEVENTY DEGREE *UP ANGLE* ON MY SIGNAL --"
ANY TIME NOW, K'KRUHK!
-- *NOW!*
EXECUTE HYPERSPACE JUMP!
COPY *THAT.*

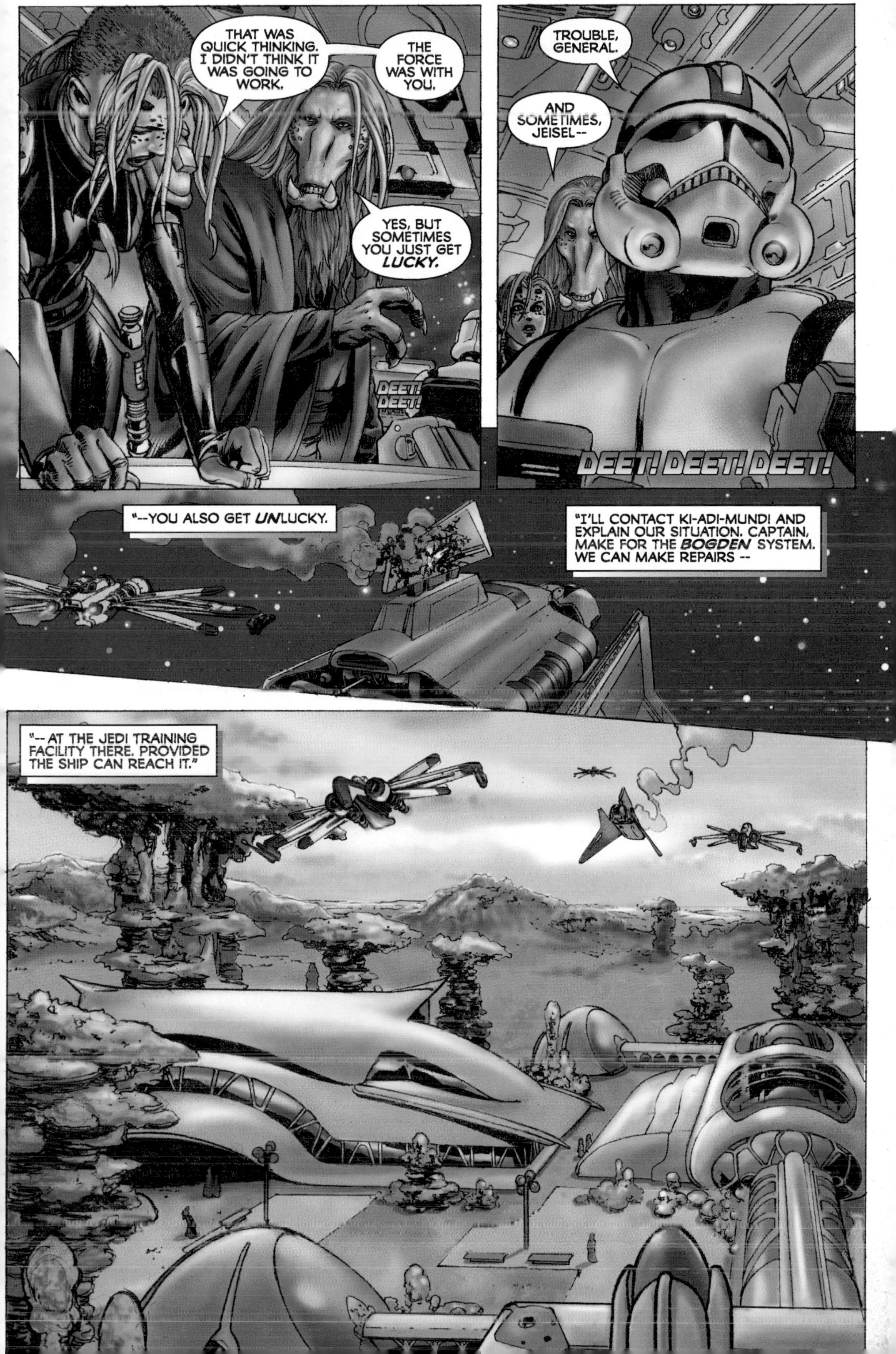
THAT WAS QUICK THINKING. I DIDN'T THINK IT WAS GOING TO WORK.
THE FORCE WAS WITH YOU.
YES, BUT SOMETIMES YOU JUST GET LUCKY.
DEET! DEET!
TROUBLE, GENERAL.
AND SOMETIMES, JEISEL--
DEET! DEET! DEET!
"--YOU ALSO GET UNLUCKY.
"I'LL CONTACT KI-ADI-MUNDI AND EXPLAIN OUR SITUATION. CAPTAIN, MAKE FOR THE BOGDEN SYSTEM. WE CAN MAKE REPAIRS --
"-- AT THE JEDI TRAINING FACILITY THERE. PROVIDED THE SHIP CAN REACH IT."

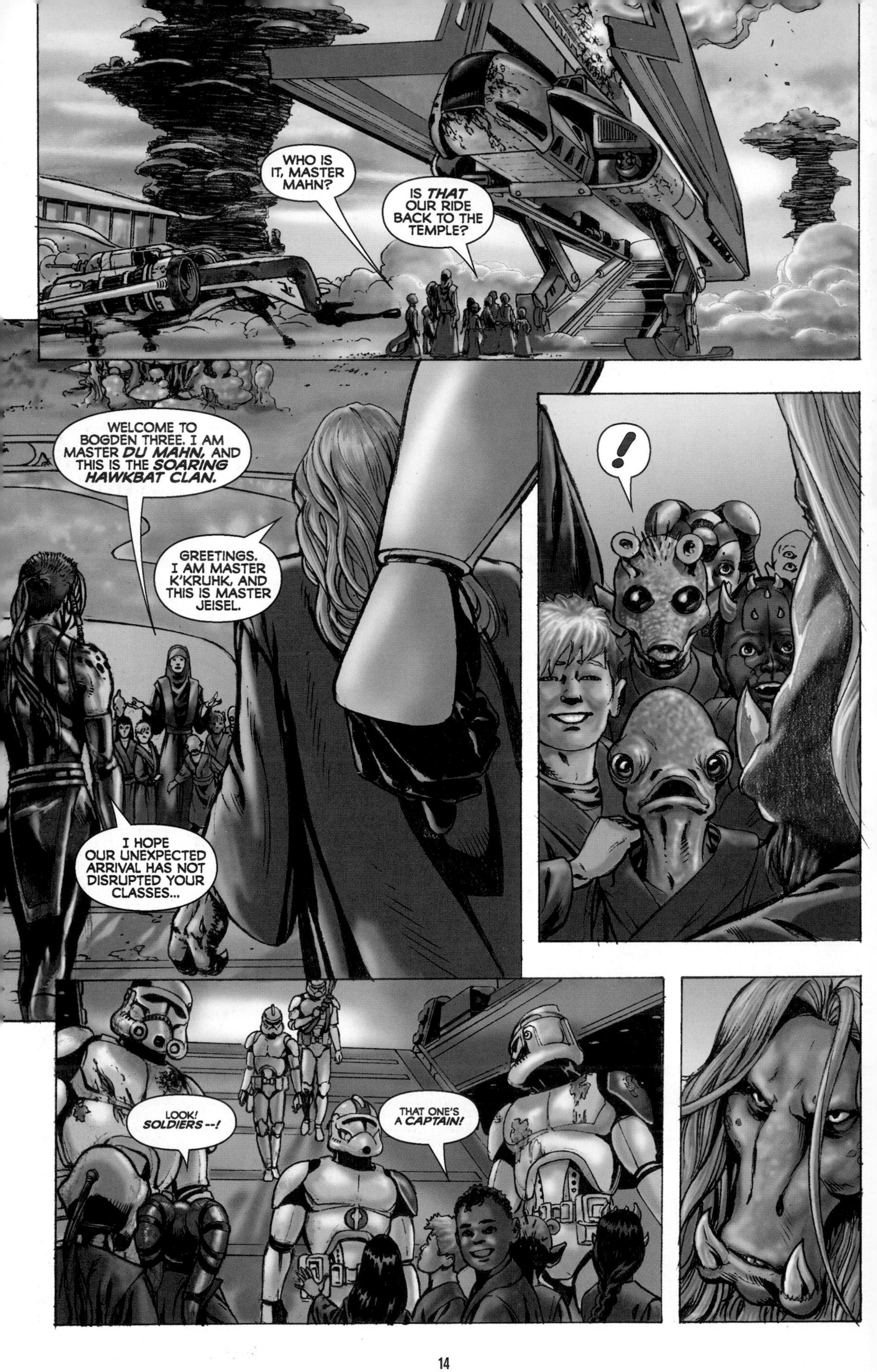
WHO IS IT, MASTER MAHN?
IS *THAT* OUR RIDE BACK TO THE TEMPLE?
WELCOME TO BOGDEN THREE. I AM MASTER *DU MAHN,* AND THIS IS THE *SOARING HAWKBAT CLAN.*
GREETINGS. I AM MASTER K'KRUHK, AND THIS IS MASTER JEISEL.
I HOPE OUR UNEXPECTED ARRIVAL HAS NOT DISRUPTED YOUR CLASSES...
!
LOOK! *SOLDIERS*--!
THAT ONE'S A *CAPTAIN!*

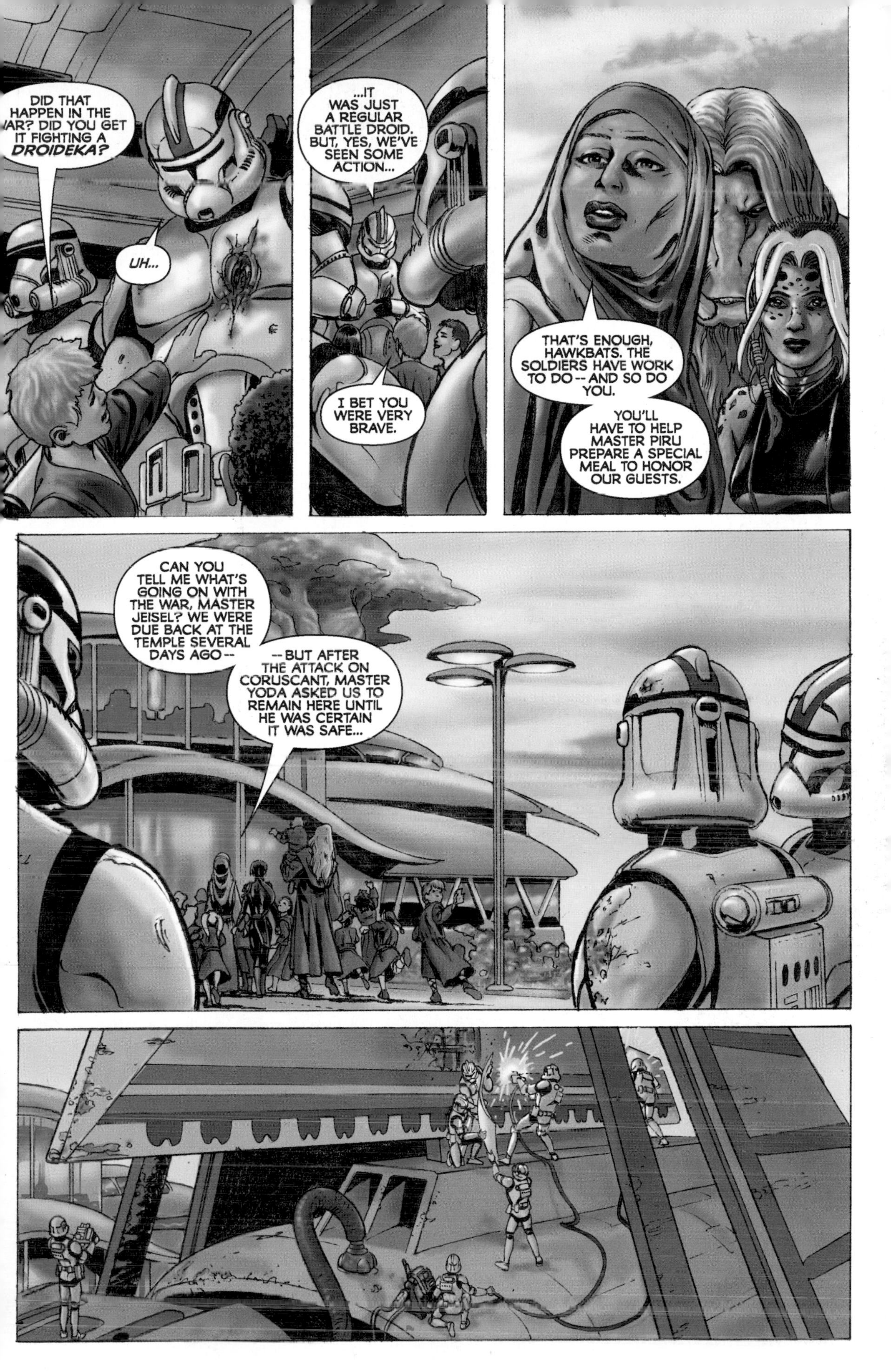
DID THAT HAPPEN IN THE WAR? DID YOU GET IT FIGHTING A DROIDEKA?
UH...
...IT WAS JUST A REGULAR BATTLE DROID. BUT, YES, WE'VE SEEN SOME ACTION...
I BET YOU WERE VERY BRAVE.
THAT'S ENOUGH, HAWKBATS. THE SOLDIERS HAVE WORK TO DO -- AND SO DO YOU.
YOU'LL HAVE TO HELP MASTER PIRU PREPARE A SPECIAL MEAL TO HONOR OUR GUESTS.
CAN YOU TELL ME WHAT'S GOING ON WITH THE WAR, MASTER JEISEL? WE WERE DUE BACK AT THE TEMPLE SEVERAL DAYS AGO --
-- BUT AFTER THE ATTACK ON CORUSCANT, MASTER YODA ASKED US TO REMAIN HERE UNTIL HE WAS CERTAIN IT WAS SAFE...

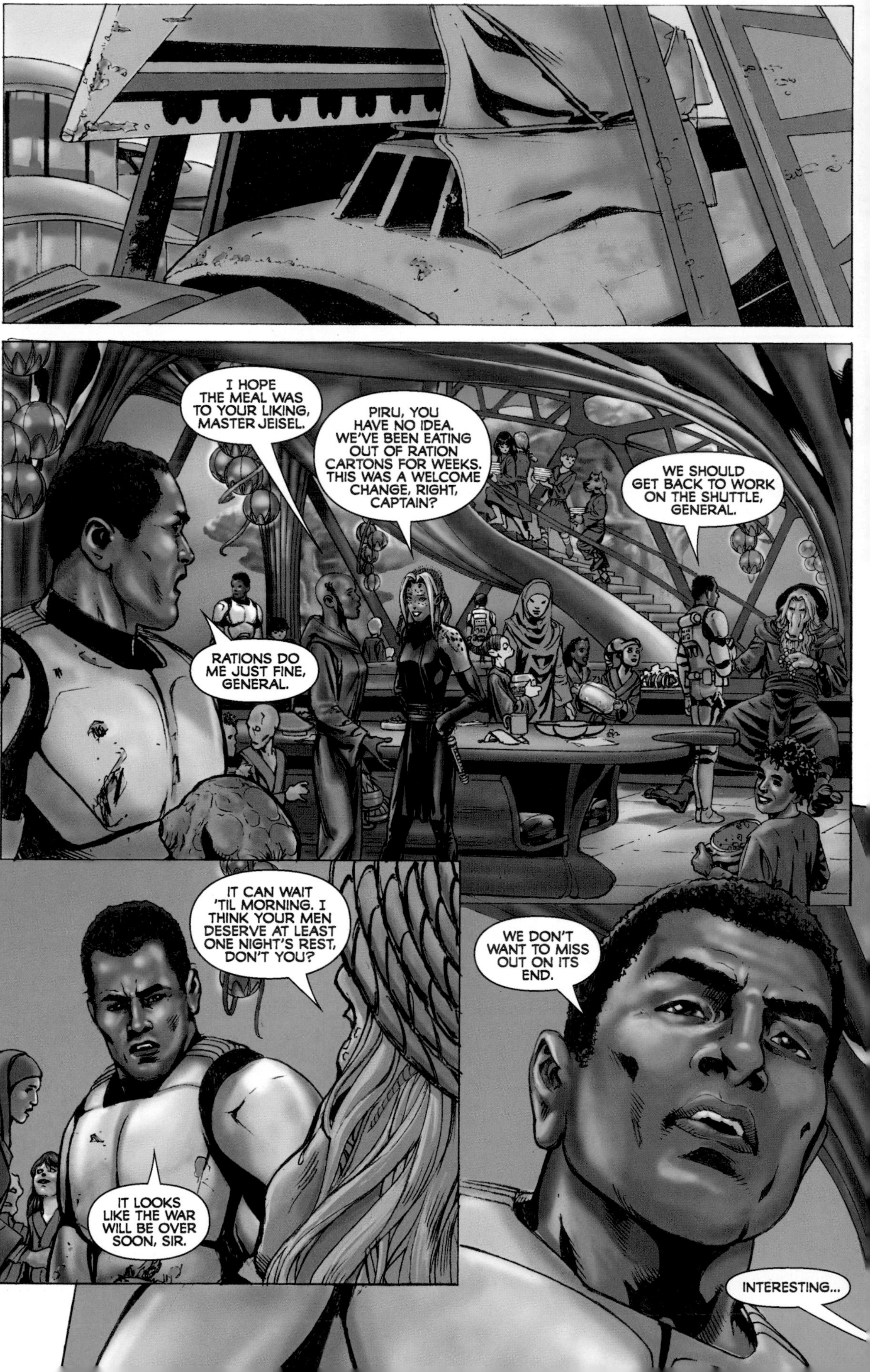
I HOPE THE MEAL WAS TO YOUR LIKING, MASTER JEISEL.
PIRU, YOU HAVE NO IDEA. WE'VE BEEN EATING OUT OF RATION CARTONS FOR WEEKS. THIS WAS A WELCOME CHANGE, RIGHT, CAPTAIN?
WE SHOULD GET BACK TO WORK ON THE SHUTTLE, GENERAL.
RATIONS DO ME JUST FINE, GENERAL.
IT CAN WAIT 'TIL MORNING. I THINK YOUR MEN DESERVE AT LEAST ONE NIGHT'S REST, DON'T YOU?
IT LOOKS LIKE THE WAR WILL BE OVER SOON, SIR.
WE DON'T WANT TO MISS OUT ON ITS END.
INTERESTING...

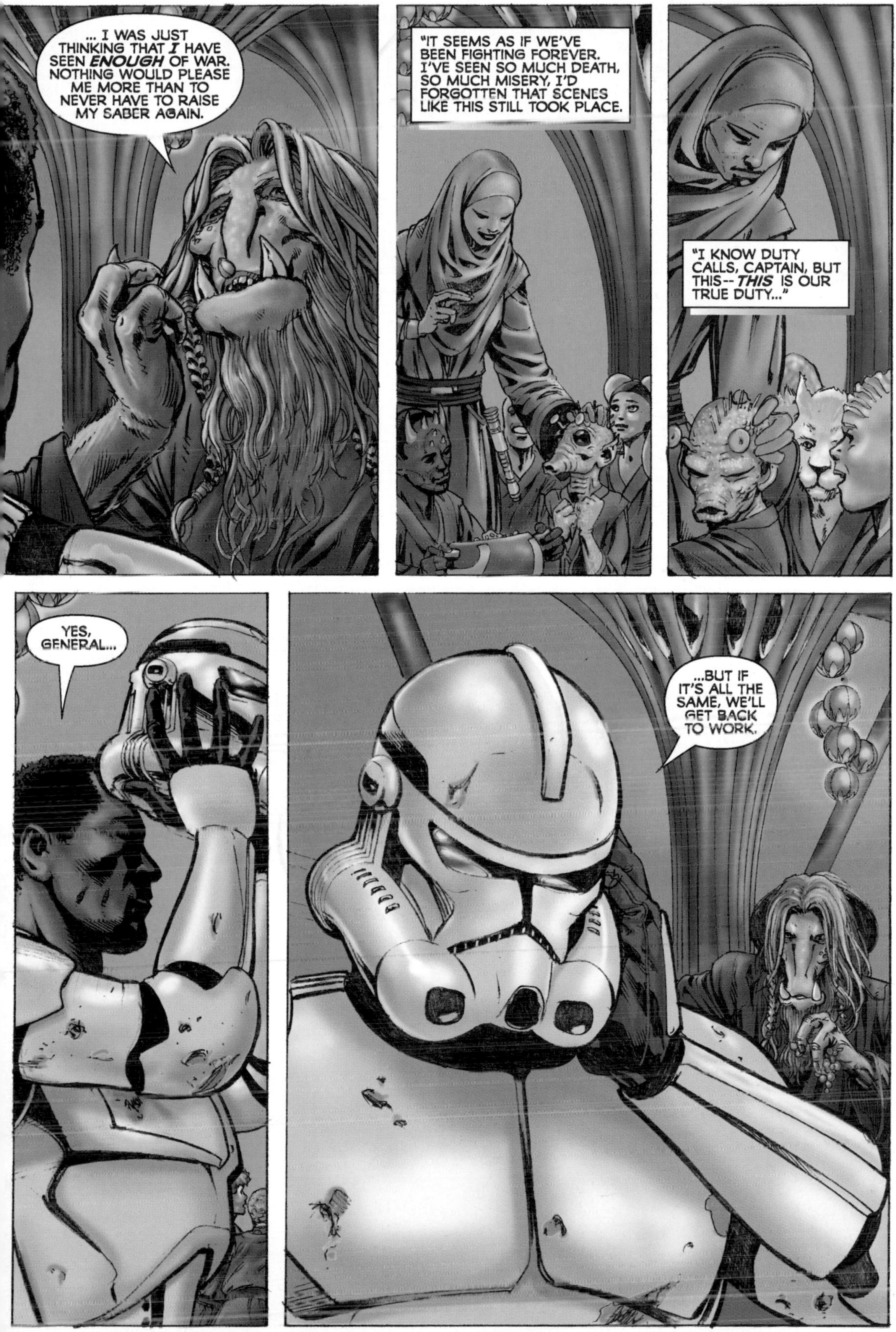
... I WAS JUST THINKING THAT I HAVE SEEN ENOUGH OF WAR. NOTHING WOULD PLEASE ME MORE THAN TO NEVER HAVE TO RAISE MY SABER AGAIN.
"IT SEEMS AS IF WE'VE BEEN FIGHTING FOREVER. I'VE SEEN SO MUCH DEATH, SO MUCH MISERY, I'D FORGOTTEN THAT SCENES LIKE THIS STILL TOOK PLACE.
"I KNOW DUTY CALLS, CAPTAIN, BUT THIS-- THIS IS OUR TRUE DUTY..."
YES, GENERAL...
...BUT IF IT'S ALL THE SAME, WE'LL GET BACK TO WORK.

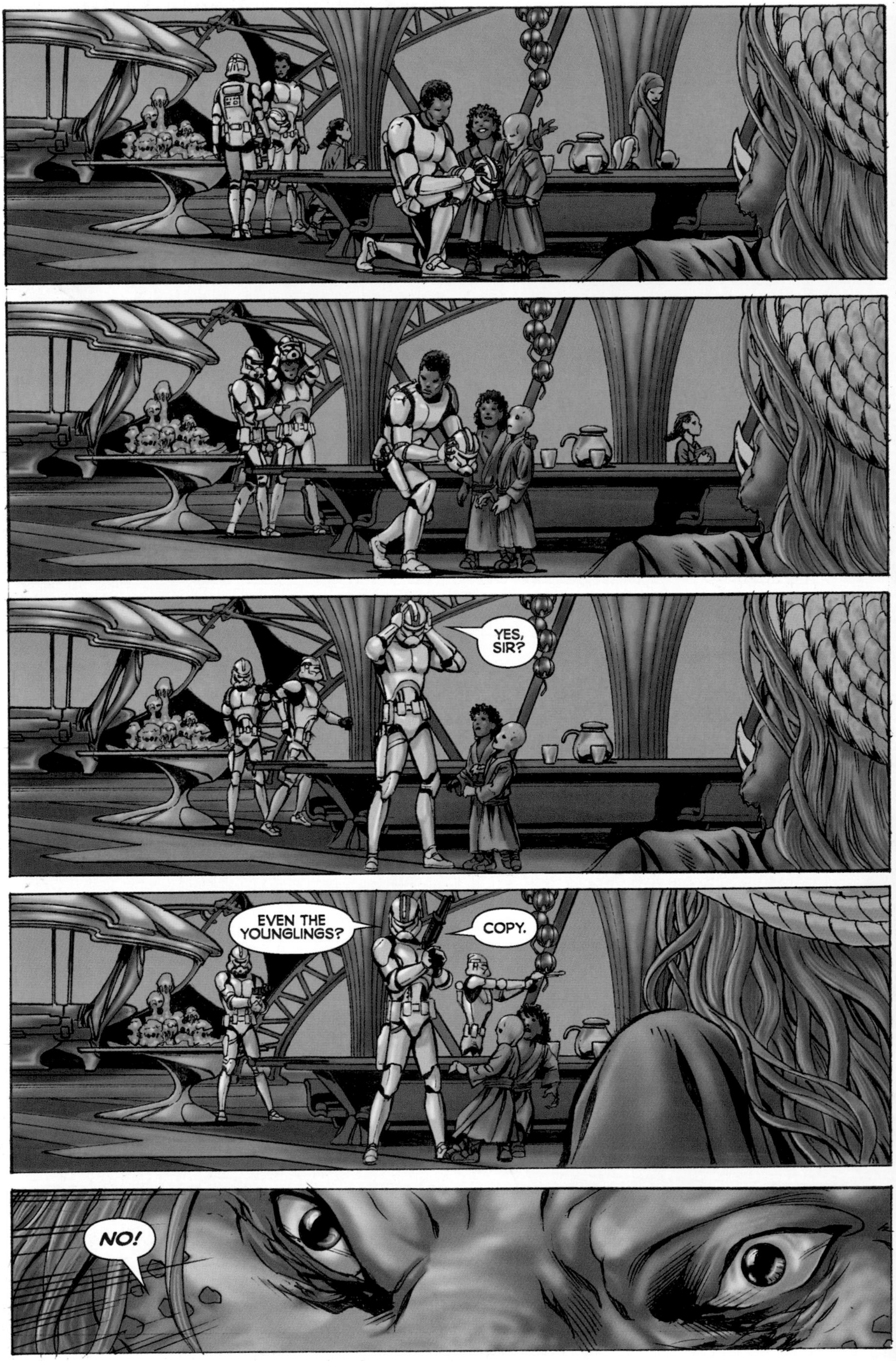
YES, SIR?
EVEN THE YOUNGLINGS?
COPY.
NO!

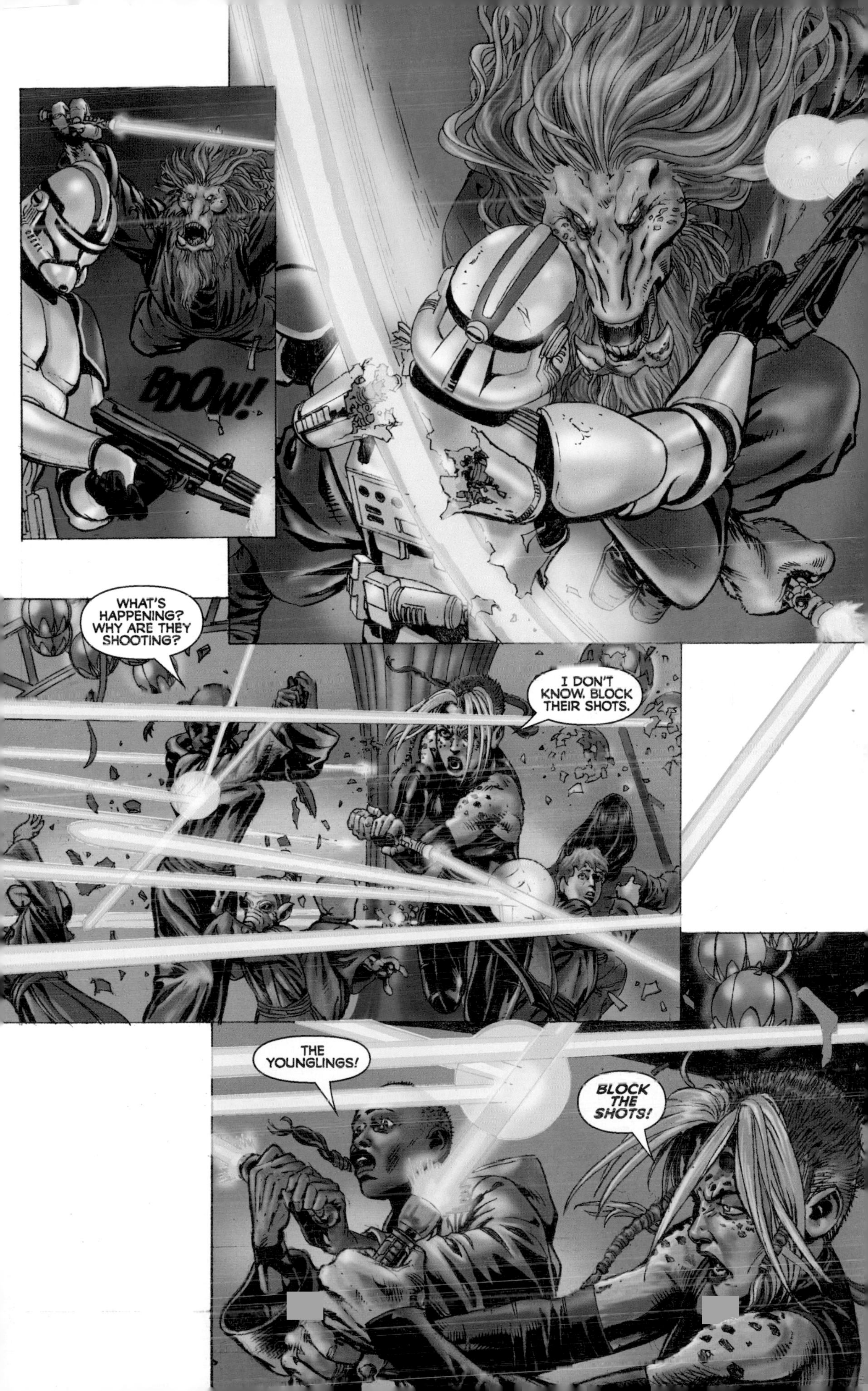
BDOW!
WHAT'S HAPPENING? WHY ARE THEY SHOOTING?
I DON'T KNOW. BLOCK THEIR SHOTS.
THE YOUNGLINGS!
BLOCK THE SHOTS!

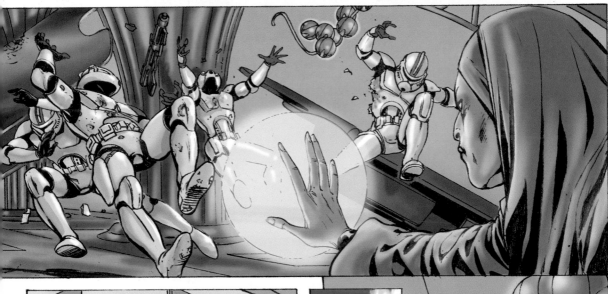

QUICKLY NOW--MAKE FOR THE DOOR.

UHN! RUN, YOUNGLINGS...

MASTER MAHN!

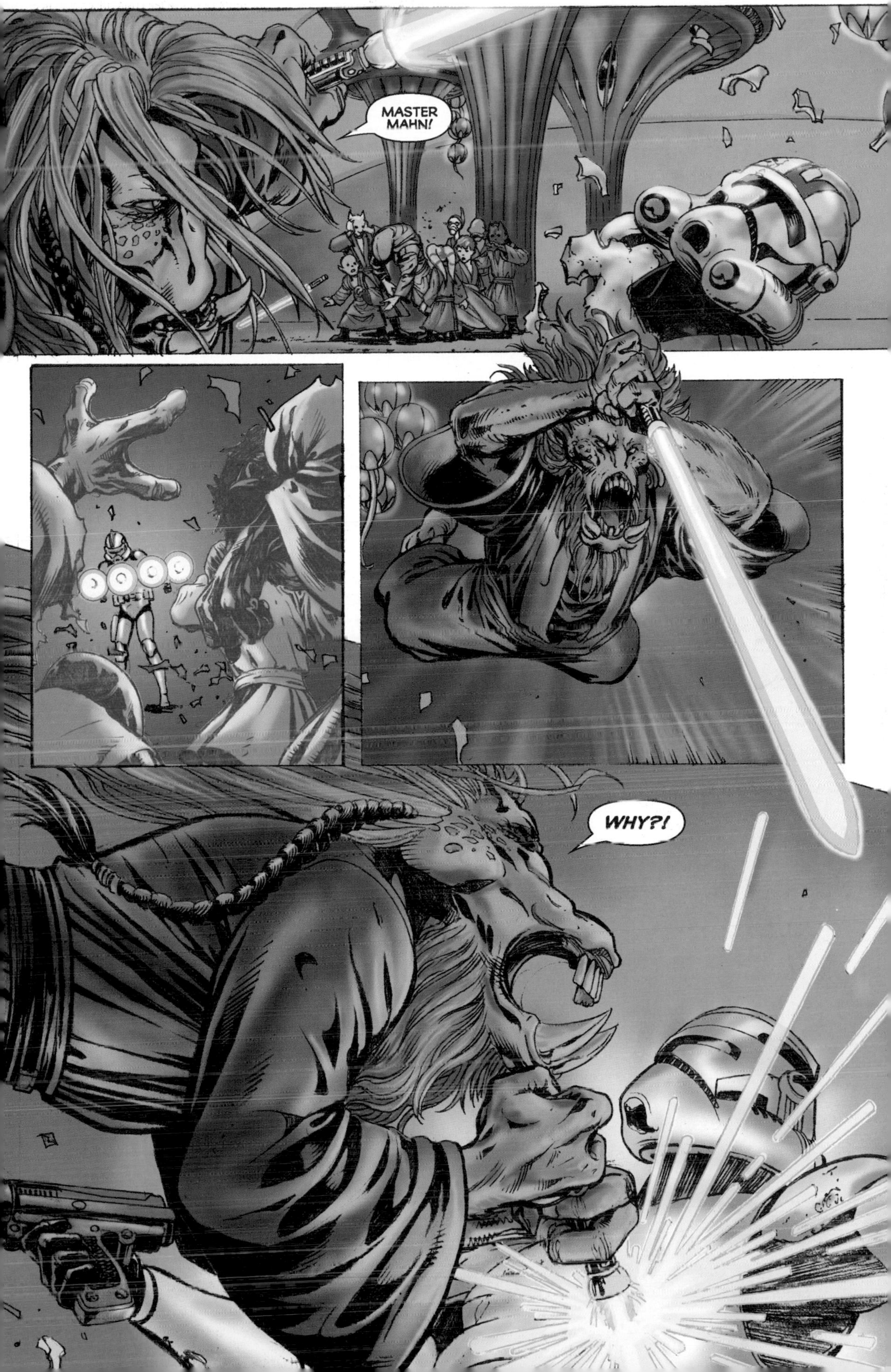
MASTER MAHN!
WHY?!

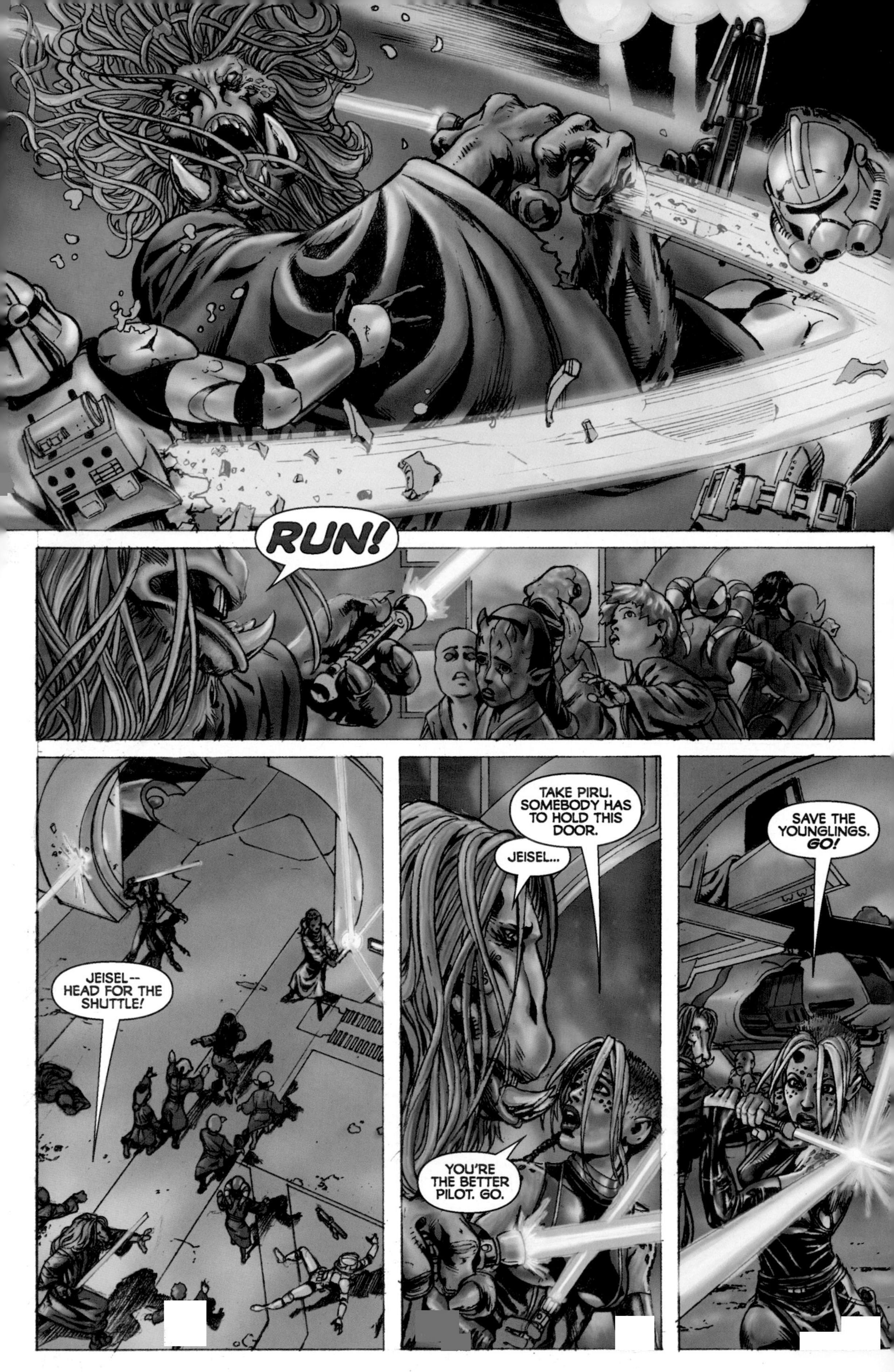
RUN!
JEISEL-- HEAD FOR THE SHUTTLE!
JEISEL...
TAKE PIRU. SOMEBODY HAS TO HOLD THIS DOOR.
YOU'RE THE BETTER PILOT. GO.
SAVE THE YOUNGLINGS. GO!

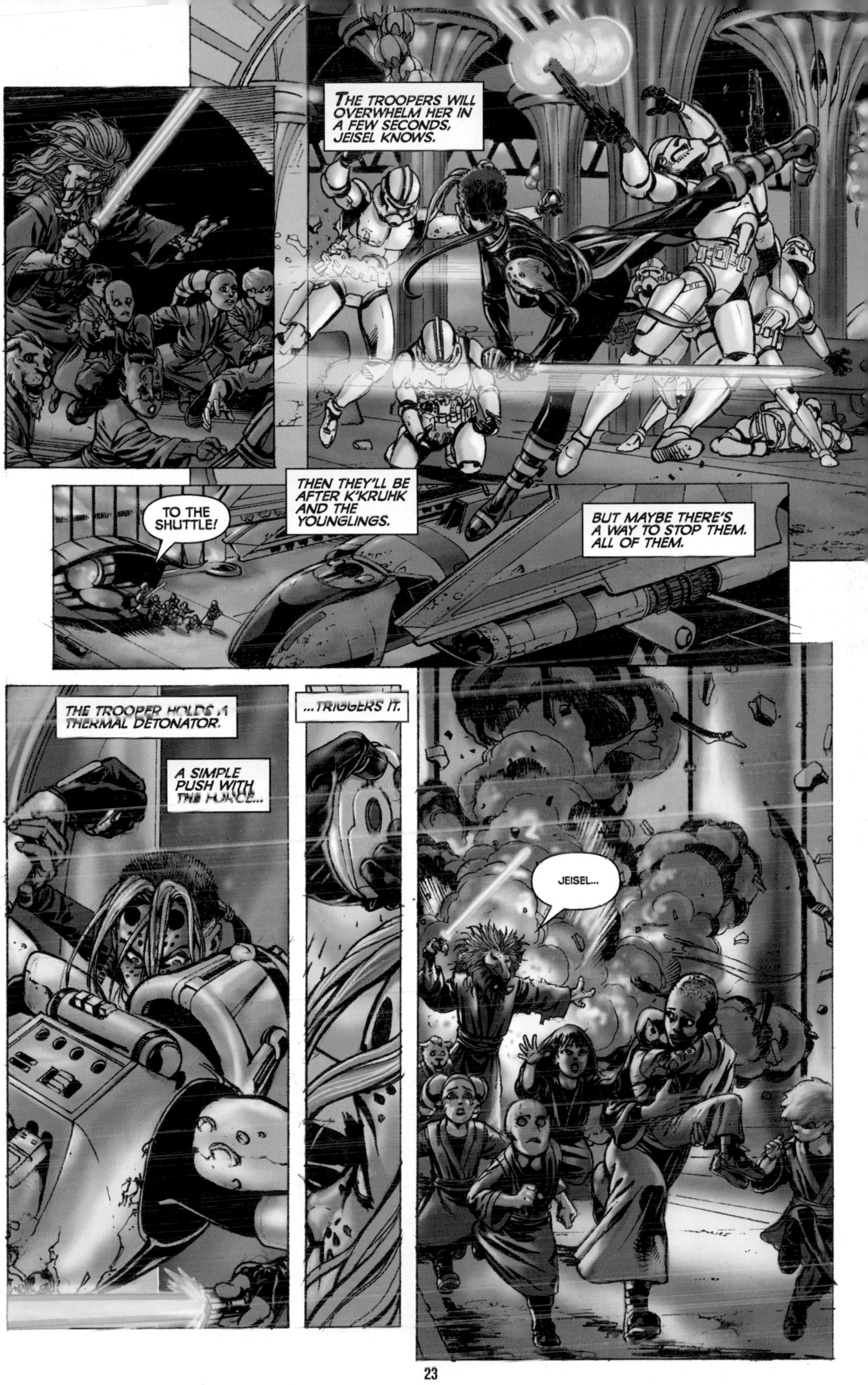
THE TROOPERS WILL OVERWHELM HER IN A FEW SECONDS, JEISEL KNOWS.
THEN THEY'LL BE AFTER K'KRUHK AND THE YOUNGLINGS.
TO THE SHUTTLE!
BUT MAYBE THERE'S A WAY TO STOP THEM. ALL OF THEM.
THE TROOPER HOLDS A THERMAL DETONATOR.
A SIMPLE PUSH WITH THE FORCE...
...TRIGGERS IT.
JEISEL...

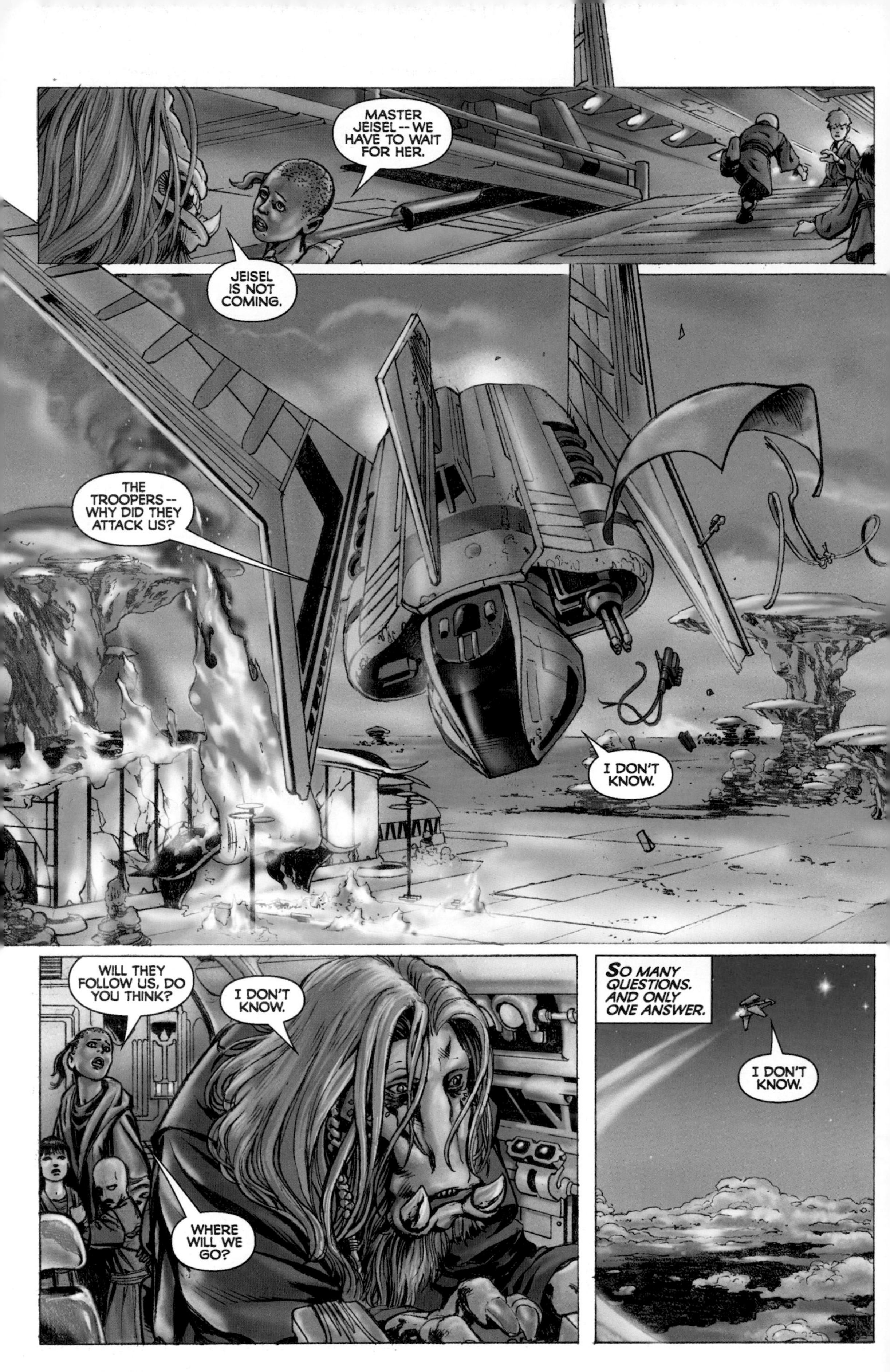
MASTER JEISEL -- WE HAVE TO WAIT FOR HER.
JEISEL IS NOT COMING.
THE TROOPERS -- WHY DID THEY ATTACK US?
I DON'T KNOW.
WILL THEY FOLLOW US, DO YOU THINK?
I DON'T KNOW.
WHERE WILL WE GO?
SO MANY QUESTIONS. AND ONLY ONE ANSWER.
I DON'T KNOW.

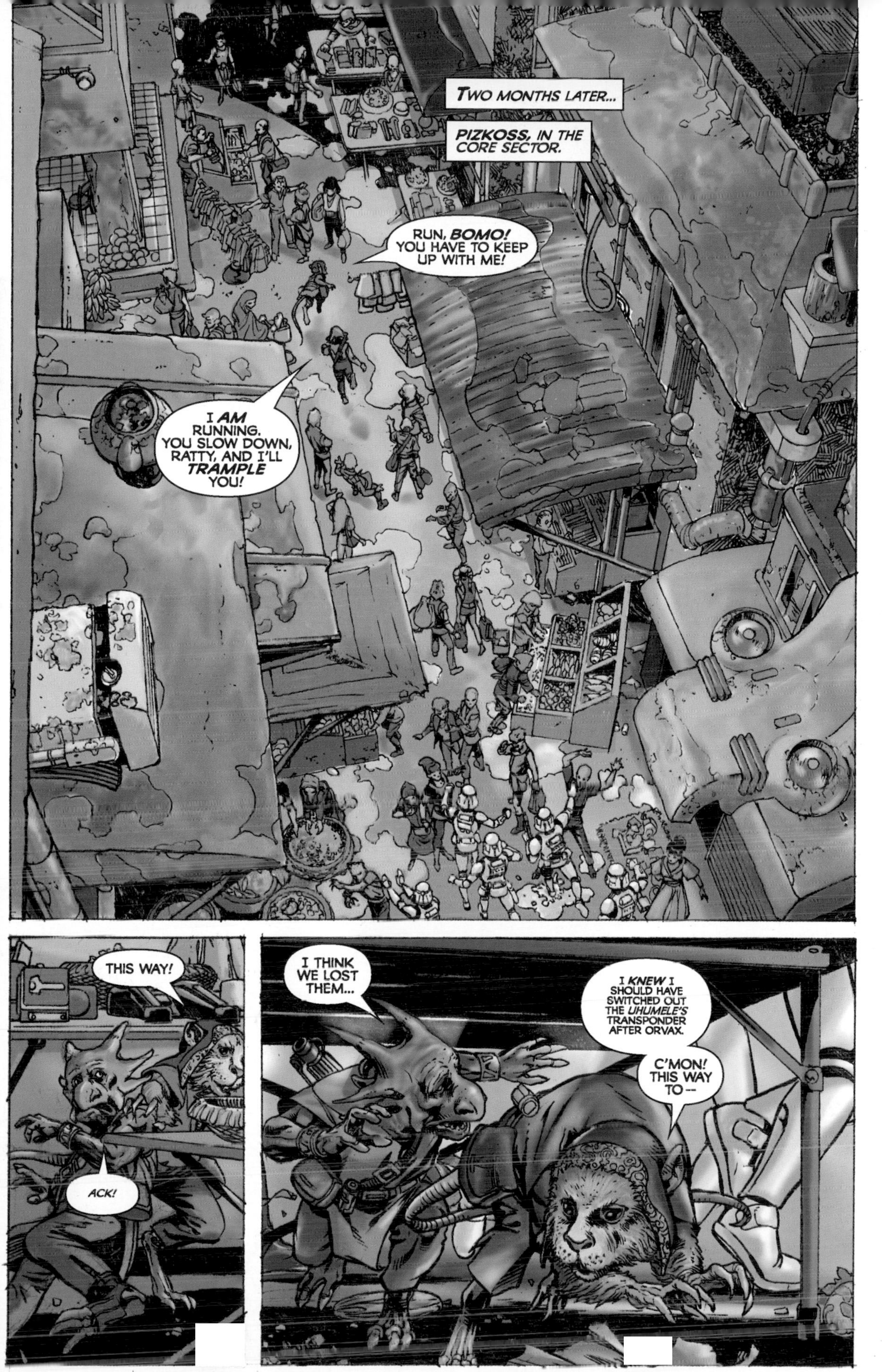
TWO MONTHS LATER...
PIZKOSS, IN THE CORE SECTOR.
RUN, BOMO! YOU HAVE TO KEEP UP WITH ME!
I AM RUNNING. YOU SLOW DOWN, RATTY, AND I'LL TRAMPLE YOU!
THIS WAY!
ACK!
I THINK WE LOST THEM...
I KNEW I SHOULD HAVE SWITCHED OUT THE UHUMELE'S TRANSPONDER AFTER ORVAX.
C'MON! THIS WAY TO--

--THE --*OOF!*

MEEKERDIN-MAA... YOU SHOULD WATCH WHERE YOU'RE GOING!

JANKS!

JANKS, GET UP!

WE HAVE TO GO!

IN GOOD TIME, GREENBARK. LET ME GET MY BAGS.

YOU SIMPLY WILL *NOT* BELIEVE WHAT I FOUND--

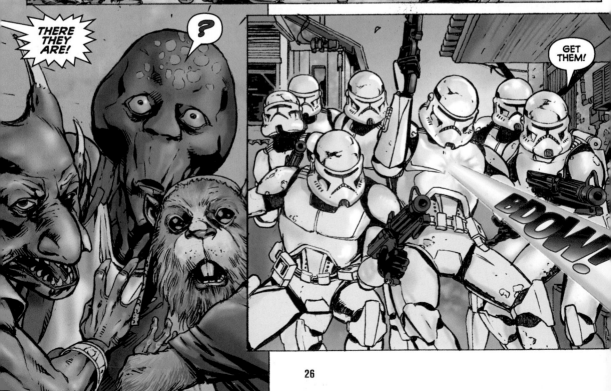

THERE THEY ARE!

?

GET THEM!

BOOM!

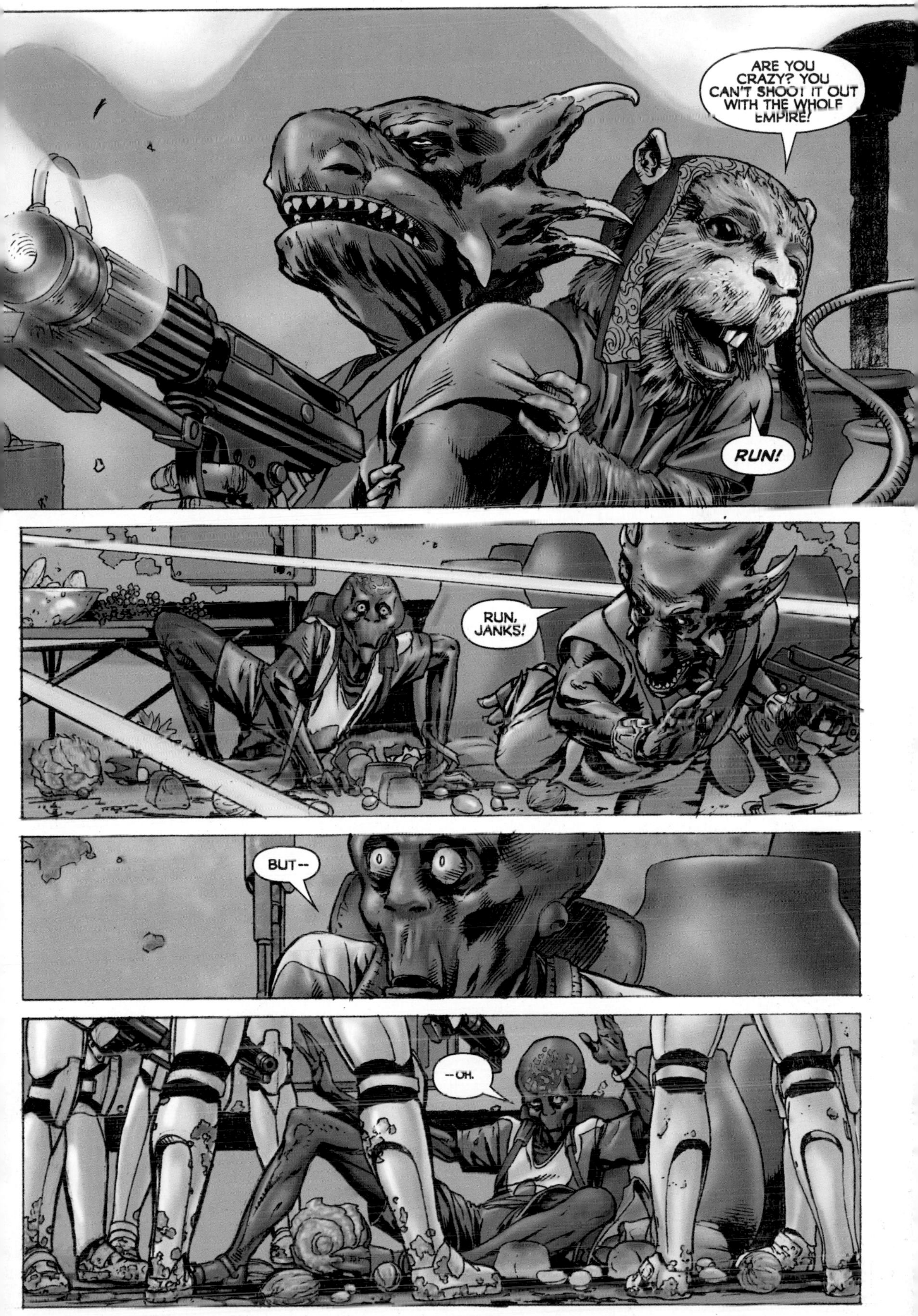

ARE YOU CRAZY? YOU CAN'T SHOOT IT OUT WITH THE WHOLE EMPIRE!
RUN!
RUN, JANKS!
BUT--
--OH.

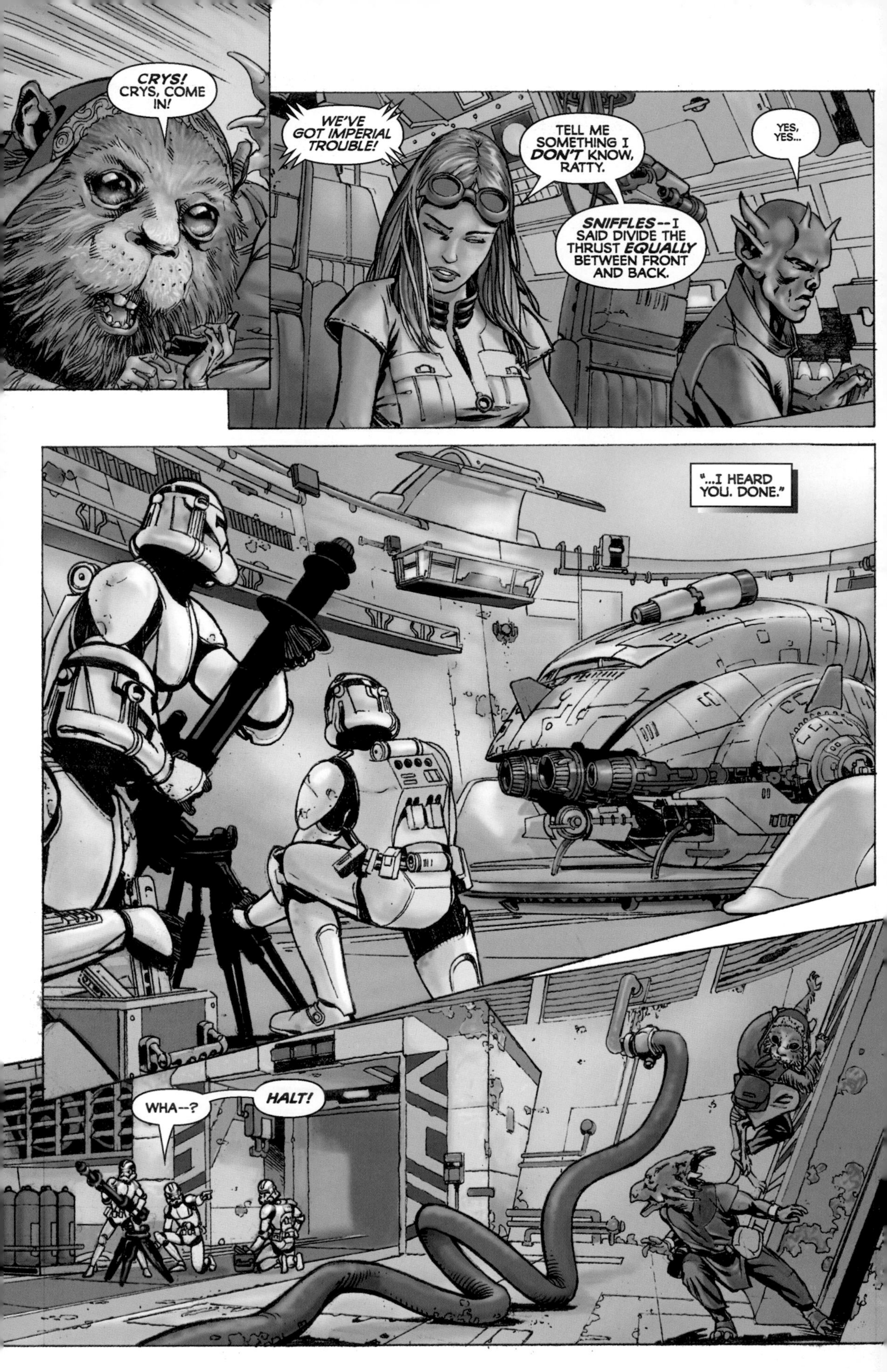
CRYS! CRYS, COME IN!
WE'VE GOT IMPERIAL TROUBLE!
TELL ME SOMETHING I DON'T KNOW, RATTY.
SNIFFLES--I SAID DIVIDE THE THRUST EQUALLY BETWEEN FRONT AND BACK.
YES, YES...
"...I HEARD YOU. DONE."
HALT!
WHA--?

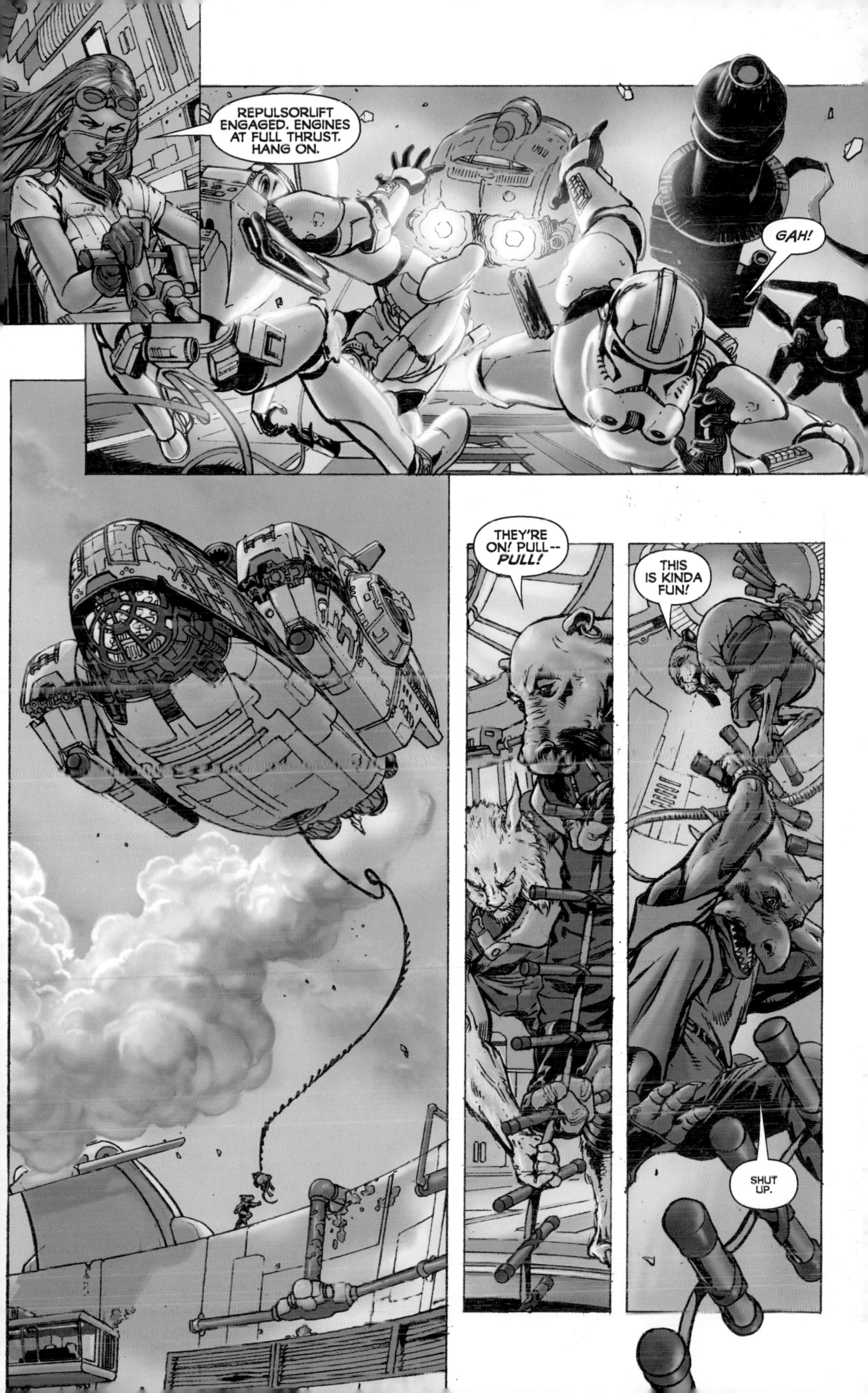

REPULSORLIFT ENGAGED. ENGINES AT FULL THRUST. HANG ON.
GAH!
THEY'RE ON! PULL-- *PULL!*
THIS IS KINDA FUN!
SHUT UP.

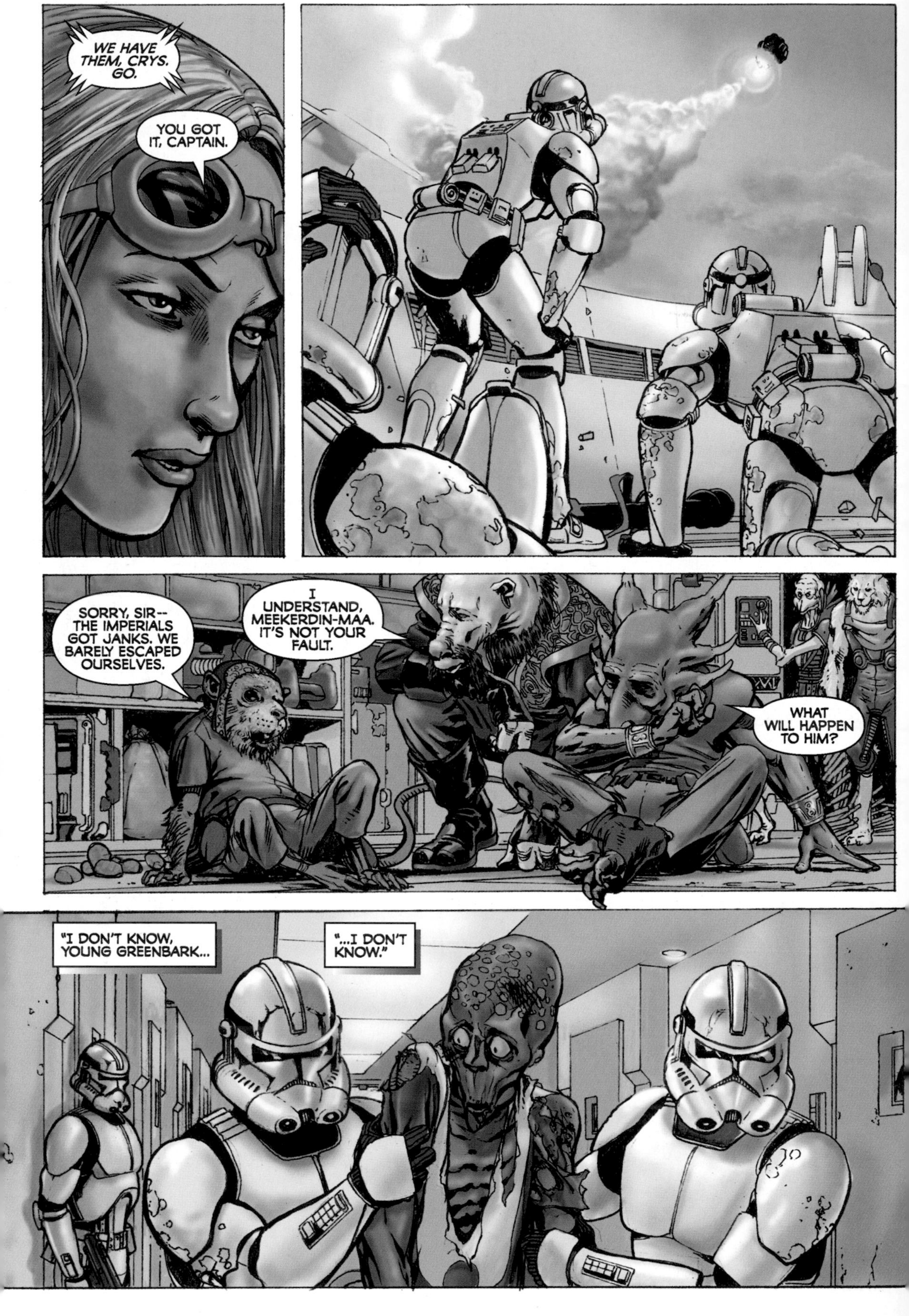
WE HAVE THEM, CRYS. GO.
YOU GOT IT, CAPTAIN.
SORRY, SIR-- THE IMPERIALS GOT JANKS. WE BARELY ESCAPED OURSELVES.
I UNDERSTAND, MEEKERDIN-MAA. IT'S NOT YOUR FAULT.
WHAT WILL HAPPEN TO HIM?
"I DON'T KNOW, YOUNG GREENBARK...
"...I DON'T KNOW."

IF YOU'VE LIVED THROUGH YOUR WORST NIGHTMARE, YOU WOULD EXPECT THAT YOUR LIFE AFTERWARD COULD ONLY GET BETTER.

BUT ROMO GREENBARK KNOWS THIS TO BE FALSE.

SUCH HOPEFUL THINKING IGNORES THE EVER-PRESENT ANGUISH AND REGRET-- THE CRUEL KNOWLEDGE THAT IF YOU HAD DONE THINGS DIFFERENTLY, MADE OTHER CHOICES, EVENTS MIGHT HAVE PLAYED OUT BETTER...

...AND YOUR WIFE AND YOUR CHILD MIGHT STILL BE ALIVE.

RESA...!

KNOWING THAT THE WORST HAS ALREADY HAPPENED AND THAT WHAT IS PAST IS BEYOND CHANGE OR REPAIR DOES NOTHING TO LESSEN THE GUILT--

--THAT YOU WEREN'T THERE WHEN YOUR WIFE DIED PROTECTING YOUR DAUGHTER...

...OR THAT YOU ARRIVED TOO LATE TO SAVE YOUR CHILD FROM...

ULP!

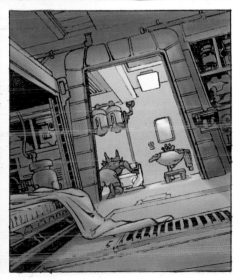

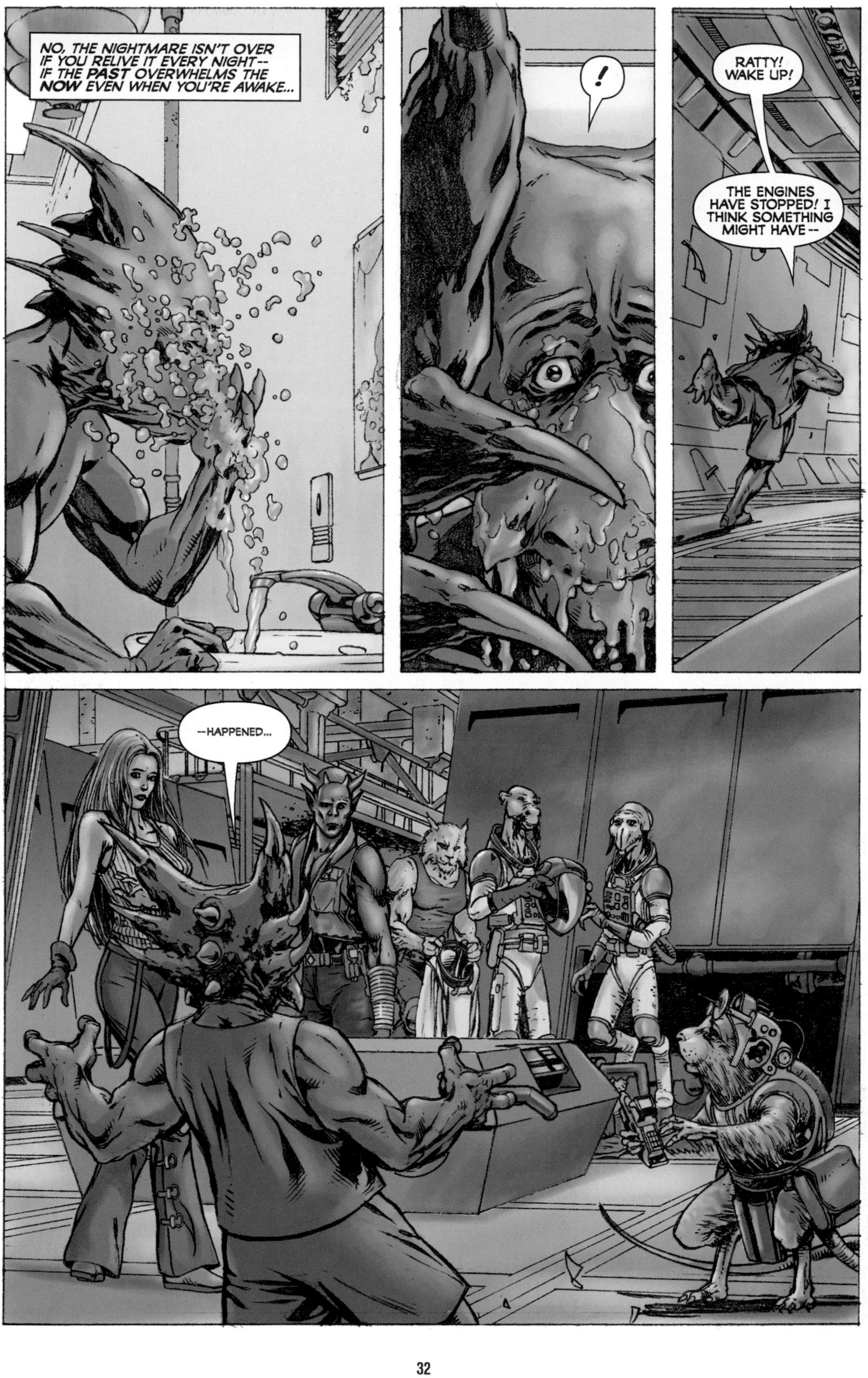
NO, THE NIGHTMARE ISN'T OVER IF YOU RELIVE IT EVERY NIGHT-- IF THE PAST OVERWHELMS THE NOW EVEN WHEN YOU'RE AWAKE...
!
RATTY! WAKE UP!
THE ENGINES HAVE STOPPED! I THINK SOMETHING MIGHT HAVE--
--HAPPENED...

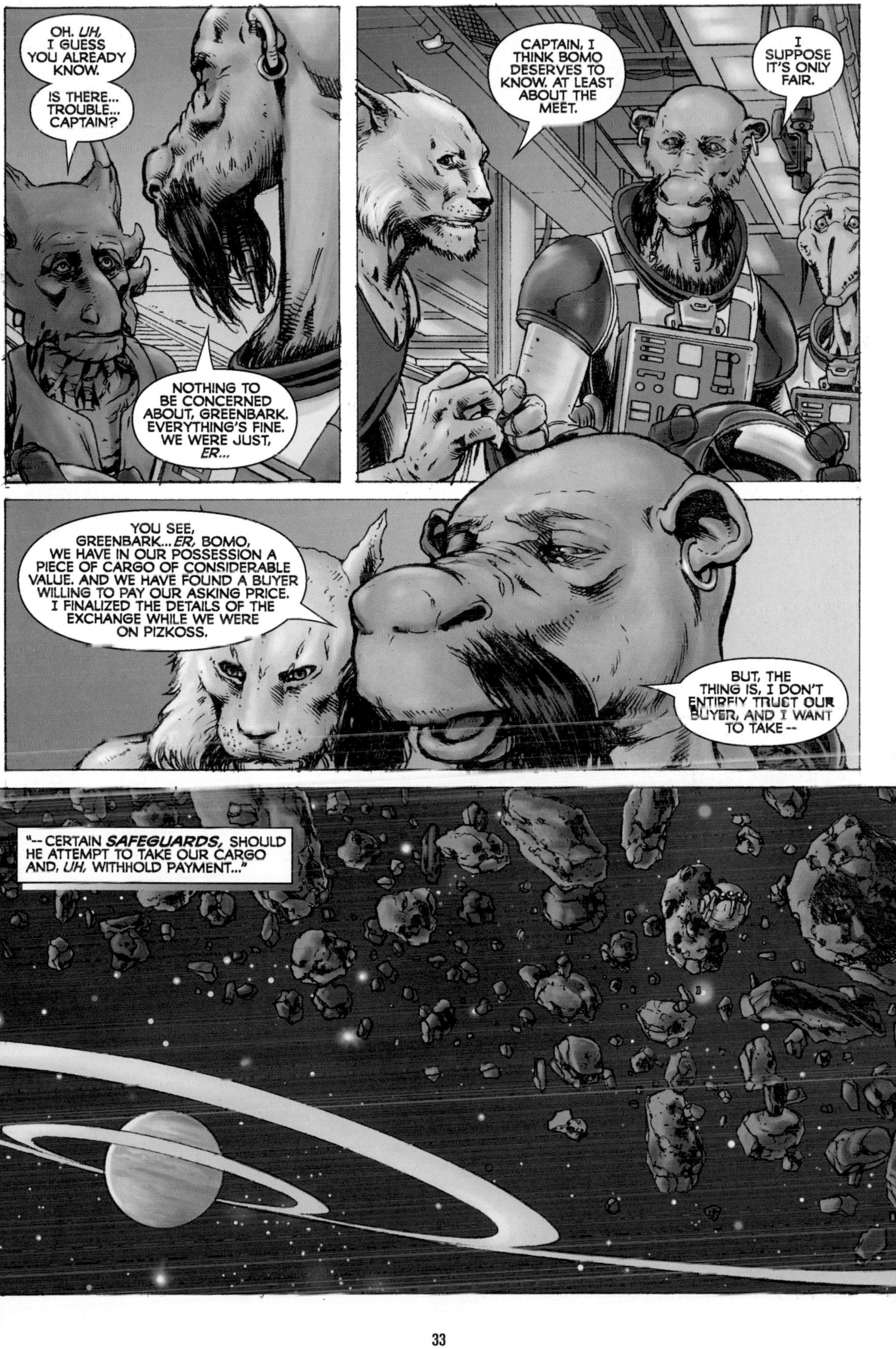
OH. UH, I GUESS YOU ALREADY KNOW.
IS THERE... TROUBLE... CAPTAIN?
NOTHING TO BE CONCERNED ABOUT, GREENBARK. EVERYTHING'S FINE. WE WERE JUST, ER...
CAPTAIN, I THINK BOMO DESERVES TO KNOW. AT LEAST ABOUT THE MEET.
I SUPPOSE IT'S ONLY FAIR.
YOU SEE, GREENBARK... ER, BOMO, WE HAVE IN OUR POSSESSION A PIECE OF CARGO OF CONSIDERABLE VALUE. AND WE HAVE FOUND A BUYER WILLING TO PAY OUR ASKING PRICE. I FINALIZED THE DETAILS OF THE EXCHANGE WHILE WE WERE ON PIZKOSS.
BUT, THE THING IS, I DON'T ENTIRELY TRUST OUR BUYER, AND I WANT TO TAKE --
"-- CERTAIN SAFEGUARDS, SHOULD HE ATTEMPT TO TAKE OUR CARGO AND, UH, WITHHOLD PAYMENT..."

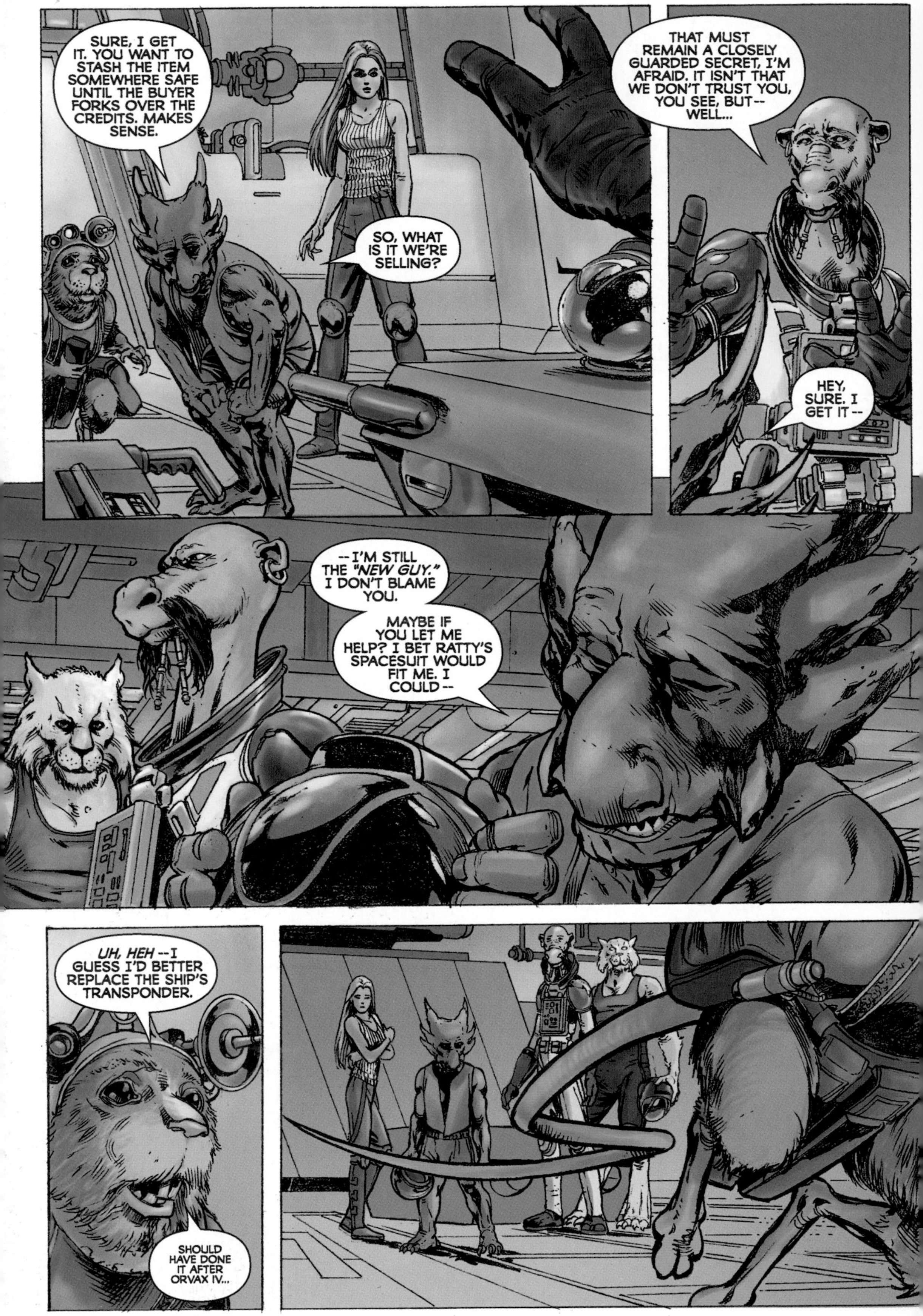
SURE, I GET IT. YOU WANT TO STASH THE ITEM SOMEWHERE SAFE UNTIL THE BUYER FORKS OVER THE CREDITS. MAKES SENSE.
SO, WHAT IS IT WE'RE SELLING?
THAT MUST REMAIN A CLOSELY GUARDED SECRET, I'M AFRAID. IT ISN'T THAT WE DON'T TRUST YOU, YOU SEE, BUT-- WELL...
HEY, SURE. I GET IT --
-- I'M STILL THE *"NEW GUY."* I DON'T BLAME YOU.
MAYBE IF YOU LET ME HELP? I BET RATTY'S SPACESUIT WOULD FIT ME. I COULD --
UH, HEH -- I GUESS I'D BETTER REPLACE THE SHIP'S TRANSPONDER.
SHOULD HAVE DONE IT AFTER ORVAX IV...

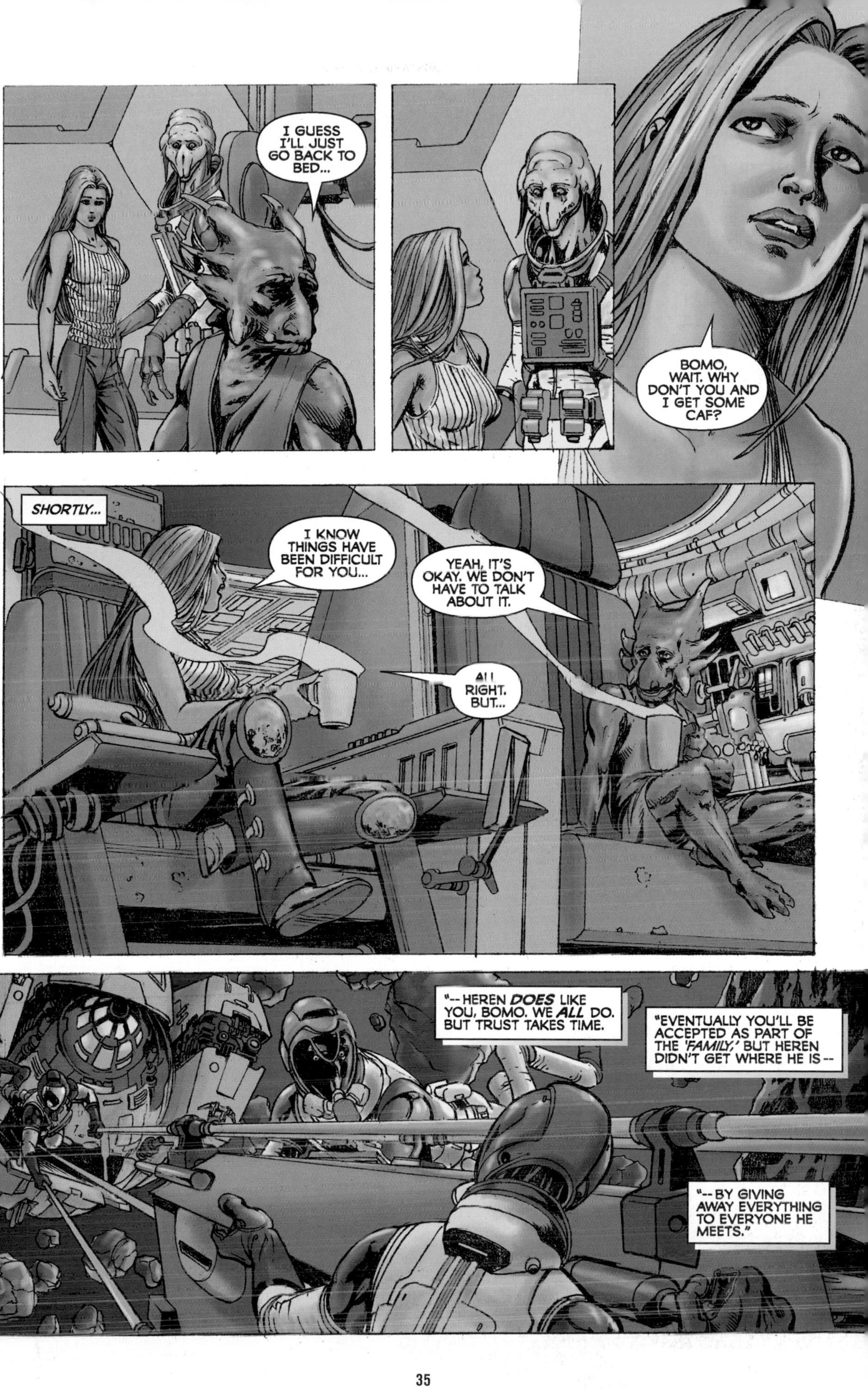
I GUESS I'LL JUST GO BACK TO BED...
BOMO, WAIT. WHY DON'T YOU AND I GET SOME CAF?
SHORTLY...
I KNOW THINGS HAVE BEEN DIFFICULT FOR YOU...
YEAH, IT'S OKAY. WE DON'T HAVE TO TALK ABOUT IT.
ALL RIGHT. BUT...
"-- HEREN *DOES* LIKE YOU, BOMO. WE *ALL* DO. BUT TRUST TAKES TIME.
"EVENTUALLY YOU'LL BE ACCEPTED AS PART OF THE *'FAMILY,'* BUT HEREN DIDN'T GET WHERE HE IS --
"-- BY GIVING AWAY EVERYTHING TO EVERYONE HE MEETS."

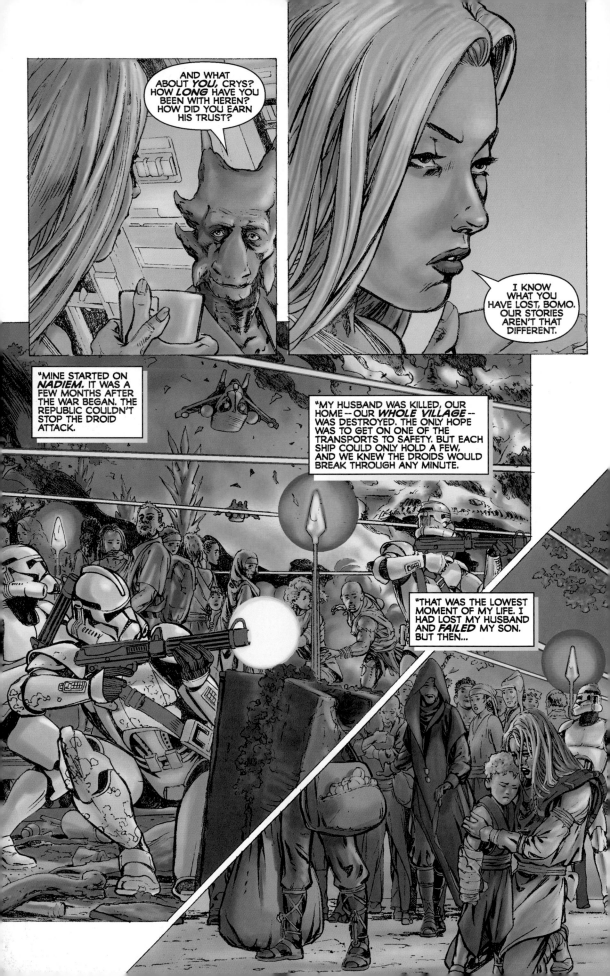

AND WHAT ABOUT *YOU*, CRYS? HOW *LONG* HAVE YOU BEEN WITH HEREN? HOW DID YOU EARN HIS TRUST?

I KNOW WHAT YOU HAVE LOST, BOMO. OUR STORIES AREN'T THAT DIFFERENT.

"MINE STARTED ON *NADIEM.* IT WAS A FEW MONTHS AFTER THE WAR BEGAN. THE REPUBLIC COULDN'T STOP THE DROID ATTACK.

"MY HUSBAND WAS KILLED, OUR HOME -- OUR *WHOLE VILLAGE* -- WAS DESTROYED. THE ONLY HOPE WAS TO GET ON ONE OF THE TRANSPORTS TO SAFETY. BUT EACH SHIP COULD ONLY HOLD A FEW, AND WE KNEW THE DROIDS WOULD BREAK THROUGH ANY MINUTE.

"THAT WAS THE LOWEST MOMENT OF MY LIFE. I HAD LOST MY HUSBAND AND *FAILED* MY SON. BUT THEN...

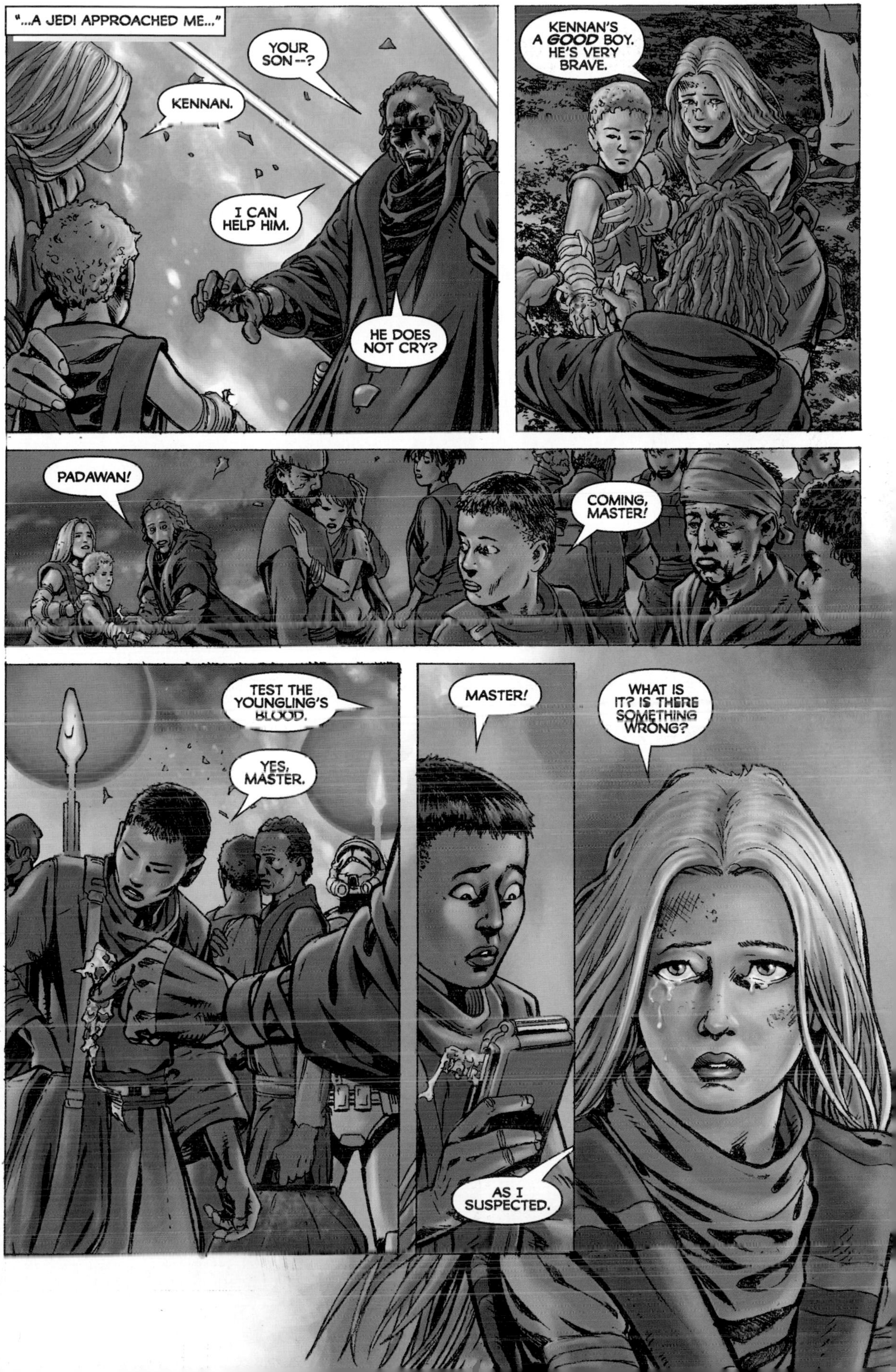
"...A JEDI APPROACHED ME..."
YOUR SON --?
KENNAN.
I CAN HELP HIM.
HE DOES NOT CRY?
KENNAN'S A GOOD BOY. HE'S VERY BRAVE.
PADAWAN!
COMING, MASTER!
TEST THE YOUNGLING'S BLOOD.
YES, MASTER.
MASTER!
WHAT IS IT? IS THERE SOMETHING WRONG?
AS I SUSPECTED.

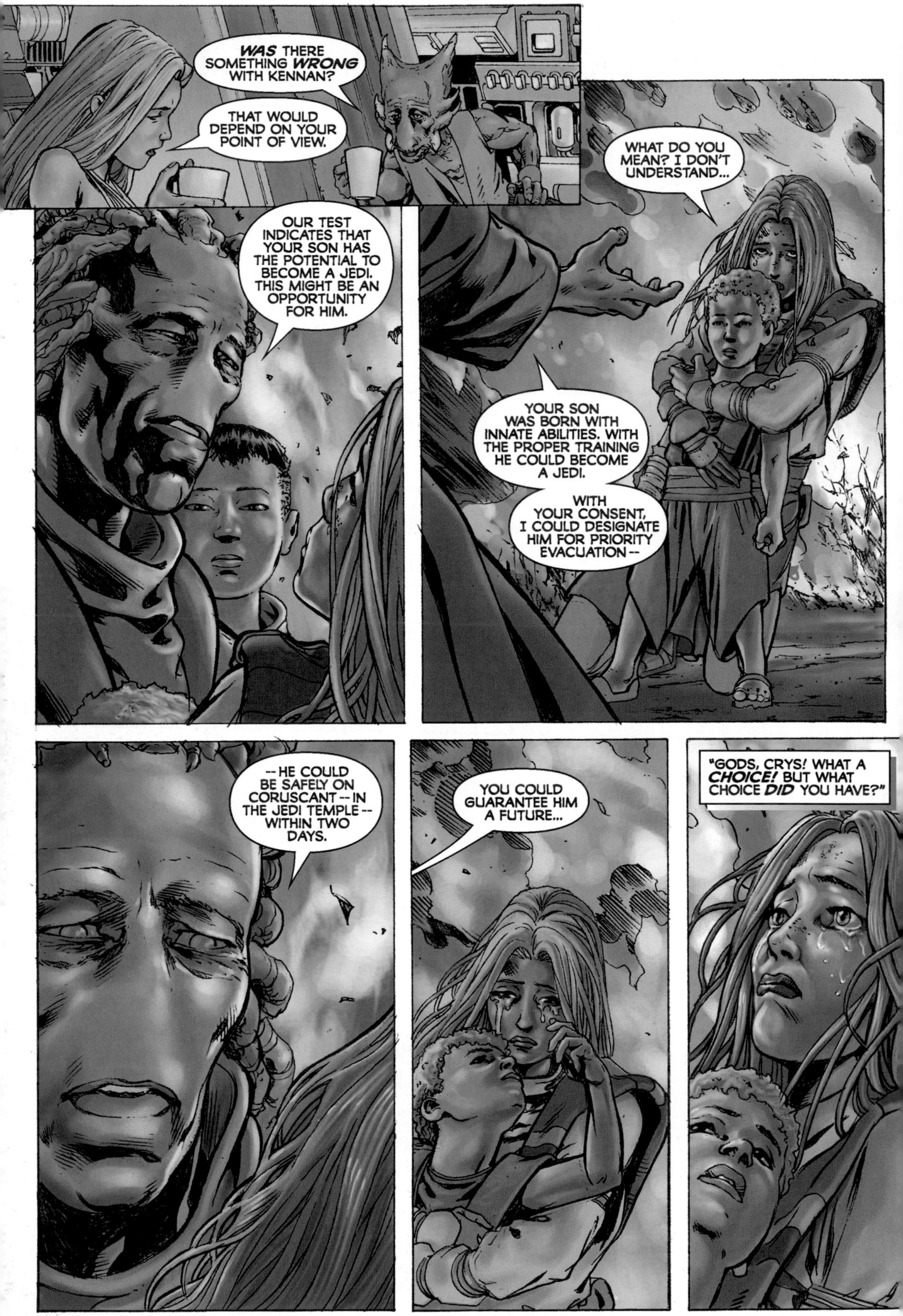
WAS THERE SOMETHING WRONG WITH KENNAN?
THAT WOULD DEPEND ON YOUR POINT OF VIEW.
WHAT DO YOU MEAN? I DON'T UNDERSTAND...
OUR TEST INDICATES THAT YOUR SON HAS THE POTENTIAL TO BECOME A JEDI. THIS MIGHT BE AN OPPORTUNITY FOR HIM.
YOUR SON WAS BORN WITH INNATE ABILITIES. WITH THE PROPER TRAINING HE COULD BECOME A JEDI.
WITH YOUR CONSENT, I COULD DESIGNATE HIM FOR PRIORITY EVACUATION --
-- HE COULD BE SAFELY ON CORUSCANT -- IN THE JEDI TEMPLE -- WITHIN TWO DAYS.
YOU COULD GUARANTEE HIM A FUTURE...
"GODS, CRYS! WHAT A CHOICE! BUT WHAT CHOICE DID YOU HAVE?"

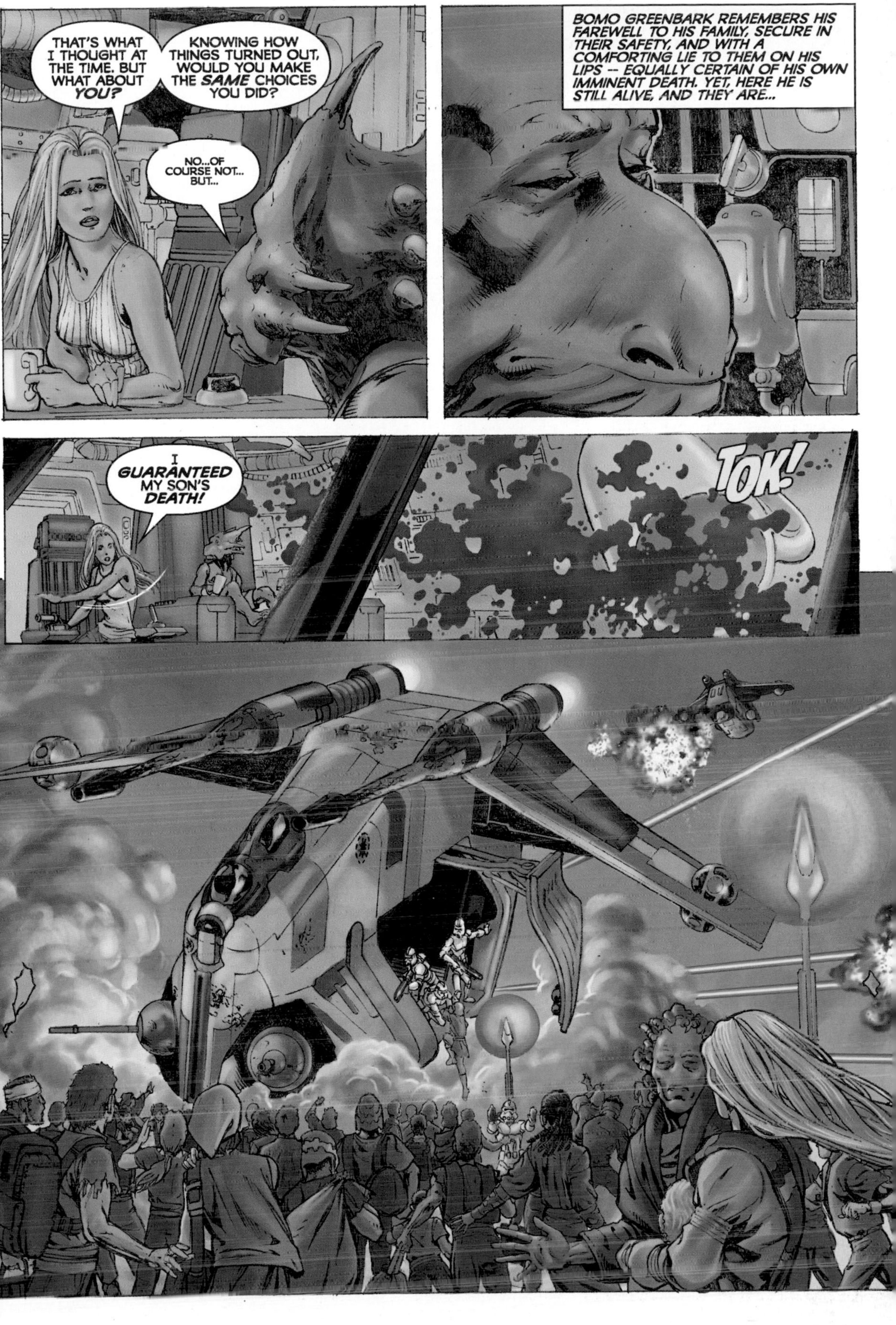
THAT'S WHAT I THOUGHT AT THE TIME. BUT WHAT ABOUT YOU?
KNOWING HOW THINGS TURNED OUT, WOULD YOU MAKE THE SAME CHOICES YOU DID?
NO...OF COURSE NOT... BUT...
BOMO GREENBARK REMEMBERS HIS FAREWELL TO HIS FAMILY, SECURE IN THEIR SAFETY, AND WITH A COMFORTING LIE TO THEM ON HIS LIPS -- EQUALLY CERTAIN OF HIS OWN IMMINENT DEATH. YET, HERE HE IS STILL ALIVE, AND THEY ARE...
I GUARANTEED MY SON'S DEATH!
TOK!

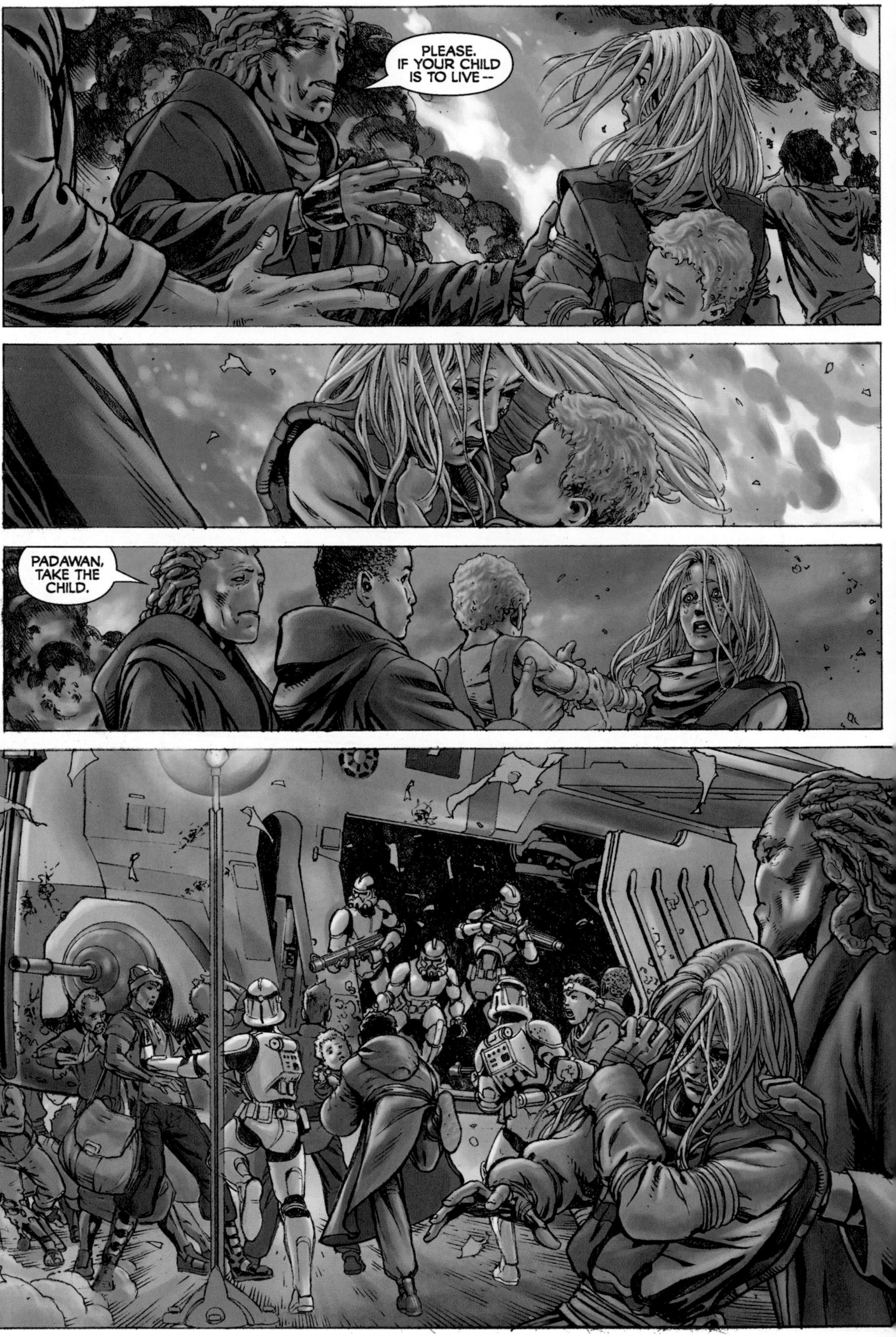
PLEASE. IF YOUR CHILD IS TO LIVE --
PADAWAN, TAKE THE CHILD.

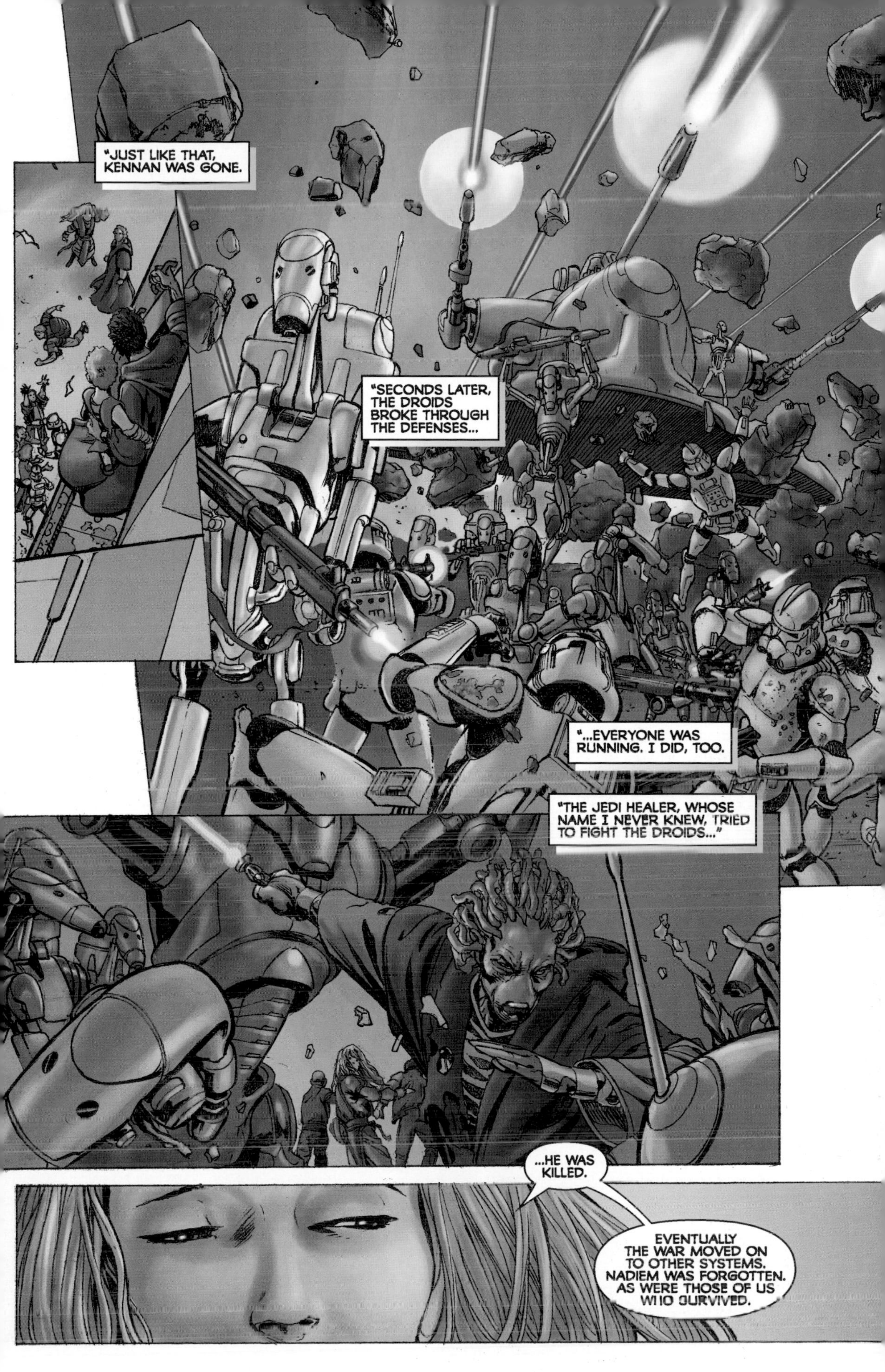
"JUST LIKE THAT, KENNAN WAS GONE.
"SECONDS LATER, THE DROIDS BROKE THROUGH THE DEFENSES...
"...EVERYONE WAS RUNNING. I DID, TOO.
"THE JEDI HEALER, WHOSE NAME I NEVER KNEW, TRIED TO FIGHT THE DROIDS..."
...HE WAS KILLED.
EVENTUALLY THE WAR MOVED ON TO OTHER SYSTEMS. NADIEM WAS FORGOTTEN. AS WERE THOSE OF US WHO SURVIVED.

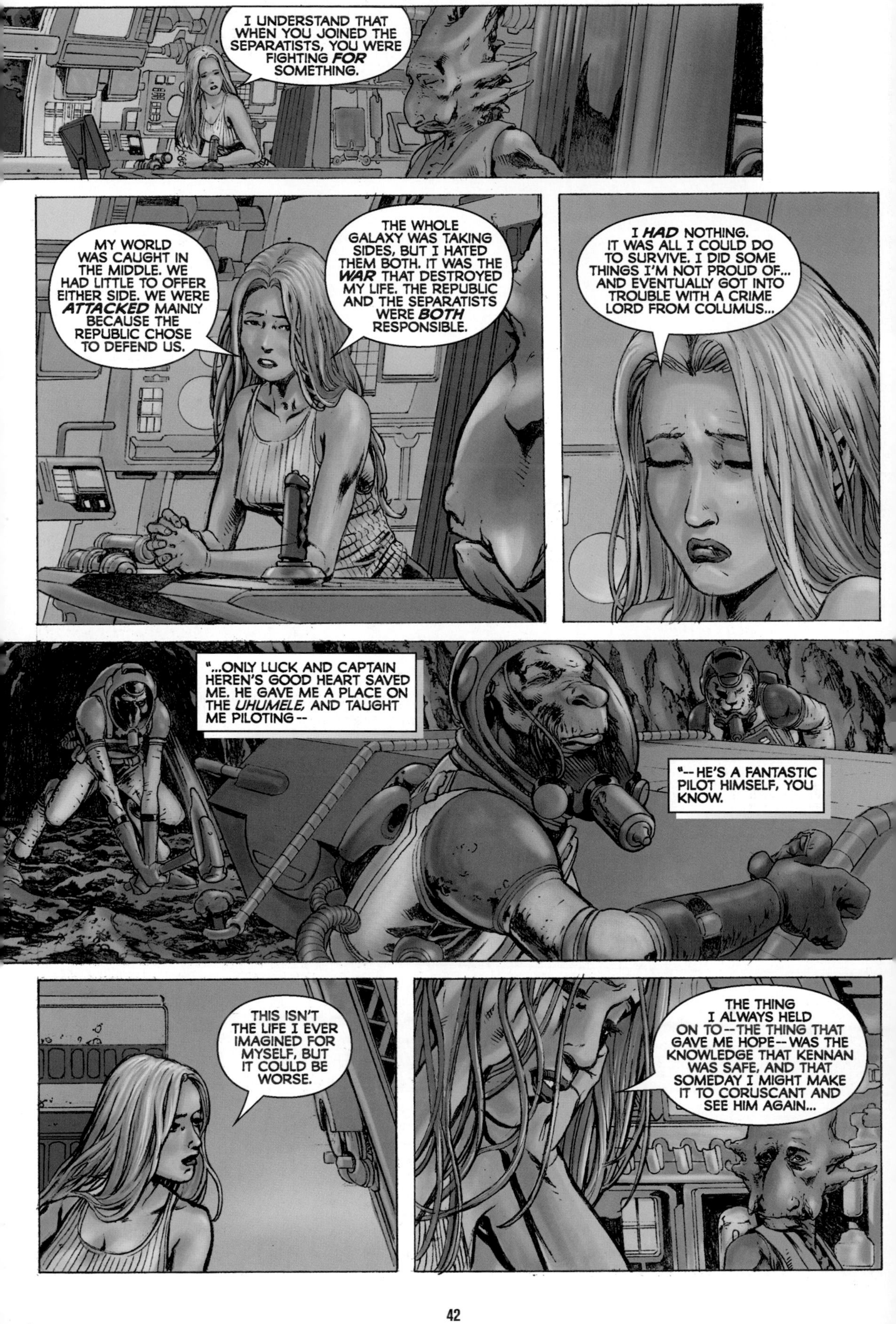
I UNDERSTAND THAT WHEN YOU JOINED THE SEPARATISTS, YOU WERE FIGHTING FOR SOMETHING.
MY WORLD WAS CAUGHT IN THE MIDDLE. WE HAD LITTLE TO OFFER EITHER SIDE. WE WERE ATTACKED MAINLY BECAUSE THE REPUBLIC CHOSE TO DEFEND US.
THE WHOLE GALAXY WAS TAKING SIDES, BUT I HATED THEM BOTH. IT WAS THE WAR THAT DESTROYED MY LIFE. THE REPUBLIC AND THE SEPARATISTS WERE BOTH RESPONSIBLE.
I HAD NOTHING. IT WAS ALL I COULD DO TO SURVIVE. I DID SOME THINGS I'M NOT PROUD OF... AND EVENTUALLY GOT INTO TROUBLE WITH A CRIME LORD FROM COLUMUS...
"...ONLY LUCK AND CAPTAIN HEREN'S GOOD HEART SAVED ME. HE GAVE ME A PLACE ON THE UHUMELE, AND TAUGHT ME PILOTING--
"--HE'S A FANTASTIC PILOT HIMSELF, YOU KNOW.
THIS ISN'T THE LIFE I EVER IMAGINED FOR MYSELF, BUT IT COULD BE WORSE.
THE THING I ALWAYS HELD ON TO--THE THING THAT GAVE ME HOPE--WAS THE KNOWLEDGE THAT KENNAN WAS SAFE, AND THAT SOMEDAY I MIGHT MAKE IT TO CORUSCANT AND SEE HIM AGAIN...

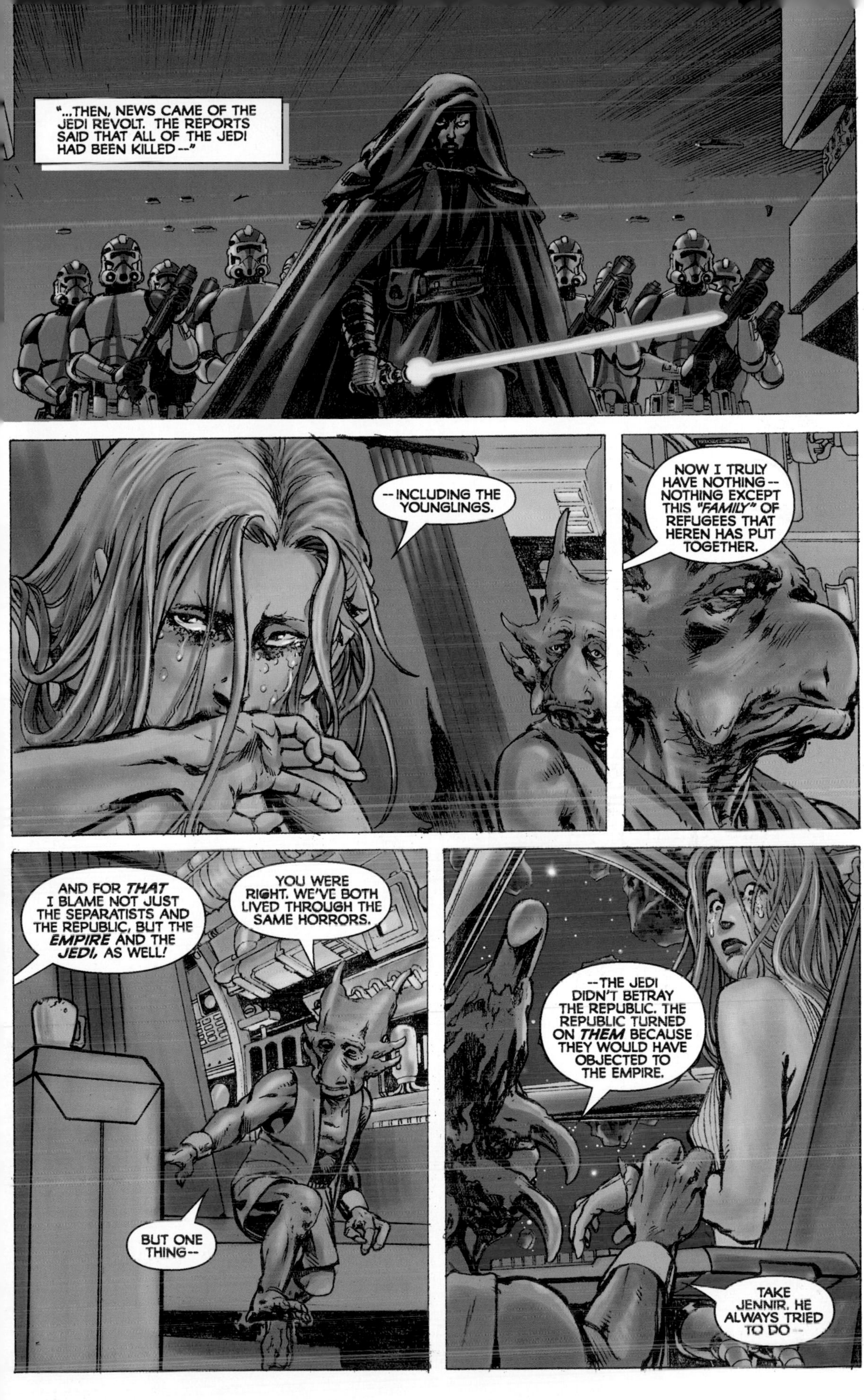
"...THEN, NEWS CAME OF THE JEDI REVOLT. THE REPORTS SAID THAT ALL OF THE JEDI HAD BEEN KILLED--"
--INCLUDING THE YOUNGLINGS.
NOW I TRULY HAVE NOTHING-- NOTHING EXCEPT THIS *"FAMILY"* OF REFUGEES THAT HEREN HAS PUT TOGETHER.
AND FOR ***THAT*** I BLAME NOT JUST THE SEPARATISTS AND THE REPUBLIC, BUT THE ***EMPIRE*** AND THE ***JEDI,*** AS WELL!
YOU WERE RIGHT. WE'VE BOTH LIVED THROUGH THE SAME HORRORS.
BUT ONE THING--
--THE JEDI DIDN'T BETRAY THE REPUBLIC. THE REPUBLIC TURNED ON ***THEM*** BECAUSE THEY WOULD HAVE OBJECTED TO THE EMPIRE.
TAKE JENNIR. HE ALWAYS TRIED TO DO--

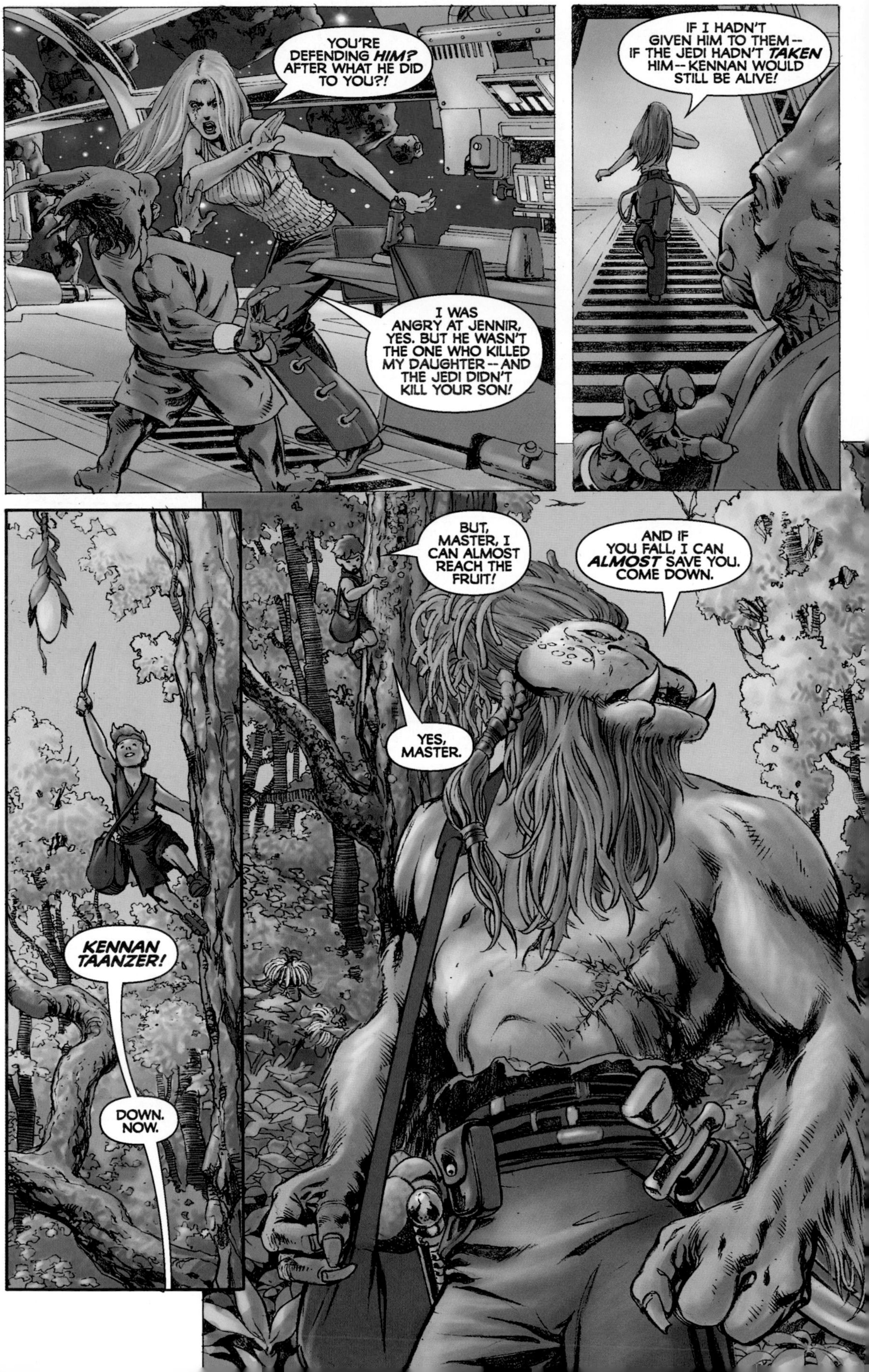
YOU'RE DEFENDING HIM? AFTER WHAT HE DID TO YOU?!
I WAS ANGRY AT JENNIR, YES. BUT HE WASN'T THE ONE WHO KILLED MY DAUGHTER -- AND THE JEDI DIDN'T KILL YOUR SON!
IF I HADN'T GIVEN HIM TO THEM -- IF THE JEDI HADN'T TAKEN HIM -- KENNAN WOULD STILL BE ALIVE!
BUT, MASTER, I CAN ALMOST REACH THE FRUIT!
AND IF YOU FALL, I CAN ALMOST SAVE YOU. COME DOWN.
KENNAN TAANZER!
DOWN. NOW.
YES, MASTER.

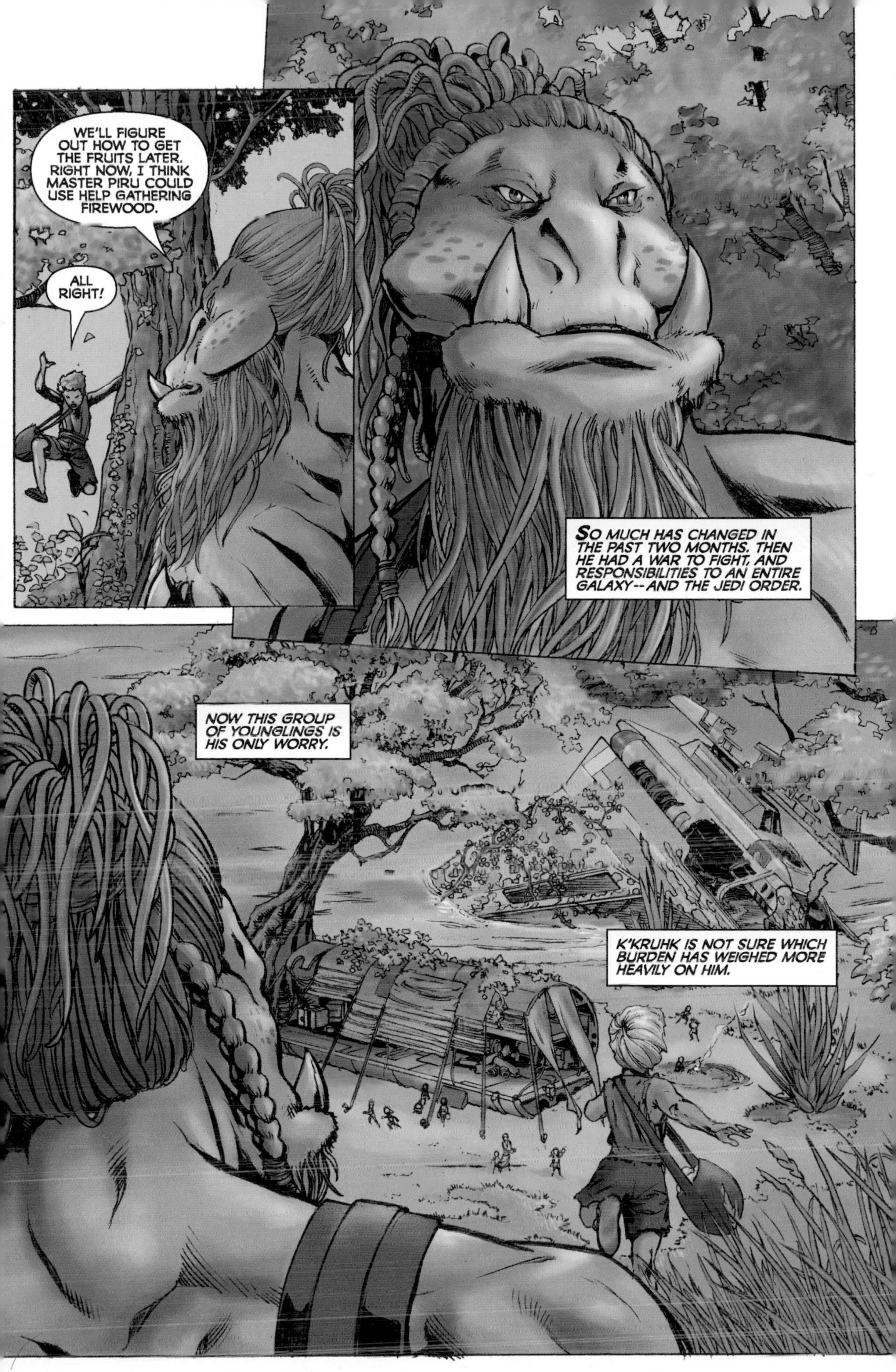
WE'LL FIGURE OUT HOW TO GET THE FRUITS LATER. RIGHT NOW, I THINK MASTER PIRU COULD USE HELP GATHERING FIREWOOD.
ALL RIGHT!
SO MUCH HAS CHANGED IN THE PAST TWO MONTHS. THEN HE HAD A WAR TO FIGHT, AND RESPONSIBILITIES TO AN ENTIRE GALAXY--AND THE JEDI ORDER.
NOW THIS GROUP OF YOUNGLINGS IS HIS ONLY WORRY.
K'KRUHK IS NOT SURE WHICH BURDEN HAS WEIGHED MORE HEAVILY ON HIM.

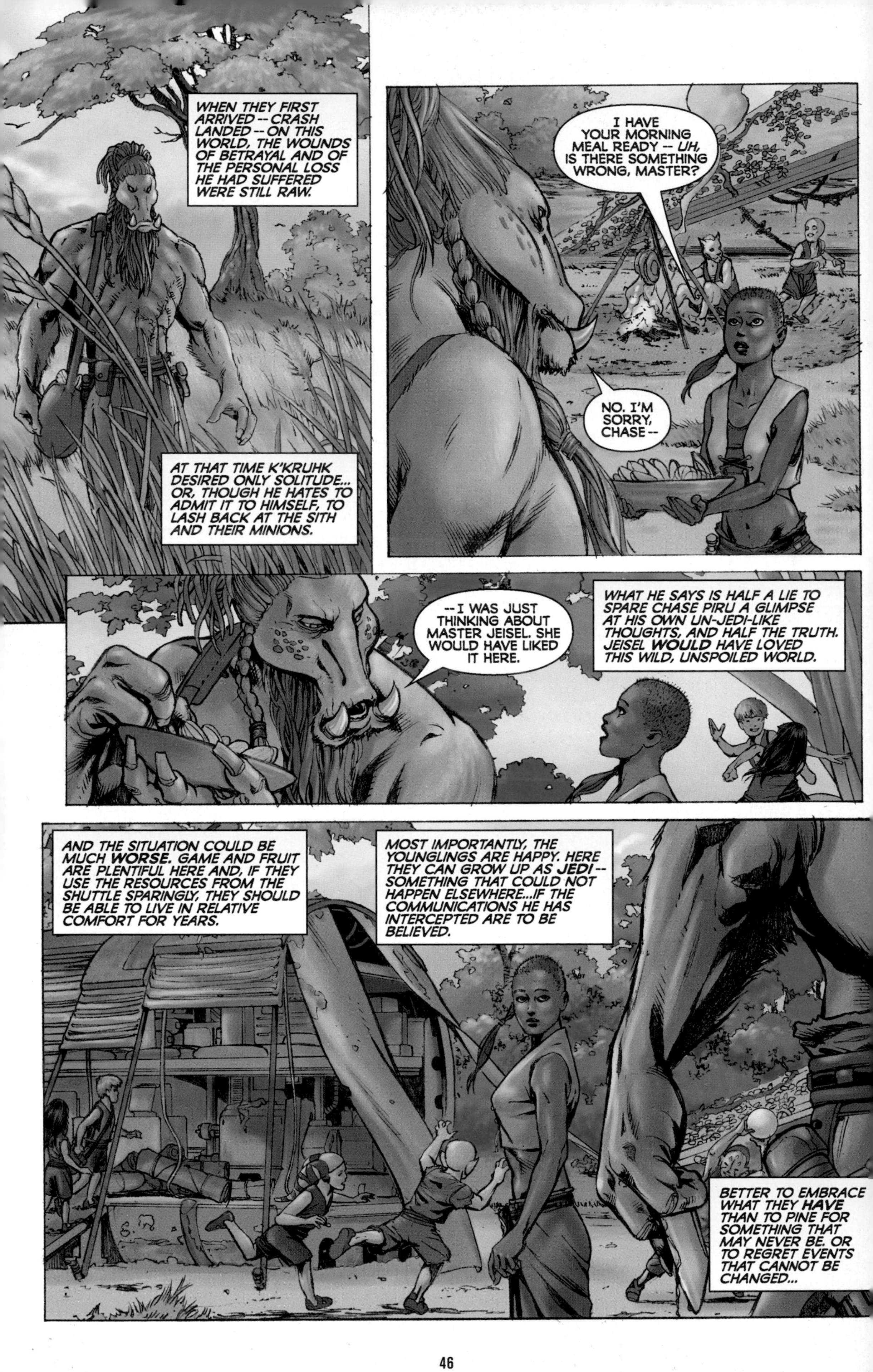
WHEN THEY FIRST ARRIVED -- CRASH LANDED -- ON THIS WORLD, THE WOUNDS OF BETRAYAL AND OF THE PERSONAL LOSS HE HAD SUFFERED WERE STILL RAW.
AT THAT TIME K'KRUHK DESIRED ONLY SOLITUDE... OR, THOUGH HE HATES TO ADMIT IT TO HIMSELF, TO LASH BACK AT THE SITH AND THEIR MINIONS.
I HAVE YOUR MORNING MEAL READY -- UH, IS THERE SOMETHING WRONG, MASTER?
NO. I'M SORRY, CHASE --
-- I WAS JUST THINKING ABOUT MASTER JEISEL. SHE WOULD HAVE LIKED IT HERE.
WHAT HE SAYS IS HALF A LIE TO SPARE CHASE PIRU A GLIMPSE AT HIS OWN UN-JEDI-LIKE THOUGHTS, AND HALF THE TRUTH. JEISEL WOULD HAVE LOVED THIS WILD, UNSPOILED WORLD.
AND THE SITUATION COULD BE MUCH WORSE. GAME AND FRUIT ARE PLENTIFUL HERE AND, IF THEY USE THE RESOURCES FROM THE SHUTTLE SPARINGLY, THEY SHOULD BE ABLE TO LIVE IN RELATIVE COMFORT FOR YEARS.
MOST IMPORTANTLY, THE YOUNGLINGS ARE HAPPY. HERE THEY CAN GROW UP AS JEDI -- SOMETHING THAT COULD NOT HAPPEN ELSEWHERE...IF THE COMMUNICATIONS HE HAS INTERCEPTED ARE TO BE BELIEVED.
BETTER TO EMBRACE WHAT THEY HAVE THAN TO PINE FOR SOMETHING THAT MAY NEVER BE. OR TO REGRET EVENTS THAT CANNOT BE CHANGED...

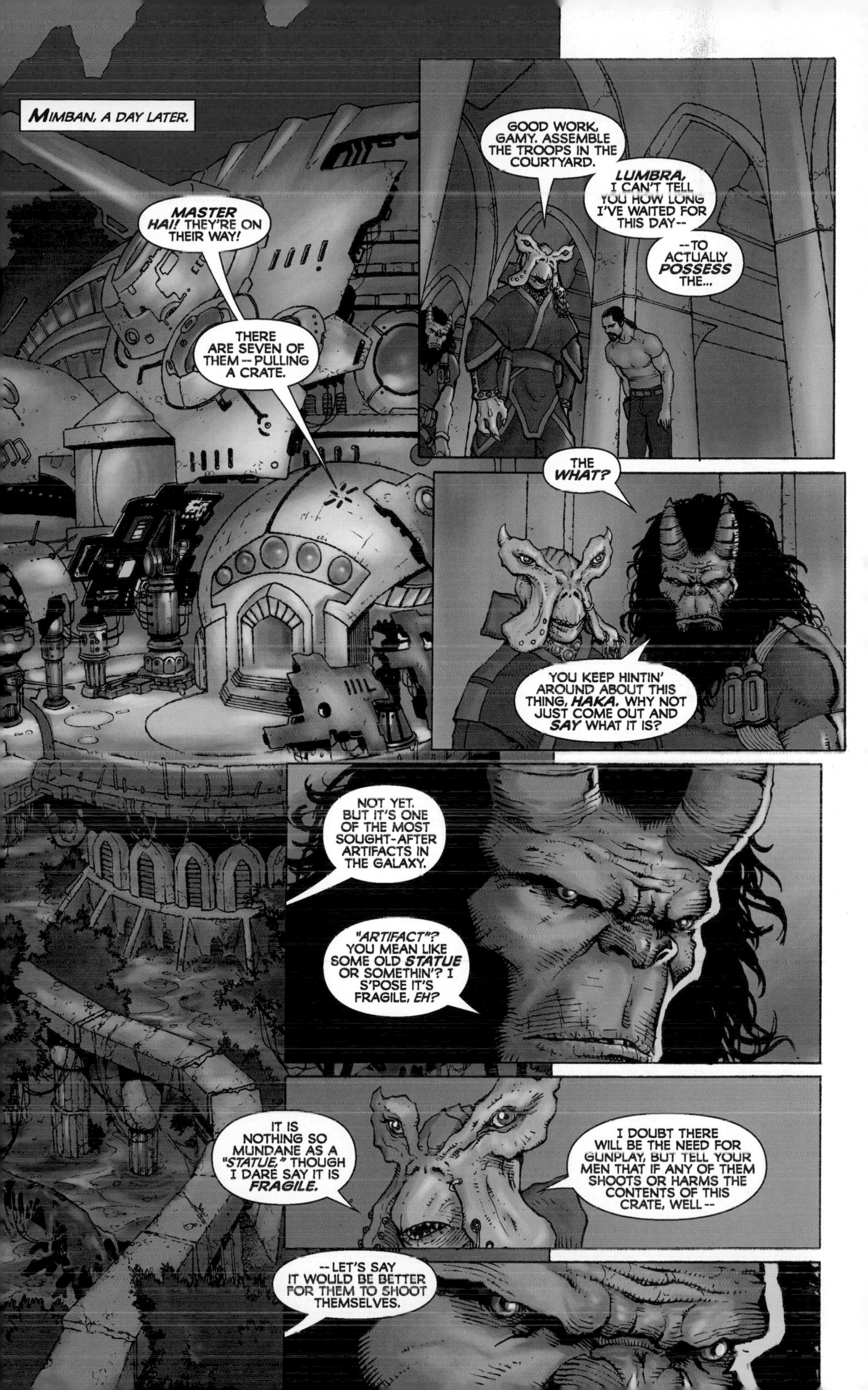
MIMBAN, A DAY LATER.
MASTER HA!! THEY'RE ON THEIR WAY!
THERE ARE SEVEN OF THEM -- PULLING A CRATE.
GOOD WORK, GAMY. ASSEMBLE THE TROOPS IN THE COURTYARD.
LUMBRA, I CAN'T TELL YOU HOW LONG I'VE WAITED FOR THIS DAY--
--TO ACTUALLY POSSESS THE...
THE WHAT?
YOU KEEP HINTIN' AROUND ABOUT THIS THING, HAKA. WHY NOT JUST COME OUT AND SAY WHAT IT IS?
NOT YET. BUT IT'S ONE OF THE MOST SOUGHT-AFTER ARTIFACTS IN THE GALAXY.
"ARTIFACT"? YOU MEAN LIKE SOME OLD STATUE OR SOMETHIN'? I S'POSE IT'S FRAGILE, EH?
IT IS NOTHING SO MUNDANE AS A "STATUE," THOUGH I DARE SAY IT IS FRAGILE.
I DOUBT THERE WILL BE THE NEED FOR GUNPLAY, BUT TELL YOUR MEN THAT IF ANY OF THEM SHOOTS OR HARMS THE CONTENTS OF THIS CRATE, WELL --
-- LET'S SAY IT WOULD BE BETTER FOR THEM TO SHOOT THEMSELVES.

THIS *STINKS!*

IT'S THE SWAMP. DECAYING VEGETATION CREATES --

NO, I MEAN THIS *SITUATION* STINKS.

HEREN, ARE YOU SURE YOU CAN TRUST THIS HAKA HAI GUY?

NO, I AM *NOT*, BOMO. BUT I KNOW HIM OF OLD, IF THAT COUNTS FOR ANYTHING. AND HE IS THE ONLY BUYER I COULD CONTACT WHO AGREED TO THE PRICE--

-- WHO *DOESN'T* HAVE IMPERIAL CONNECTIONS.

LET US HOPE FOR THE BEST...AND BE READY FOR ANYTHING.

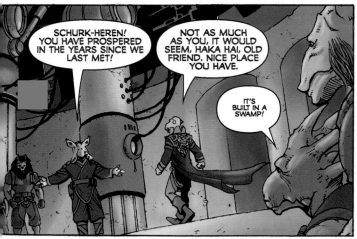

SCHURK-HEREN! YOU HAVE PROSPERED IN THE YEARS SINCE WE LAST MET!

NOT AS MUCH AS YOU, IT WOULD SEEM, HAKA HAI, OLD FRIEND. NICE PLACE YOU HAVE.

IT'S BUILT IN A SWAMP!

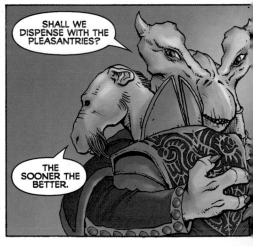

SHALL WE DISPENSE WITH THE PLEASANTRIES?

THE SOONER THE BETTER.

CLAP!

THE PAYMENT YOU REQUESTED.

YOU WON'T OBJECT IF I WISH TO EXAMINE THE CONTENTS?

-SIGH- I EXPECTED THAT YOU WOULD WANT TO.

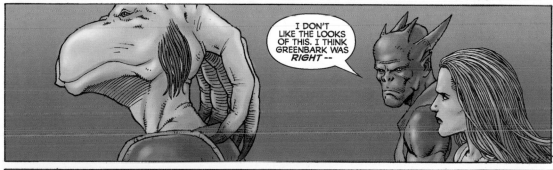

I DON'T LIKE THE LOOKS OF THIS. I THINK GREENBARK WAS *RIGHT* --

--THIS STINKS.

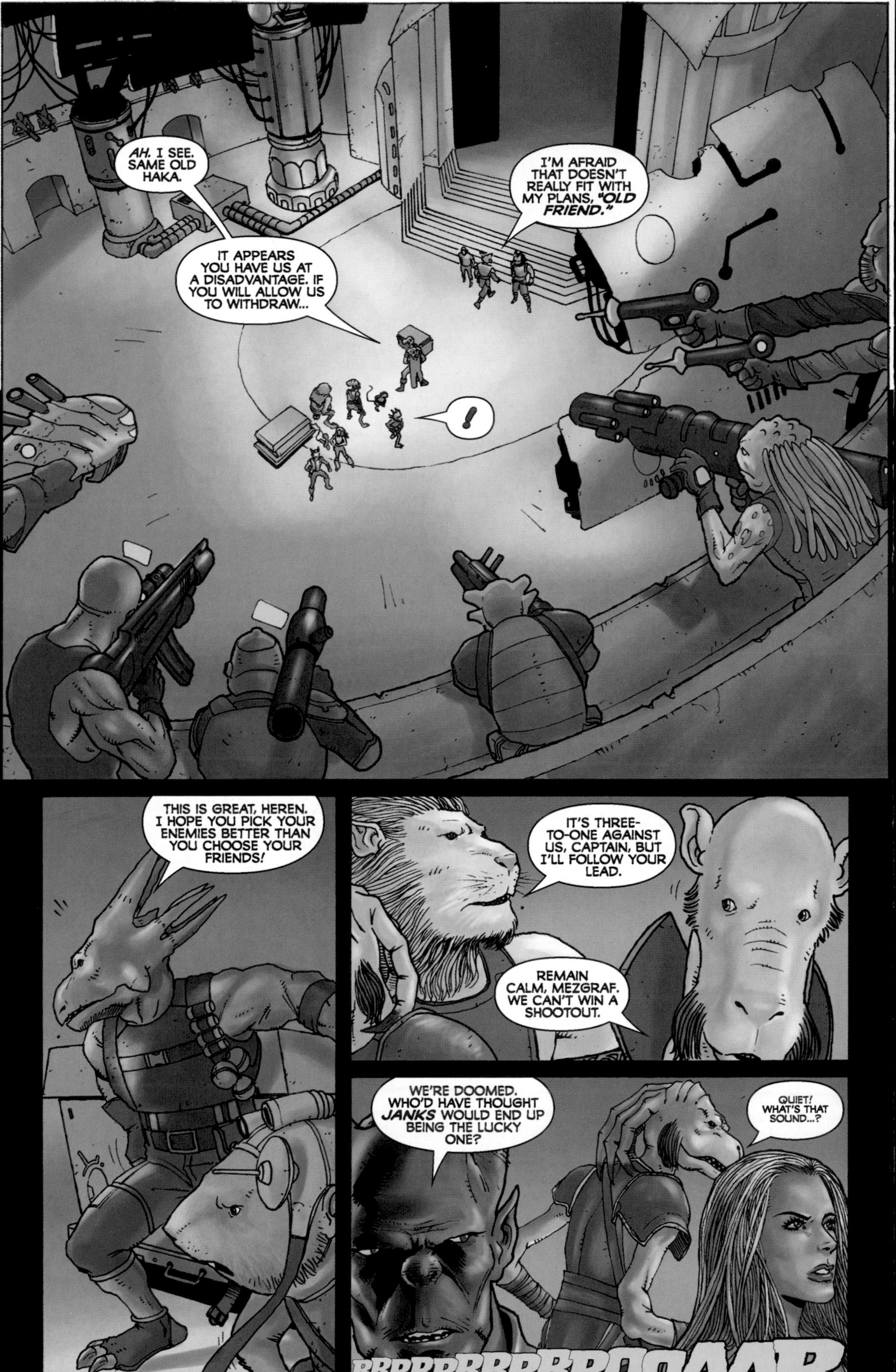
AH. I SEE. SAME OLD HAKA.
IT APPEARS YOU HAVE US AT A DISADVANTAGE. IF YOU WILL ALLOW US TO WITHDRAW...
I'M AFRAID THAT DOESN'T REALLY FIT WITH MY PLANS, "OLD FRIEND."
!
THIS IS GREAT, HEREN. I HOPE YOU PICK YOUR ENEMIES BETTER THAN YOU CHOOSE YOUR FRIENDS!
IT'S THREE-TO-ONE AGAINST US, CAPTAIN, BUT I'LL FOLLOW YOUR LEAD.
REMAIN CALM, MEZGRAF. WE CAN'T WIN A SHOOTOUT.
WE'RE DOOMED. WHO'D HAVE THOUGHT JANKS WOULD END UP BEING THE LUCKY ONE?
QUIET! WHAT'S THAT SOUND...?
RRRRRRRRRRRROOAAR

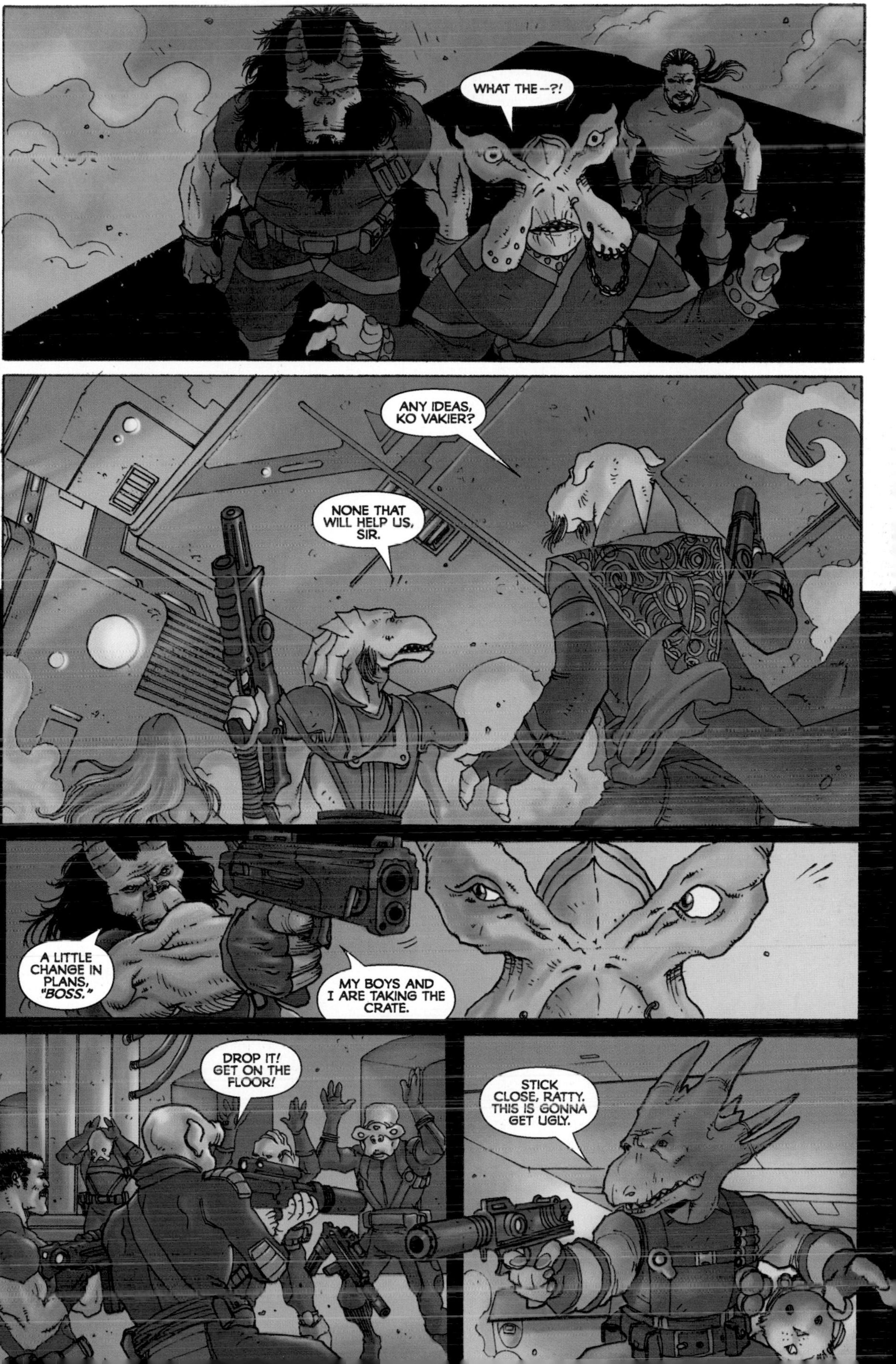
WHAT THE--?!
ANY IDEAS, KO VAKIER?
NONE THAT WILL HELP US, SIR.
A LITTLE CHANGE IN PLANS, "BOSS."
MY BOYS AND I ARE TAKING THE CRATE.
DROP IT! GET ON THE FLOOR!
STICK CLOSE, RATTY. THIS IS GONNA GET UGLY.

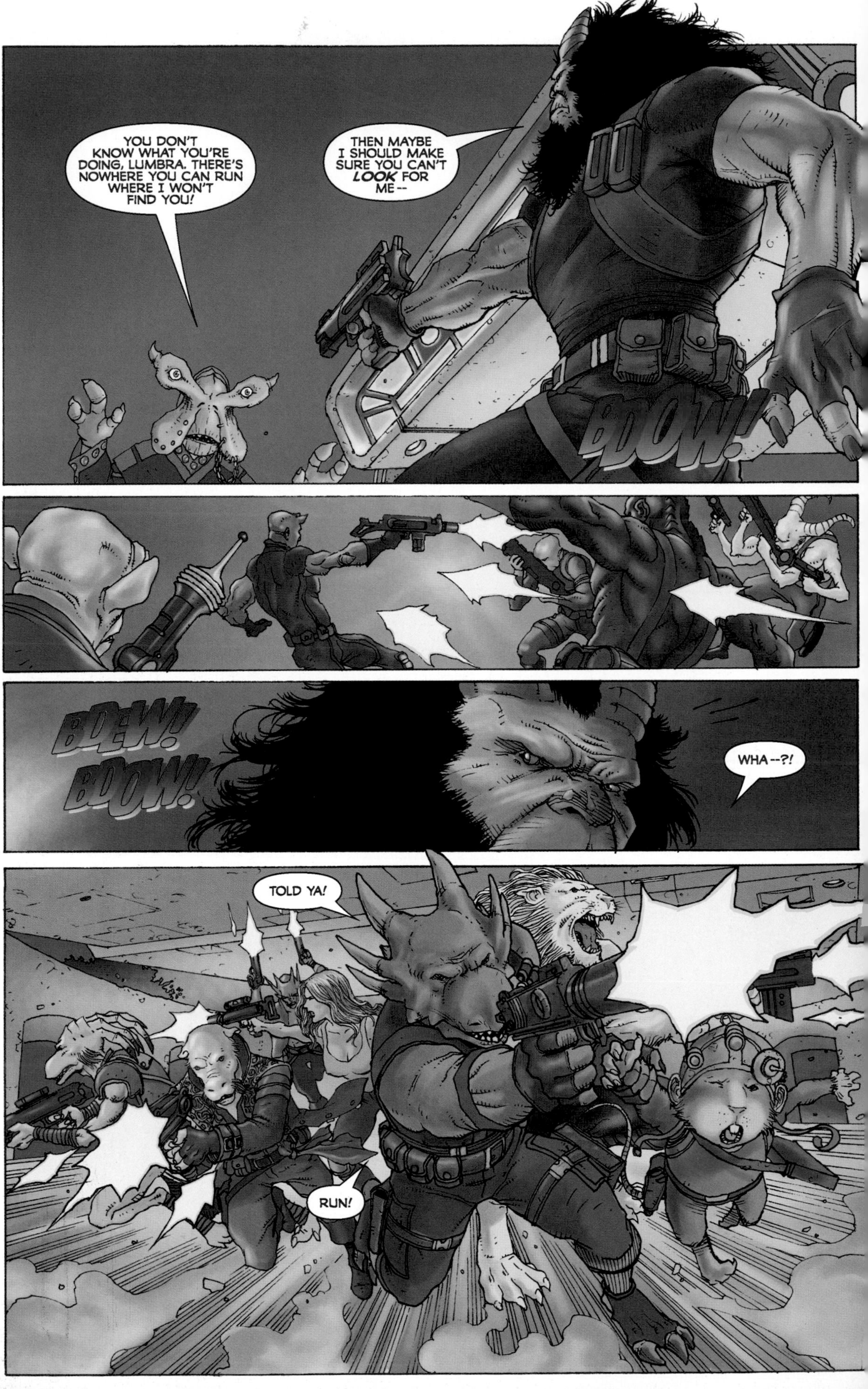
YOU DON'T KNOW WHAT YOU'RE DOING, LUMBRA. THERE'S NOWHERE YOU CAN RUN WHERE I WON'T FIND YOU!
THEN MAYBE I SHOULD MAKE SURE YOU CAN'T *LOOK* FOR ME--
BDOW!
BDEW! BDOW!
WHA--?!
TOLD YA!
RUN!

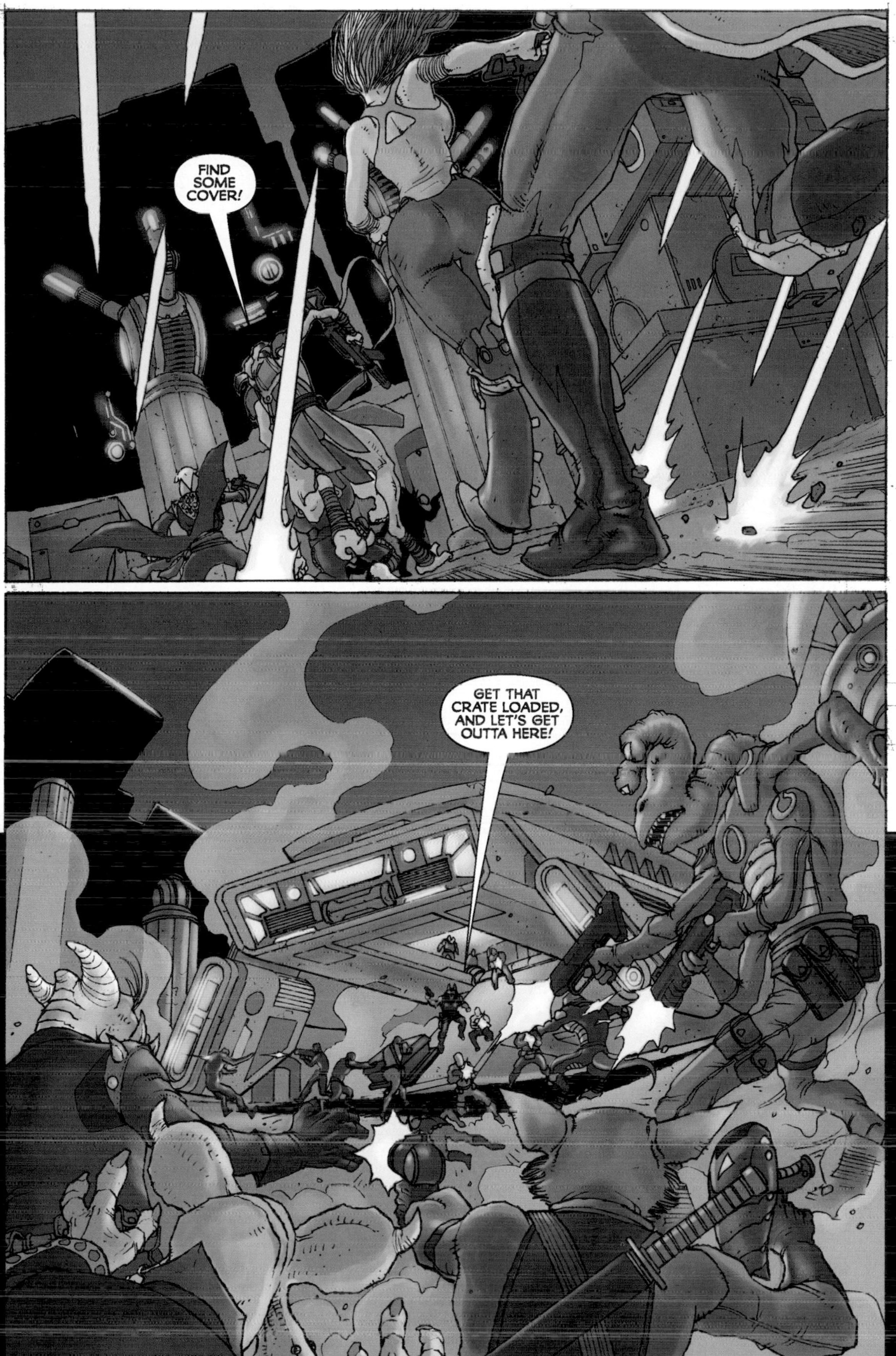
FIND SOME COVER!
GET THAT CRATE LOADED, AND LET'S GET OUTTA HERE!

CRYS! SNIFFLES! *RUN!*

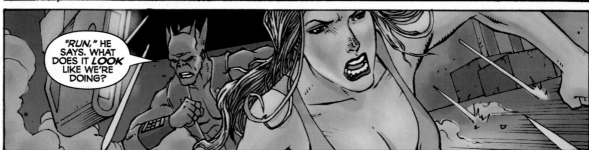

"RUN," HE SAYS. WHAT DOES IT *LOOK* LIKE WE'RE DOING?

WHA --?!

BDOW!

CRYS! GET DOWN!

SNIFFLES!

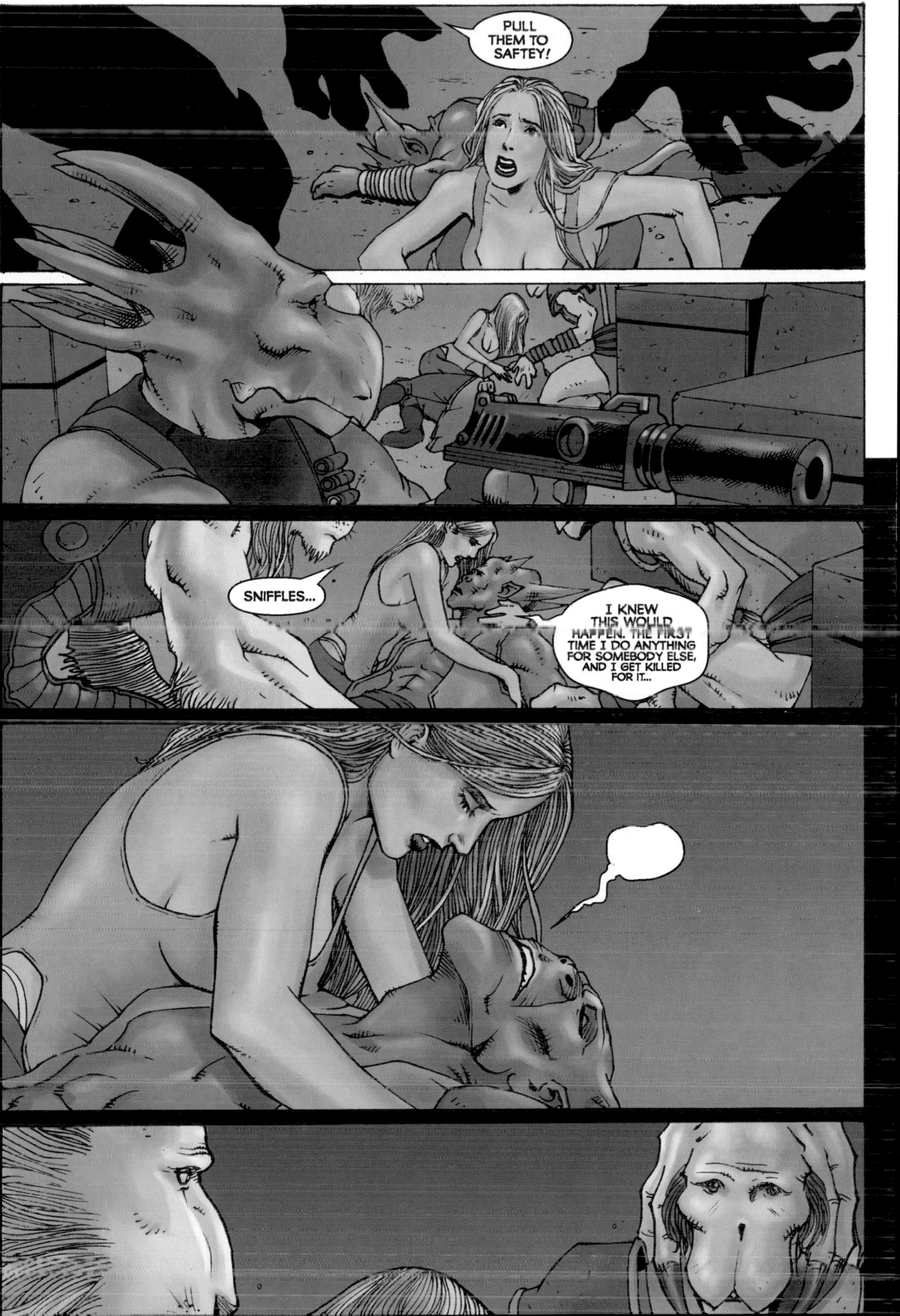
PULL THEM TO SAFTEY!
SNIFFLES...
I KNEW THIS WOULD HAPPEN. THE FIRST TIME I DO ANYTHING FOR SOMEBODY ELSE, AND I GET KILLED FOR IT...

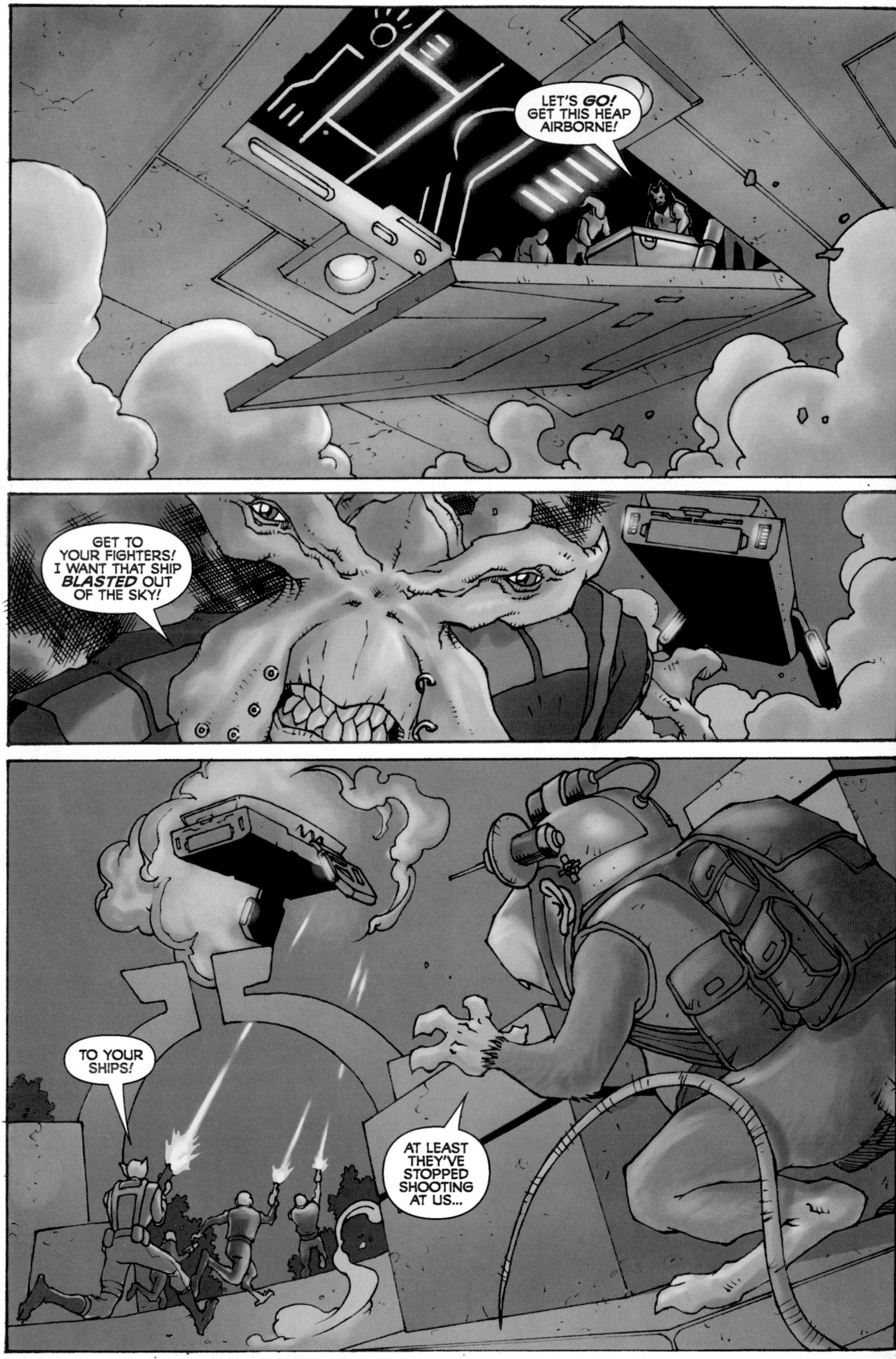
LET'S GO! GET THIS HEAP AIRBORNE!
GET TO YOUR FIGHTERS! I WANT THAT SHIP BLASTED OUT OF THE SKY!
TO YOUR SHIPS!
AT LEAST THEY'VE STOPPED SHOOTING AT US...

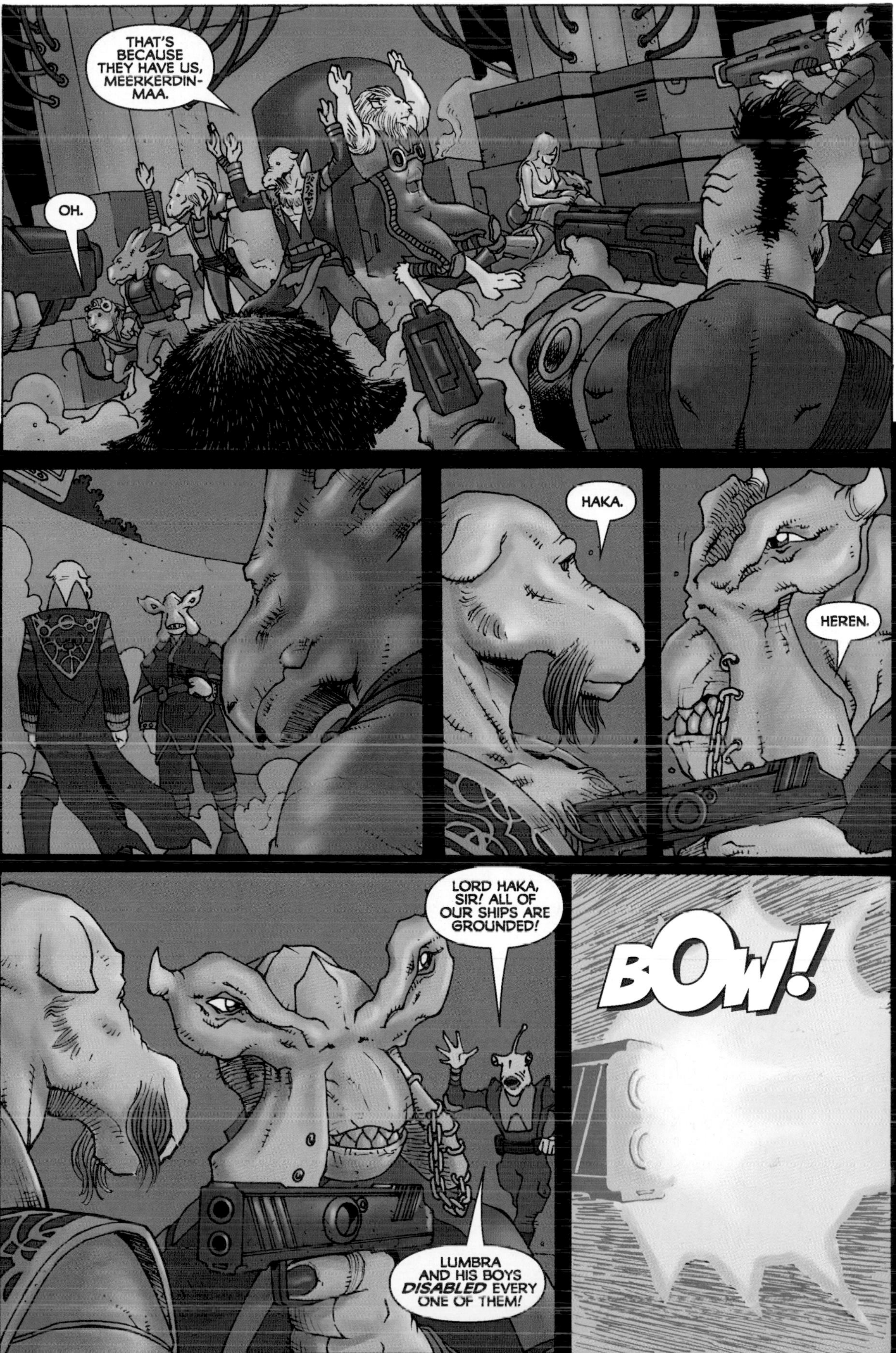
THAT'S BECAUSE THEY HAVE US, MEERKERDIN-MAA.
OH.
HAKA.
HEREN.
LORD HAKA, SIR! ALL OF OUR SHIPS ARE GROUNDED!
LUMBRA AND HIS BOYS DISABLED EVERY ONE OF THEM!
BOW!

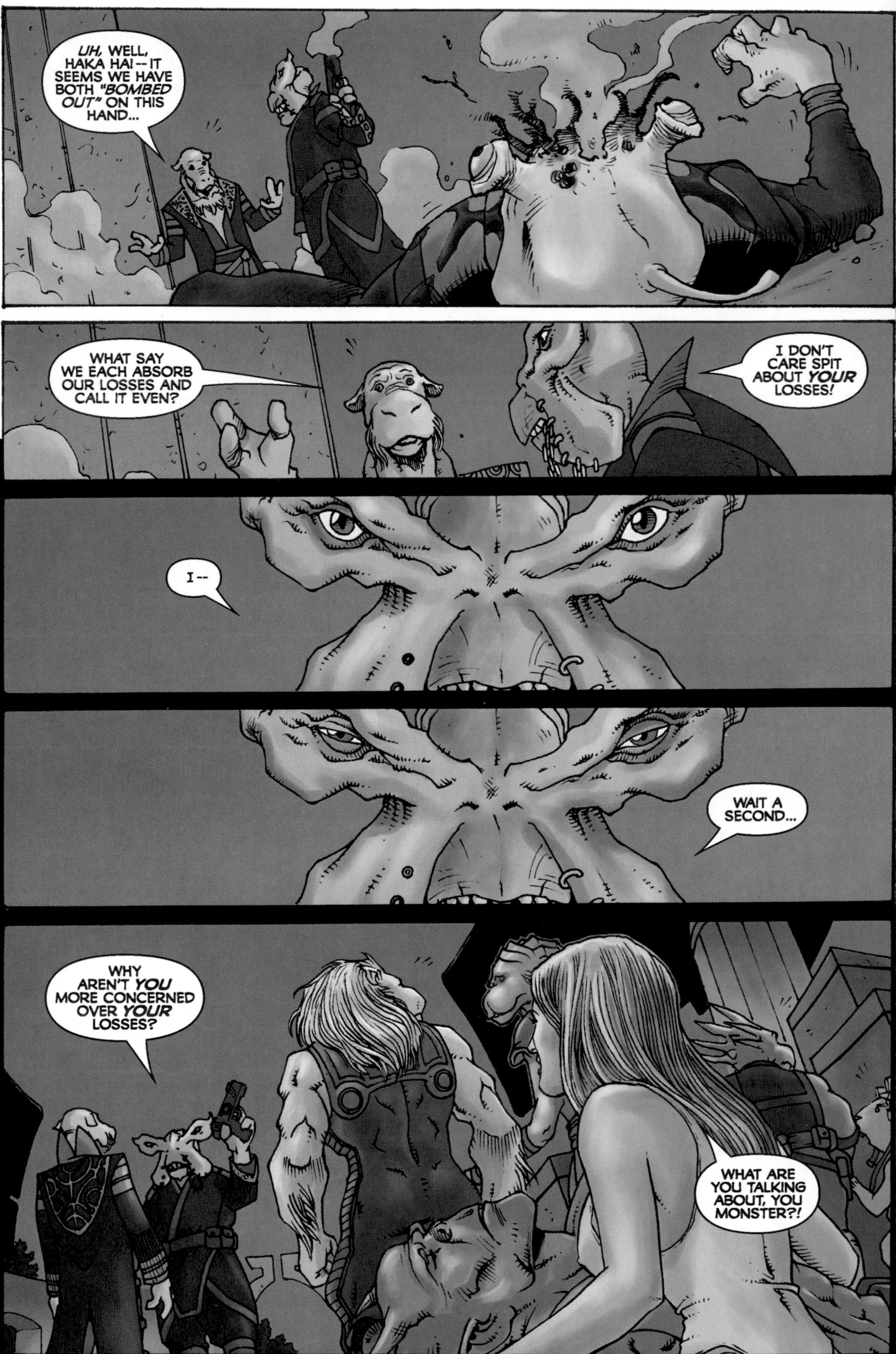

UH, WELL, HAKA HAI -- IT SEEMS WE HAVE BOTH "BOMBED OUT" ON THIS HAND...
WHAT SAY WE EACH ABSORB OUR LOSSES AND CALL IT EVEN?
I DON'T CARE SPIT ABOUT YOUR LOSSES!
I --
WAIT A SECOND...
WHY AREN'T YOU MORE CONCERNED OVER YOUR LOSSES?
WHAT ARE YOU TALKING ABOUT, YOU MONSTER?!

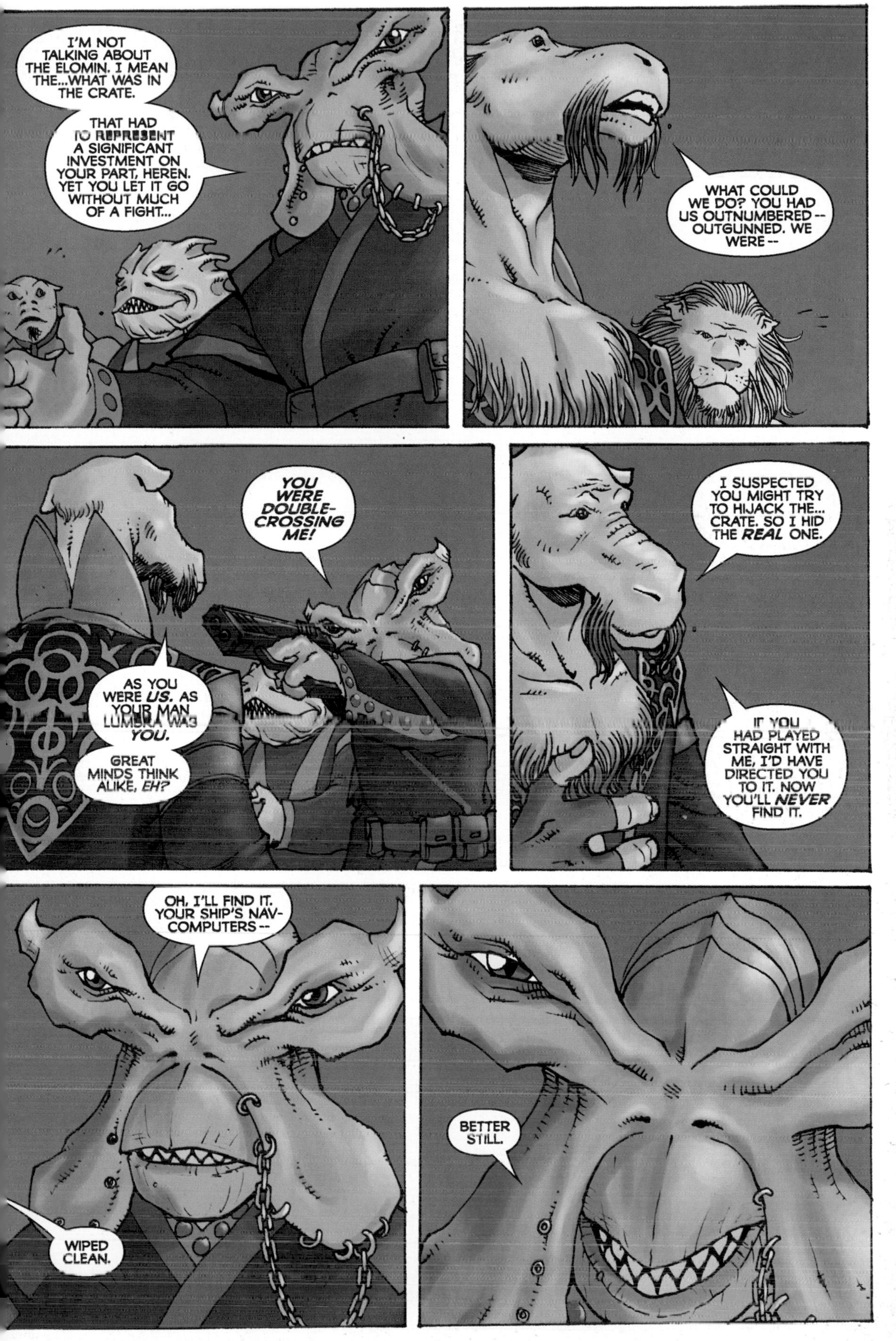
I'M NOT TALKING ABOUT THE ELOMIN. I MEAN THE...WHAT WAS IN THE CRATE.
THAT HAD TO REPRESENT A SIGNIFICANT INVESTMENT ON YOUR PART, HEREN. YET YOU LET IT GO WITHOUT MUCH OF A FIGHT...
WHAT COULD WE DO? YOU HAD US OUTNUMBERED -- OUTGUNNED. WE WERE --
YOU WERE DOUBLE-CROSSING ME!
AS YOU WERE US. AS YOUR MAN LUMBRA WAS YOU.
GREAT MINDS THINK ALIKE, EH?
I SUSPECTED YOU MIGHT TRY TO HIJACK THE... CRATE. SO I HID THE REAL ONE.
IF YOU HAD PLAYED STRAIGHT WITH ME, I'D HAVE DIRECTED YOU TO IT. NOW YOU'LL NEVER FIND IT.
OH, I'LL FIND IT. YOUR SHIP'S NAV-COMPUTERS --
WIPED CLEAN.
BETTER STILL.

HAH! I'VE BEEN WORKED OVER BY THE SLAVERS OF ORVAX. YOU WON'T BREAK *ME!*

NOR *ME!*

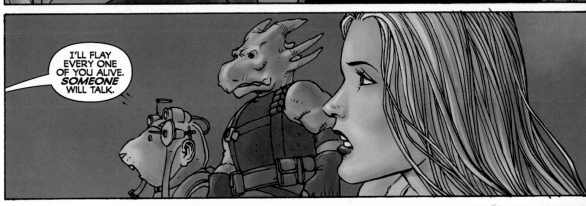

I'LL FLAY EVERY ONE OF YOU ALIVE. *SOMEONE* WILL TALK.

THEY ALWAYS DO --

ONLY *FOUR* OF US -- ME, MEZGRAF, KO VAKIER AND THE CAPTAIN -- KNOW WHERE THE *REAL* CRATE IS HIDDEN.

AND WE'VE SWORN TO TAKE THE COORDINATES TO OUR GRAVES.

WE'LL SEE --

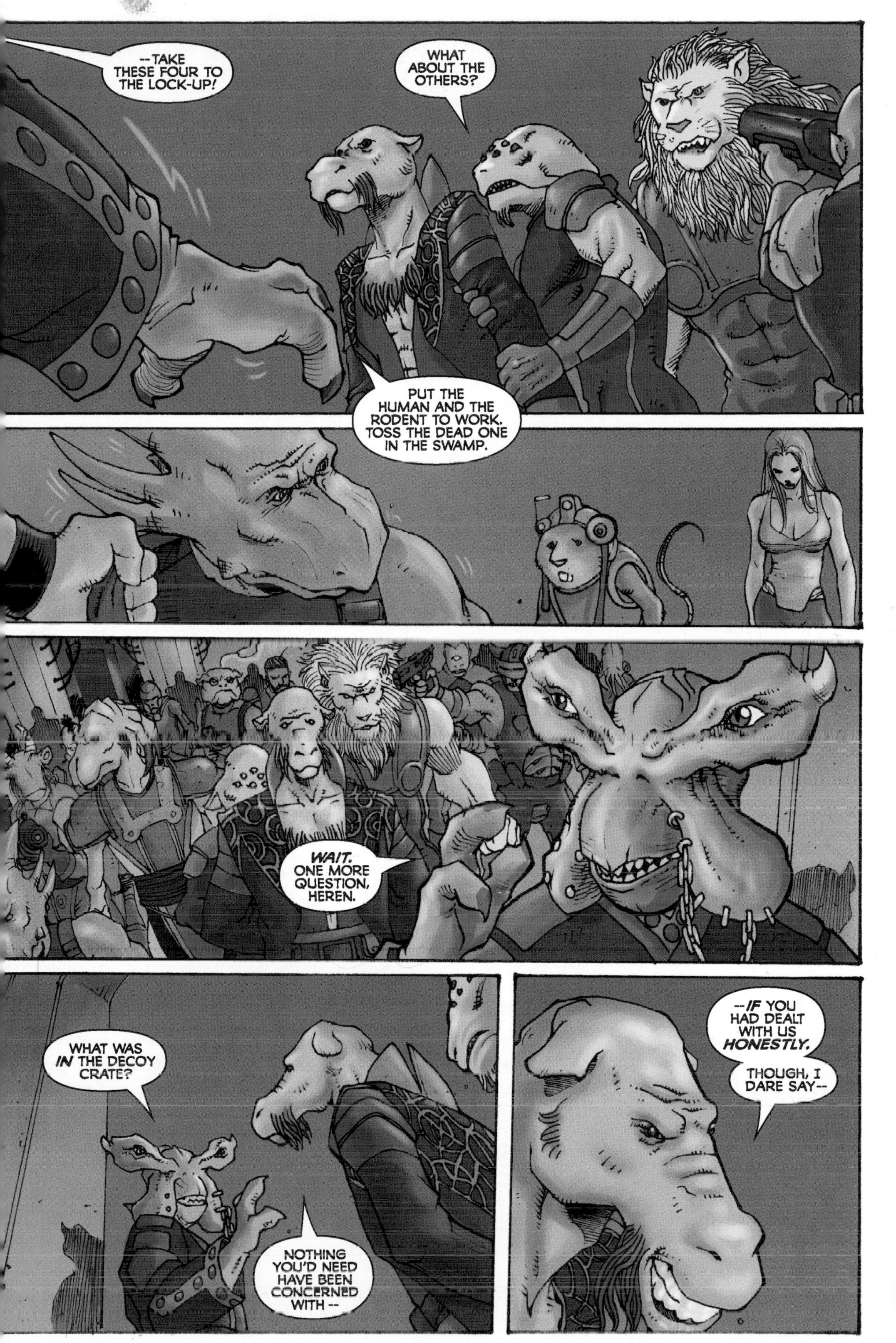
--TAKE THESE FOUR TO THE LOCK-UP!
WHAT ABOUT THE OTHERS?
PUT THE HUMAN AND THE RODENT TO WORK. TOSS THE DEAD ONE IN THE SWAMP.
WAIT. ONE MORE QUESTION, HEREN.
WHAT WAS *IN* THE DECOY CRATE?
NOTHING YOU'D NEED HAVE BEEN CONCERNED WITH --
--*IF* YOU HAD DEALT WITH US *HONESTLY.*
THOUGH, I DARE SAY--

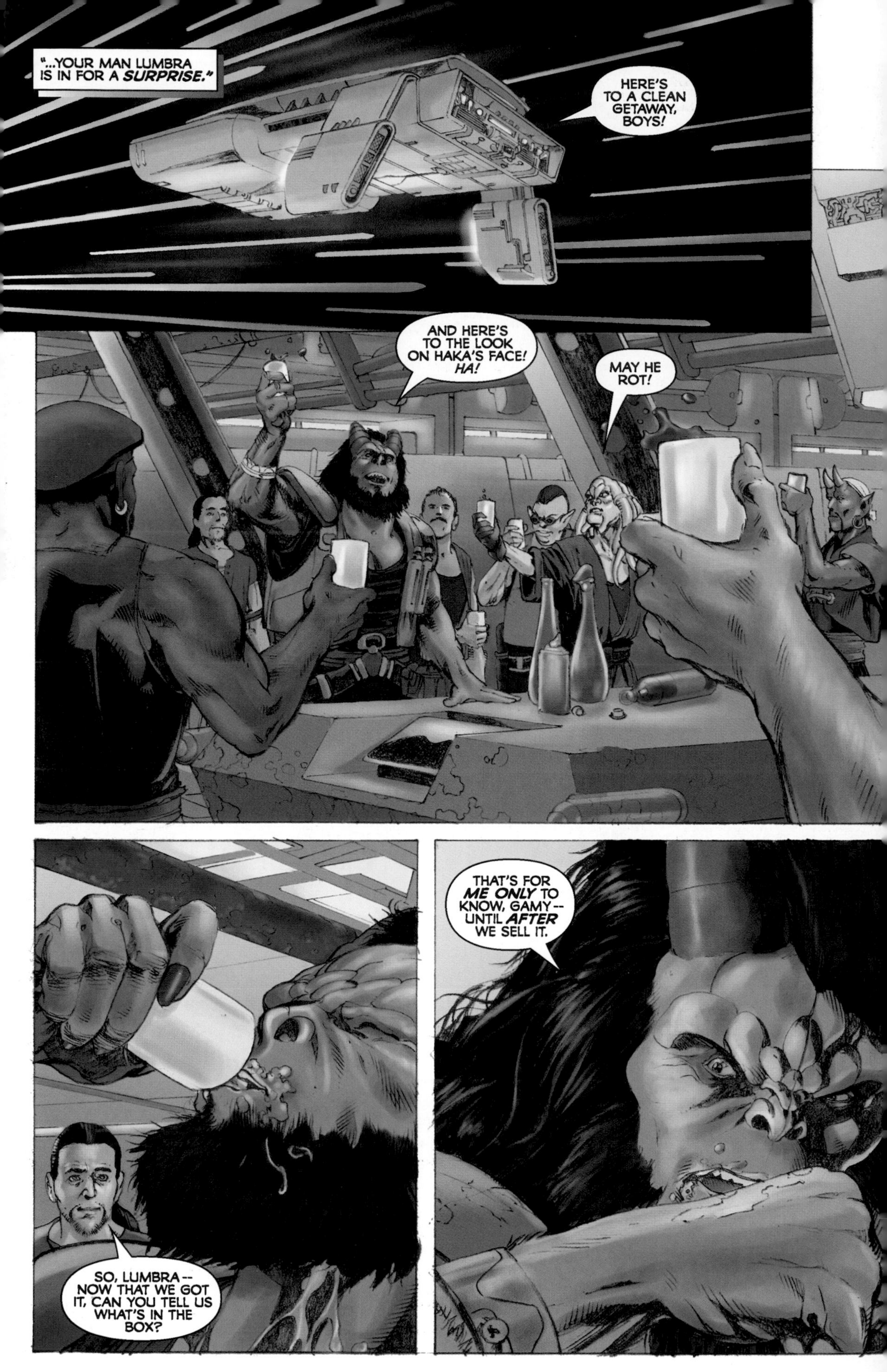
"...YOUR MAN LUMBRA IS IN FOR A SURPRISE."
HERE'S TO A CLEAN GETAWAY, BOYS!
AND HERE'S TO THE LOOK ON HAKA'S FACE! HA!
MAY HE ROT!
SO, LUMBRA -- NOW THAT WE GOT IT, CAN YOU TELL US WHAT'S IN THE BOX?
THAT'S FOR ME ONLY TO KNOW, GAMY -- UNTIL AFTER WE SELL IT.

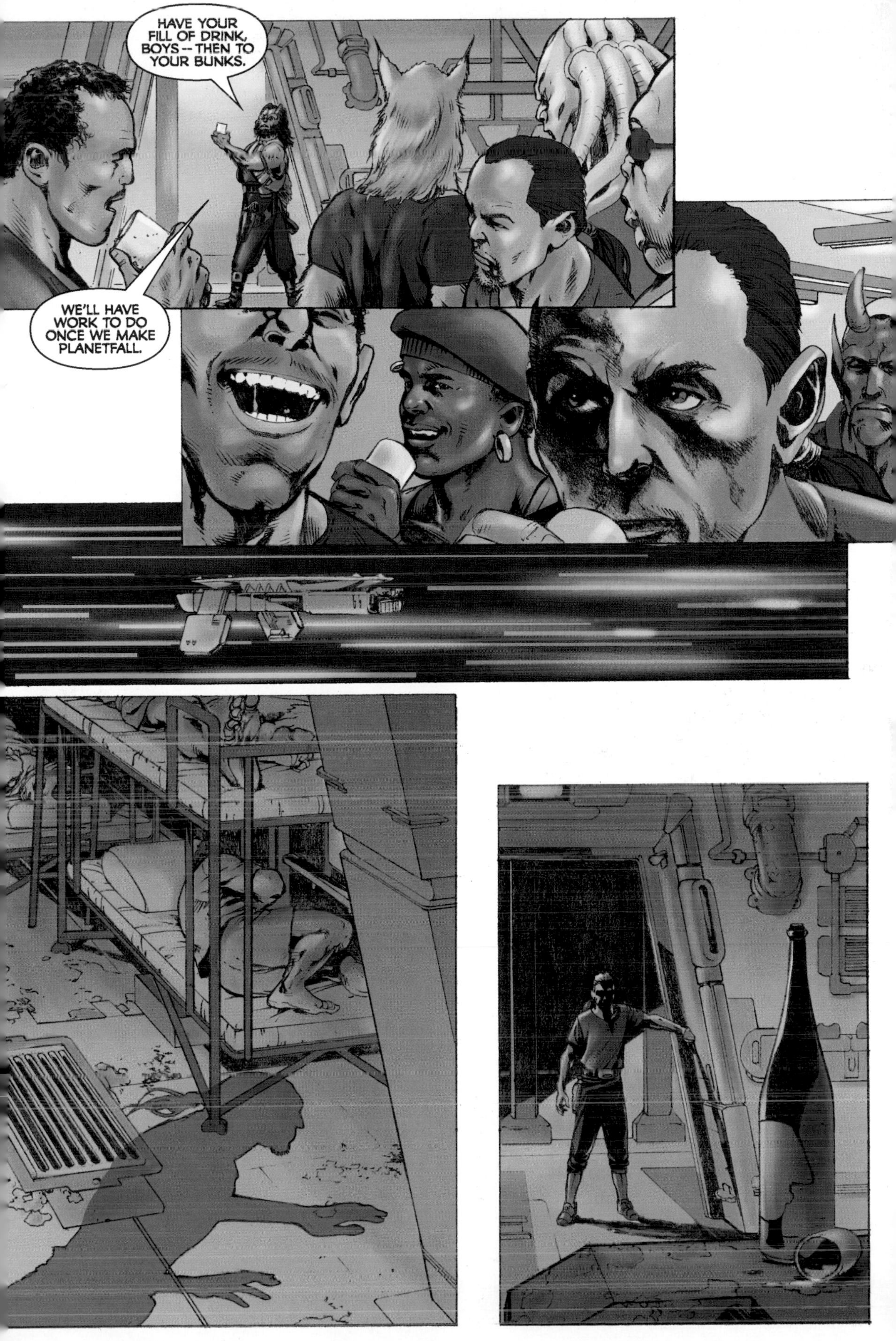
HAVE YOUR FILL OF DRINK, BOYS -- THEN TO YOUR BUNKS.
WE'LL HAVE WORK TO DO ONCE WE MAKE PLANETFALL.

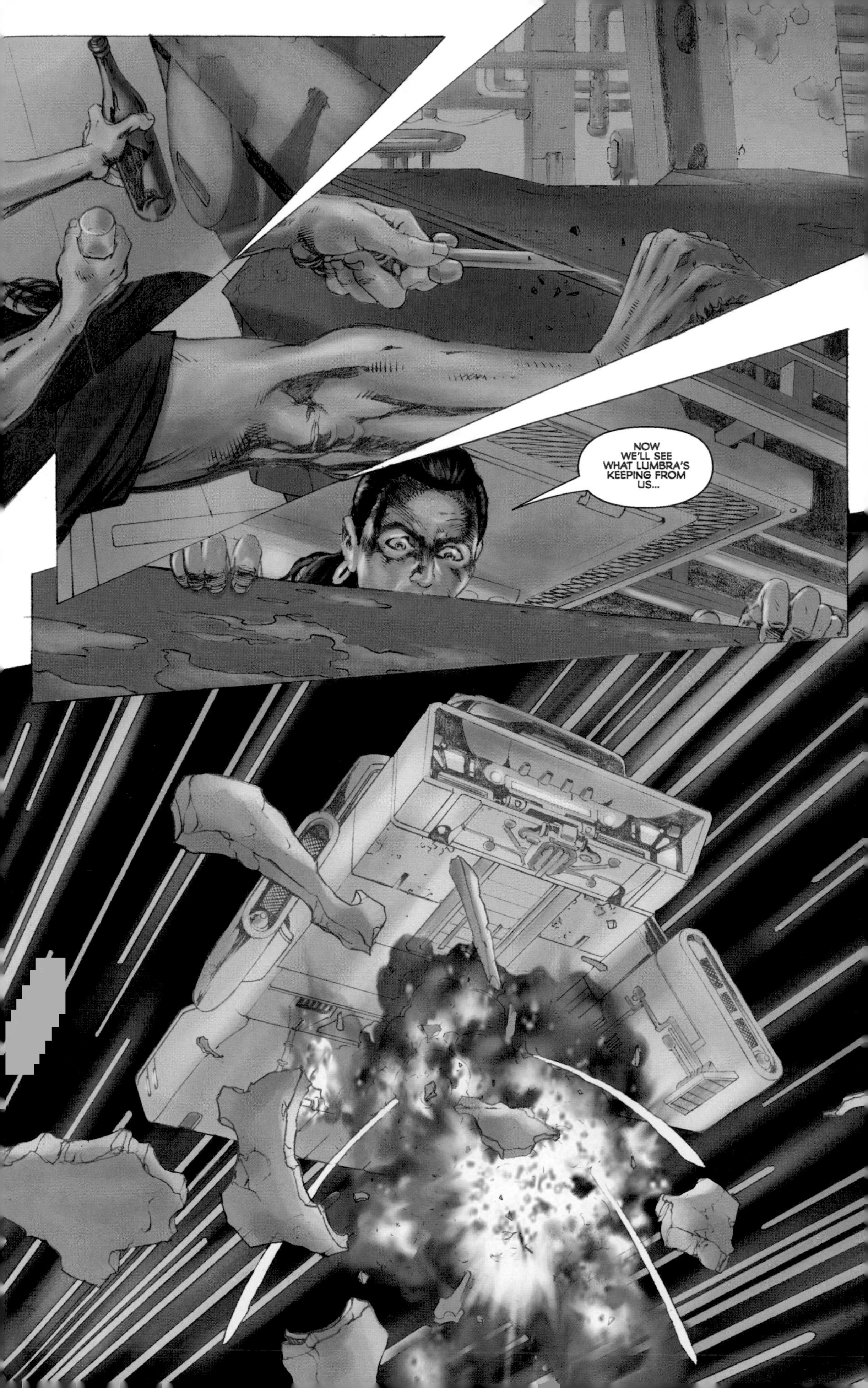
NOW WE'LL SEE WHAT LUMBRA'S KEEPING FROM US...

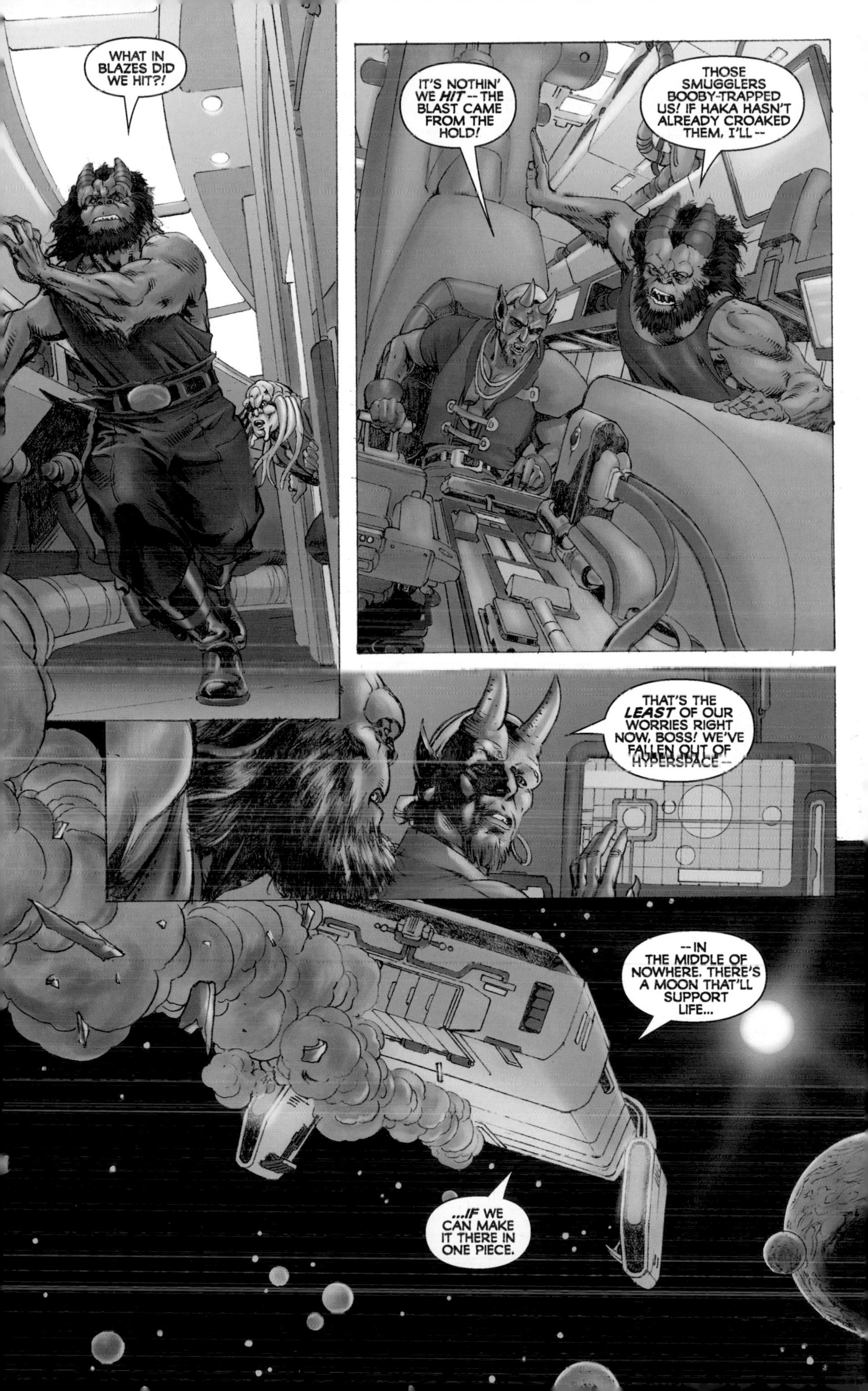
WHAT IN BLAZES DID WE HIT?!
IT'S NOTHIN' WE HIT -- THE BLAST CAME FROM THE HOLD!
THOSE SMUGGLERS BOOBY-TRAPPED US! IF HAKA HASN'T ALREADY CROAKED THEM, I'LL --
THAT'S THE LEAST OF OUR WORRIES RIGHT NOW, BOSS! WE'VE FALLEN OUT OF HYPERSPACE --
-- IN THE MIDDLE OF NOWHERE. THERE'S A MOON THAT'LL SUPPORT LIFE...
...IF WE CAN MAKE IT THERE IN ONE PIECE.

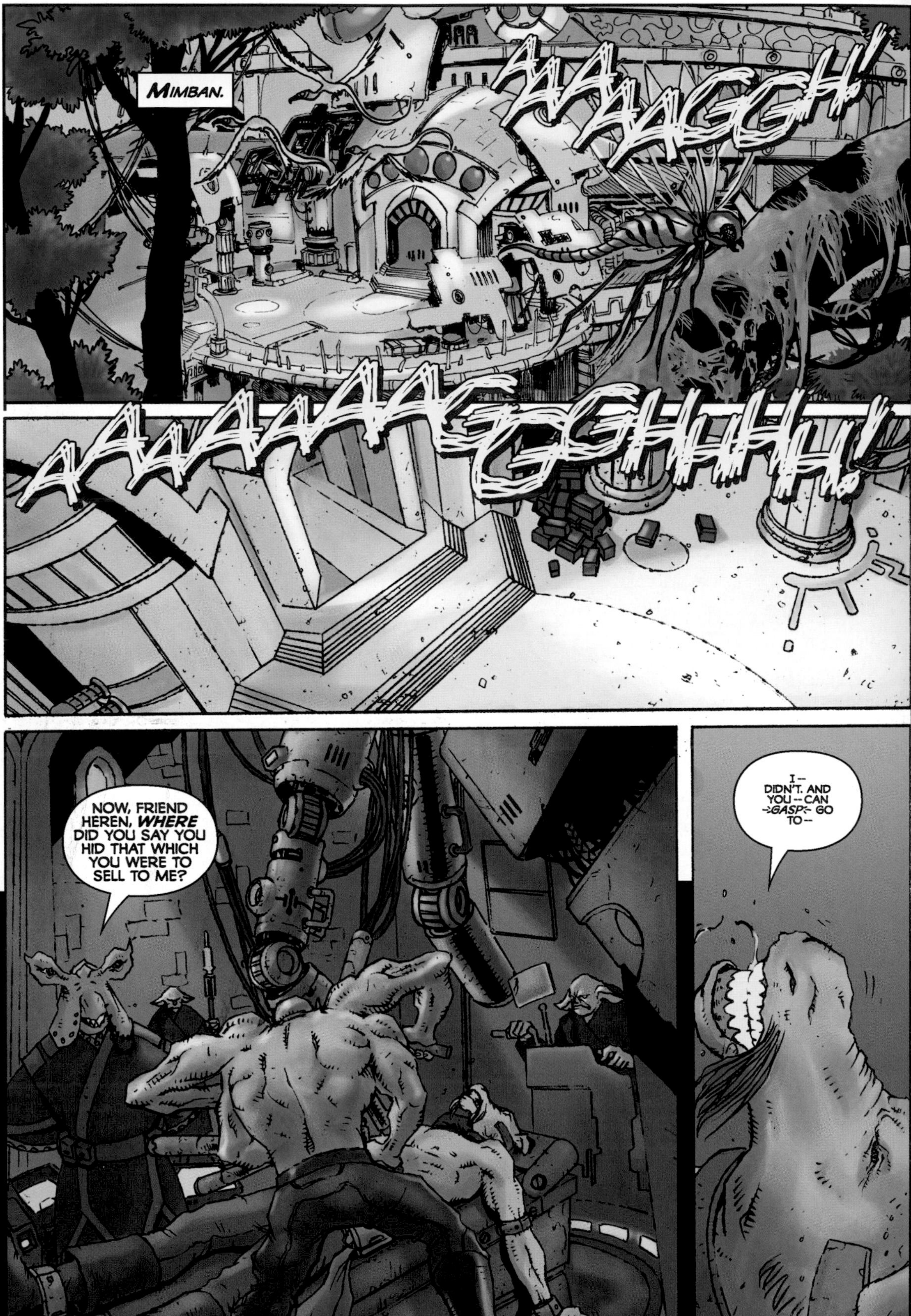
MIMBAN.
AAAAGGGH!
AAAAAAAGGGHHHHH!
NOW, FRIEND HEREN, WHERE DID YOU SAY YOU HID THAT WHICH YOU WERE TO SELL TO ME?
I -- DIDN'T. AND YOU -- CAN -GASP- GO TO --

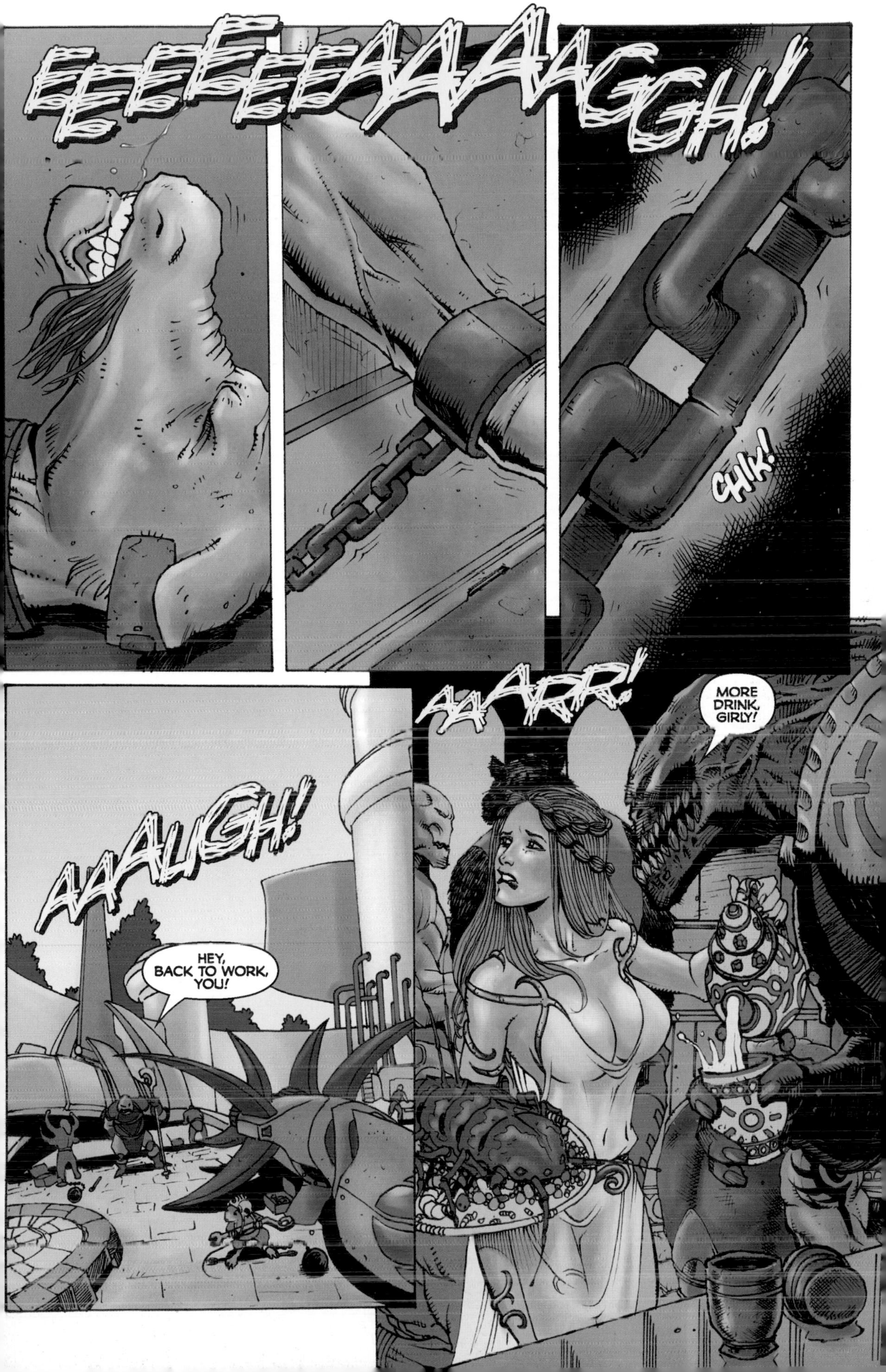
EEEEEEEAAAAAGGH!
CHIK!
AAARR!
MORE DRINK, GIRLY!
AAAUGH!
HEY, BACK TO WORK, YOU!

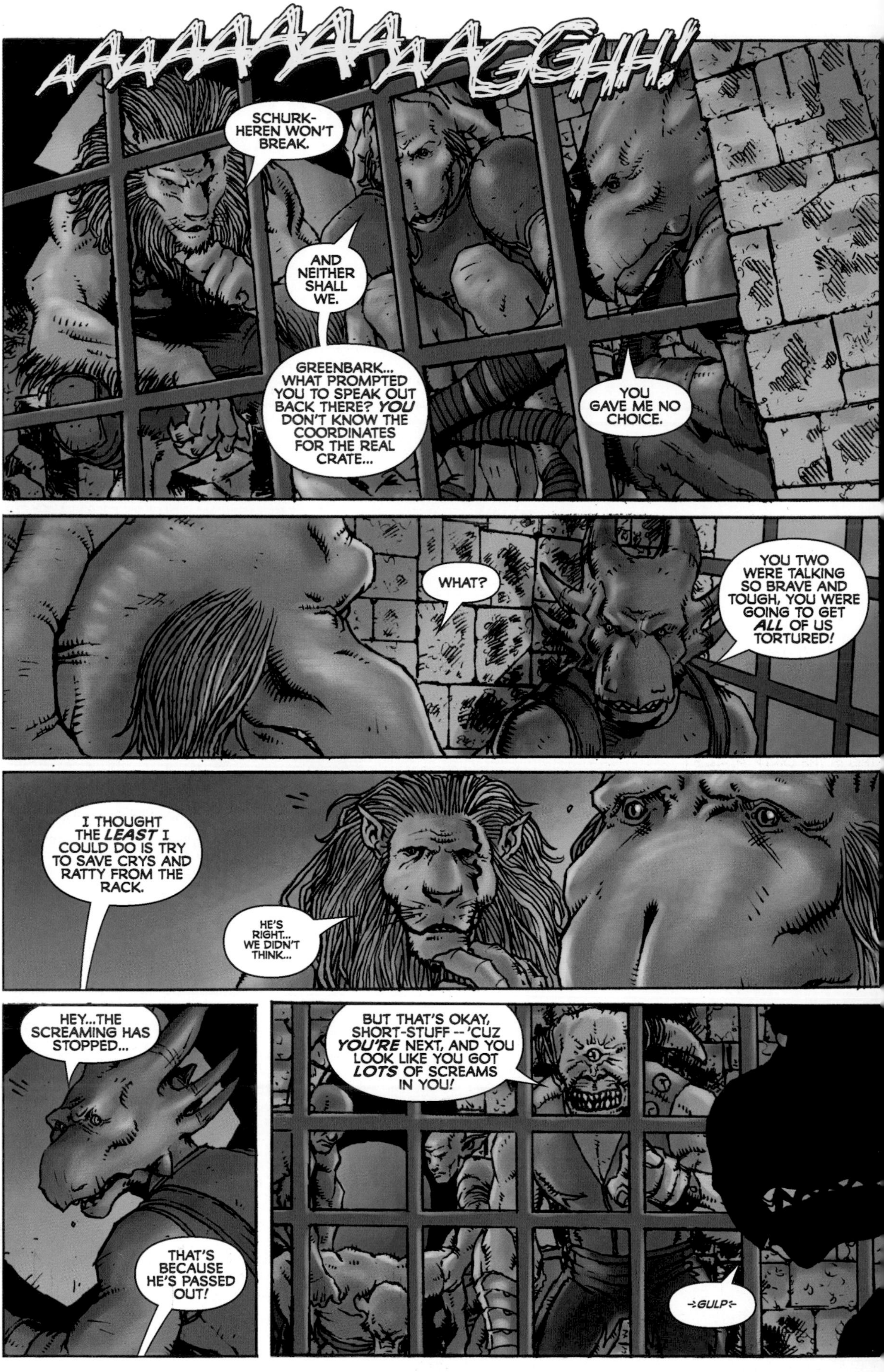
AAAAAAAAAAGGHH!
SCHURK-HEREN WON'T BREAK.
AND NEITHER SHALL WE.
GREENBARK... WHAT PROMPTED YOU TO SPEAK OUT BACK THERE? *YOU* DON'T KNOW THE COORDINATES FOR THE REAL CRATE...
YOU GAVE ME NO CHOICE.
WHAT?
YOU TWO WERE TALKING SO BRAVE AND TOUGH, YOU WERE GOING TO GET *ALL* OF US TORTURED!
I THOUGHT THE *LEAST* I COULD DO IS TRY TO SAVE CRYS AND RATTY FROM THE RACK.
HE'S RIGHT... WE DIDN'T THINK...
HEY...THE SCREAMING HAS STOPPED...
THAT'S BECAUSE HE'S PASSED OUT!
BUT THAT'S OKAY, SHORT-STUFF -- 'CUZ *YOU'RE* NEXT, AND YOU LOOK LIKE YOU GOT *LOTS* OF SCREAMS IN YOU!
GULP

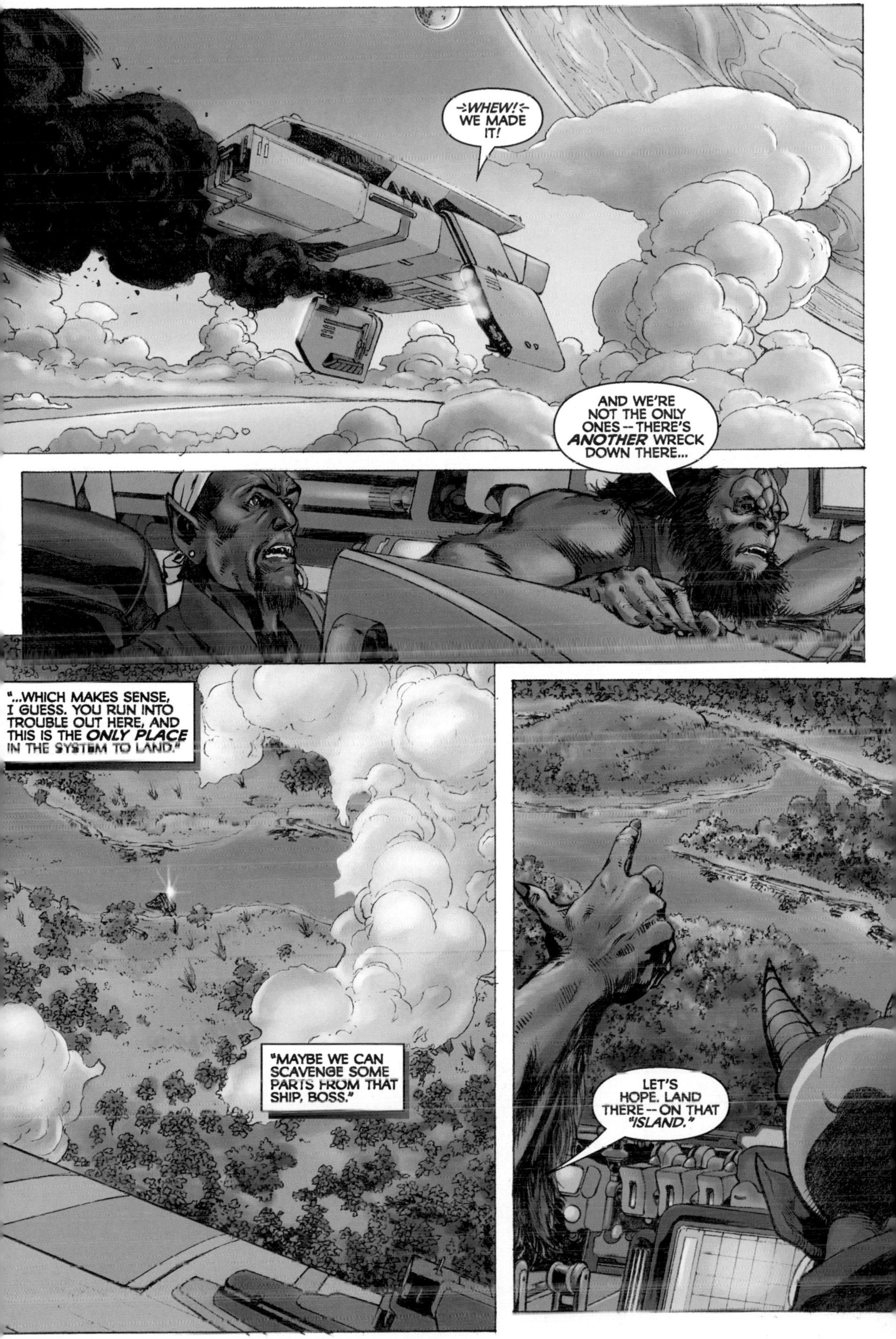

WHEW! WE MADE IT!
AND WE'RE NOT THE ONLY ONES -- THERE'S ANOTHER WRECK DOWN THERE...
"...WHICH MAKES SENSE, I GUESS. YOU RUN INTO TROUBLE OUT HERE, AND THIS IS THE ONLY PLACE IN THE SYSTEM TO LAND."
"MAYBE WE CAN SCAVENGE SOME PARTS FROM THAT SHIP, BOSS."
LET'S HOPE. LAND THERE -- ON THAT "ISLAND."

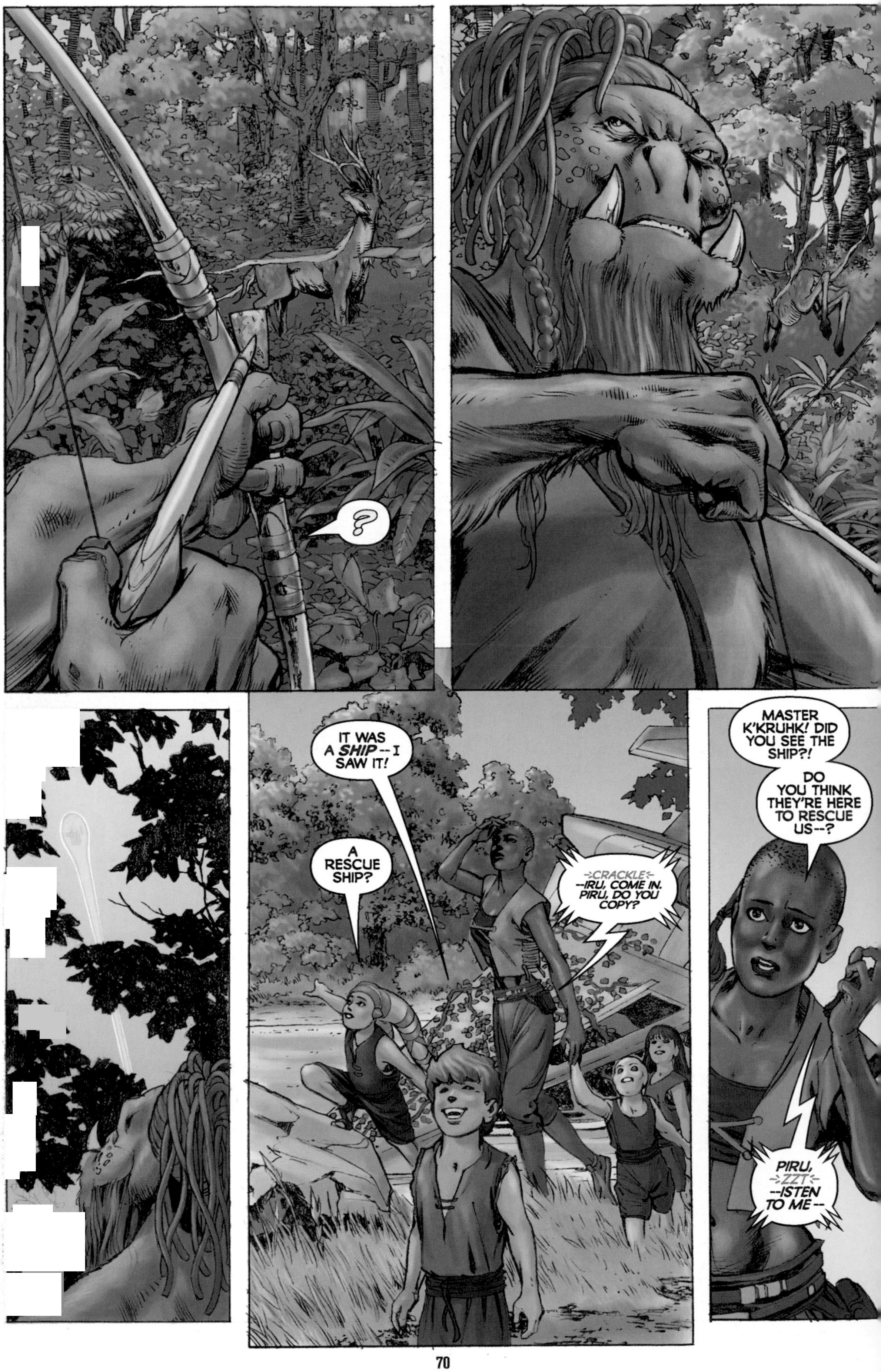
?
IT WAS A SHIP -- I SAW IT!
A RESCUE SHIP?
-CRACKLE- --IRU, COME IN. PIRU, DO YOU COPY?
MASTER K'KRUHK! DID YOU SEE THE SHIP?!
DO YOU THINK THEY'RE HERE TO RESCUE US--?
PIRU, -ZZT- --ISTEN TO ME--

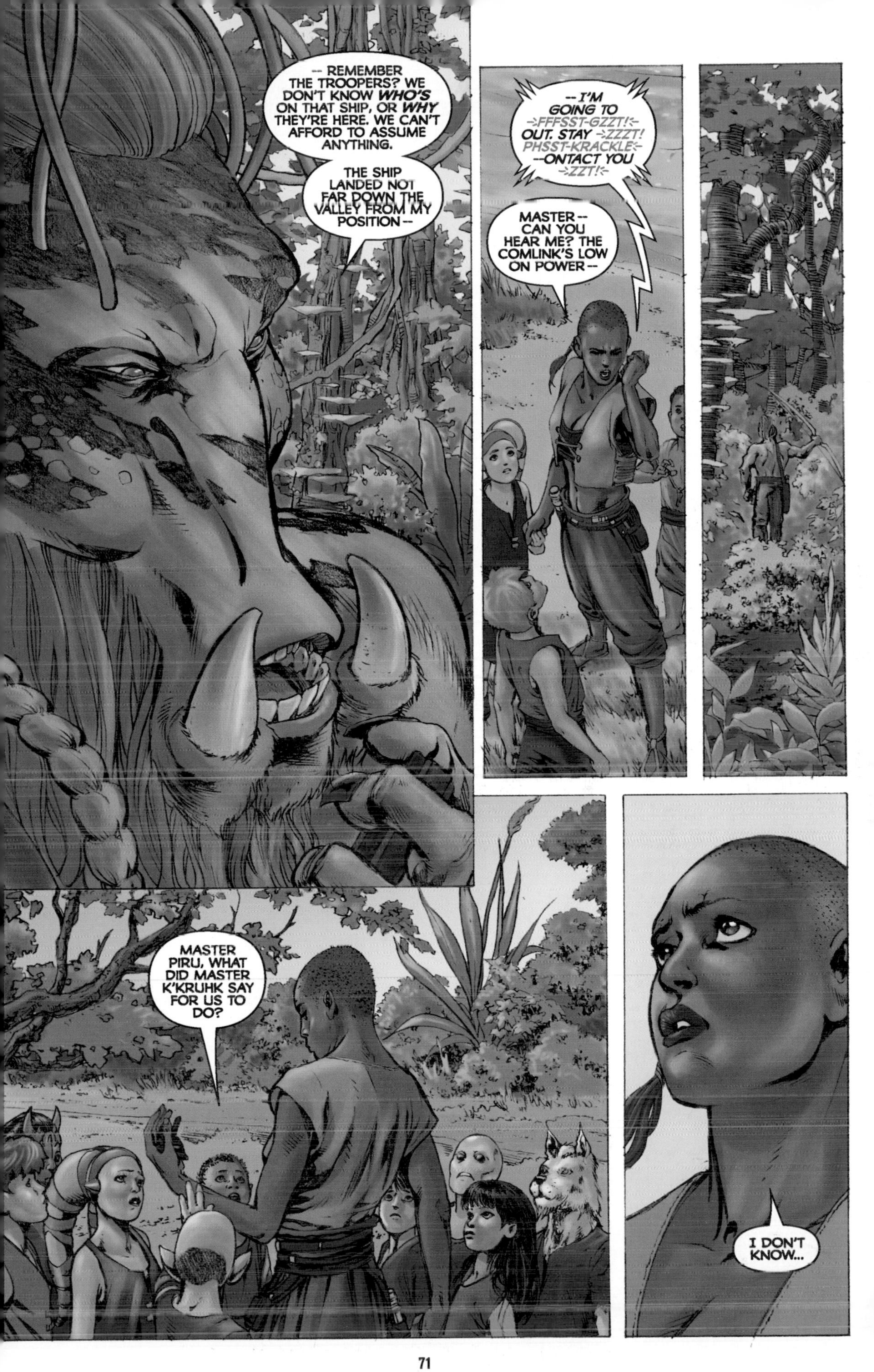
-- REMEMBER THE TROOPERS? WE DON'T KNOW WHO'S ON THAT SHIP, OR WHY THEY'RE HERE. WE CAN'T AFFORD TO ASSUME ANYTHING.
THE SHIP LANDED NOT FAR DOWN THE VALLEY FROM MY POSITION --
-- I'M GOING TO ~FFFSST-GZZT!~ OUT. STAY ~ZZZT! PHSST-KRACKLE~ --ONTACT YOU ~ZZT!~
MASTER -- CAN YOU HEAR ME? THE COMLINK'S LOW ON POWER --
MASTER PIRU, WHAT DID MASTER K'KRUHK SAY FOR US TO DO?
I DON'T KNOW...

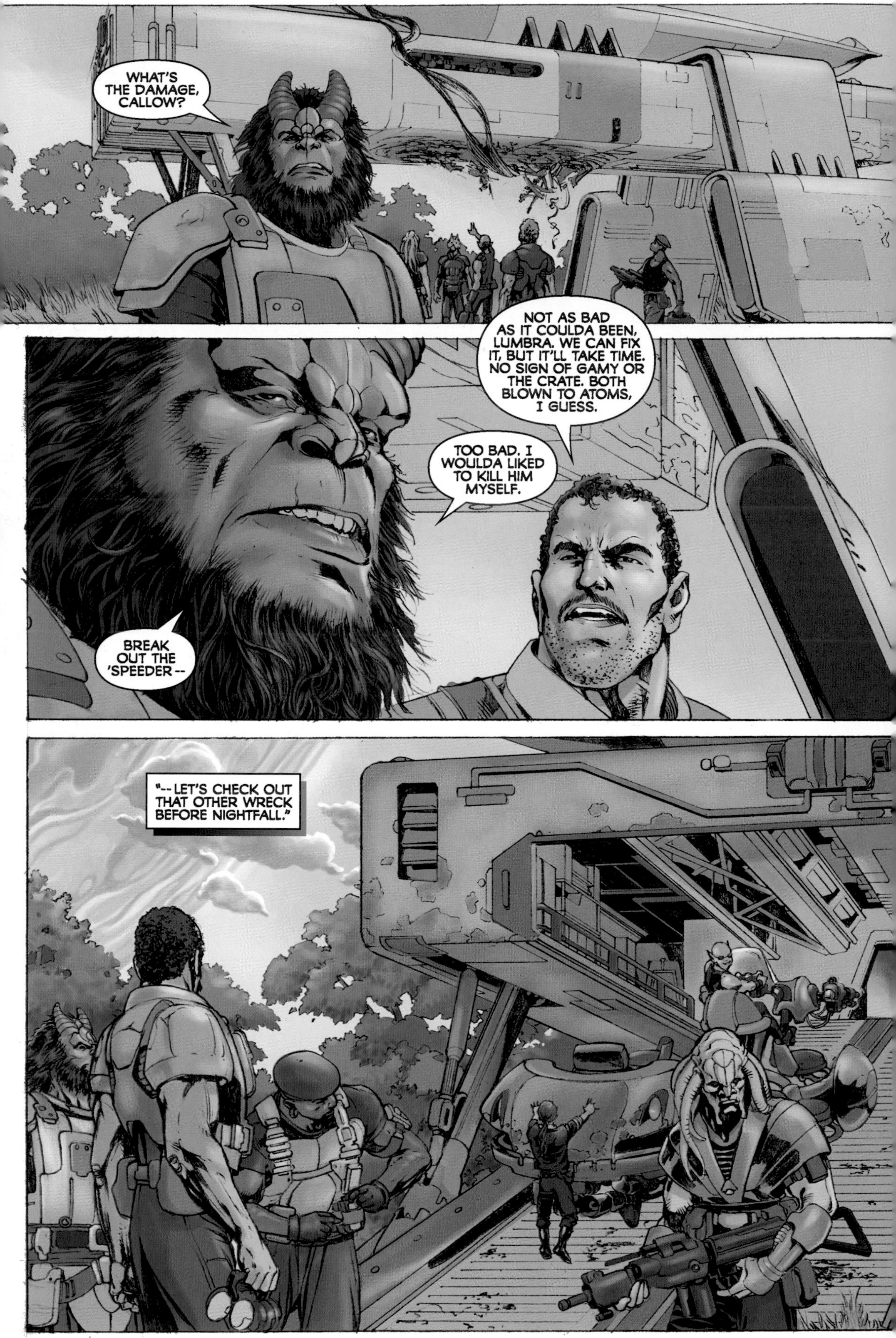
WHAT'S THE DAMAGE, CALLOW?
NOT AS BAD AS IT COULDA BEEN, LUMBRA. WE CAN FIX IT, BUT IT'LL TAKE TIME. NO SIGN OF GAMY OR THE CRATE. BOTH BLOWN TO ATOMS, I GUESS.
TOO BAD. I WOULDA LIKED TO KILL HIM MYSELF.
BREAK OUT THE 'SPEEDER --
"-- LET'S CHECK OUT THAT OTHER WRECK BEFORE NIGHTFALL."

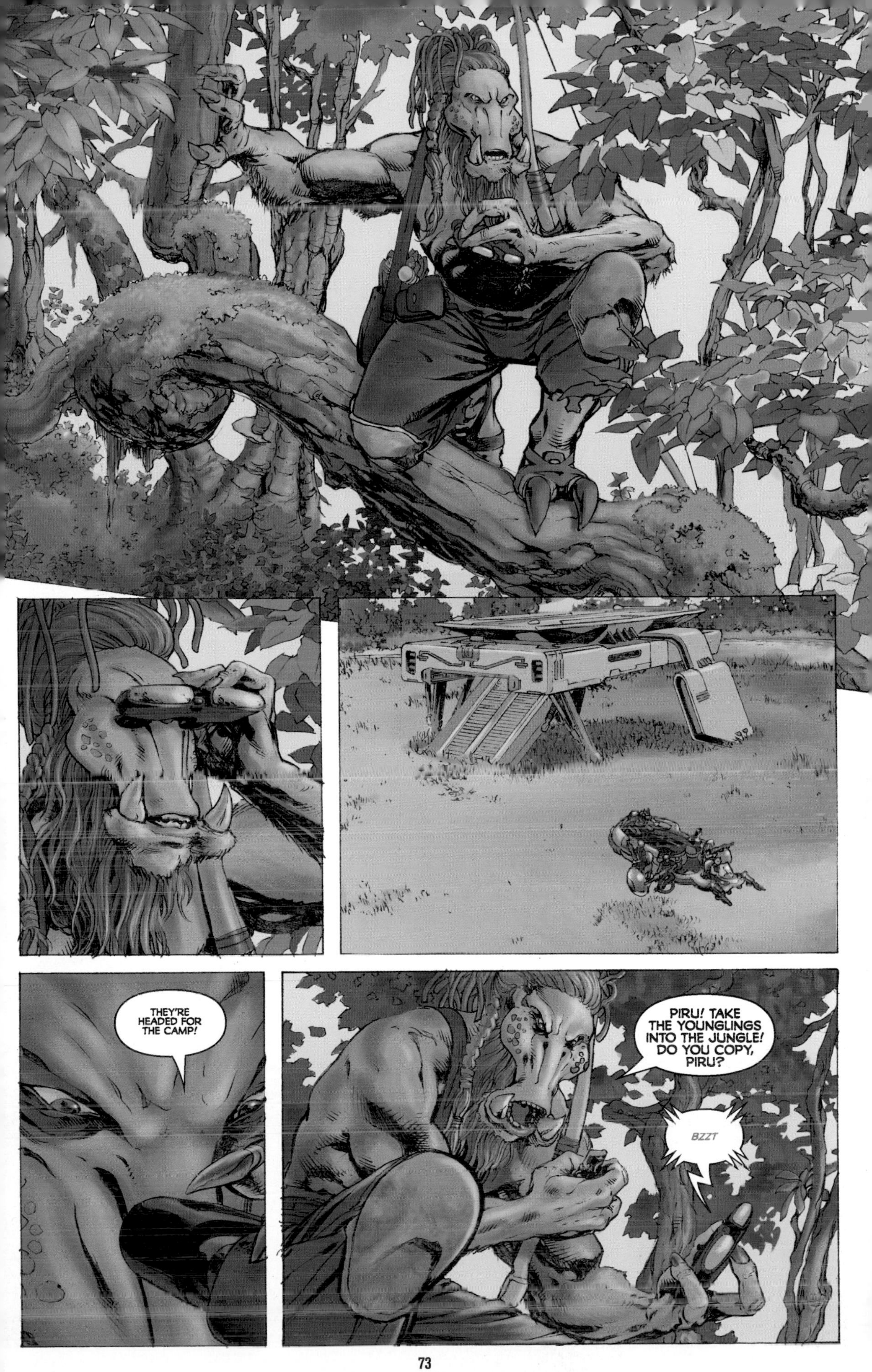
THEY'RE HEADED FOR THE CAMP!
PIRU! TAKE THE YOUNGLINGS INTO THE JUNGLE! DO YOU COPY, PIRU?
BZZT

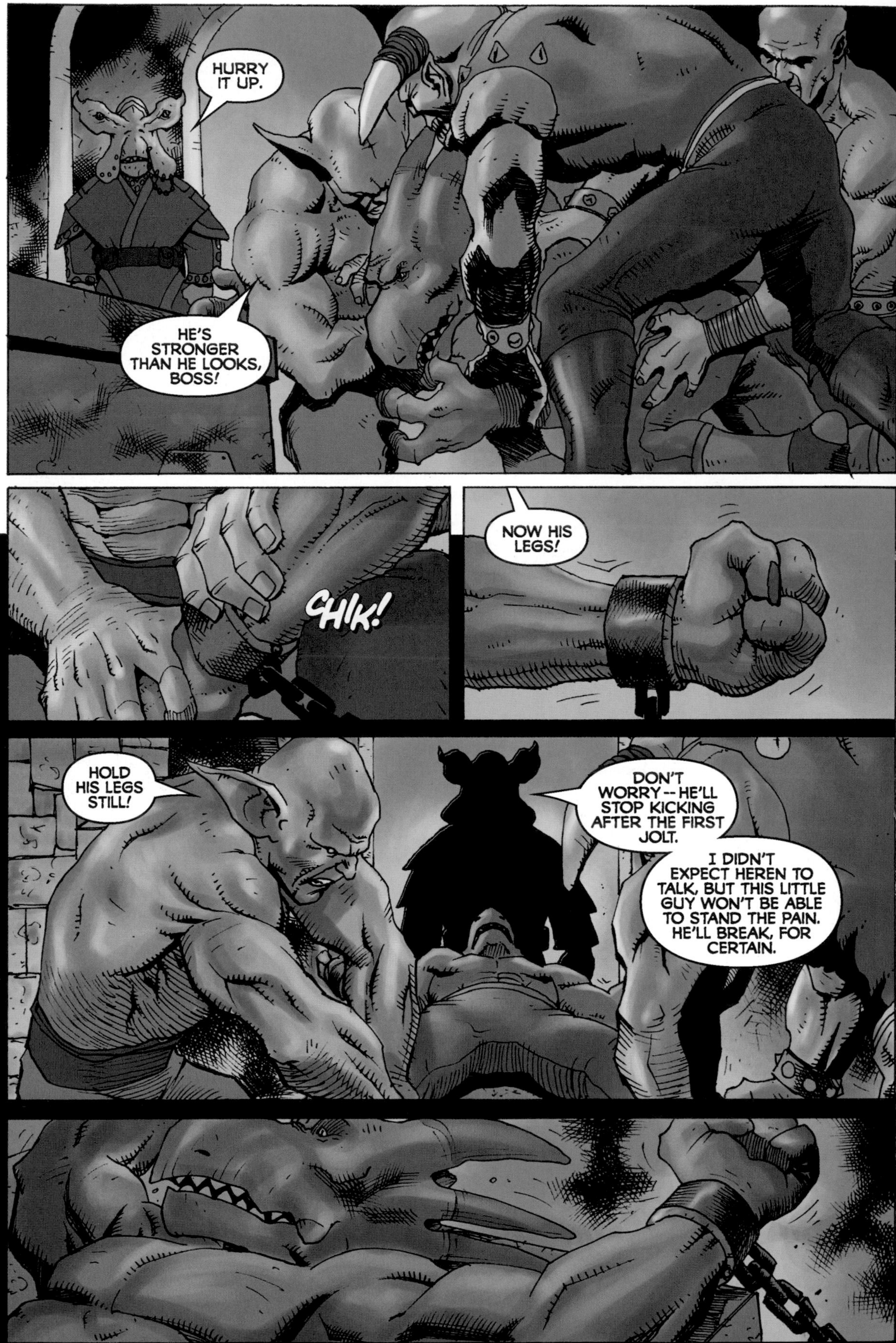
HURRY IT UP.
HE'S STRONGER THAN HE LOOKS, BOSS!
CHIK!
NOW HIS LEGS!
HOLD HIS LEGS STILL!
DON'T WORRY--HE'LL STOP KICKING AFTER THE FIRST JOLT.
I DIDN'T EXPECT HEREN TO TALK, BUT THIS LITTLE GUY WON'T BE ABLE TO STAND THE PAIN. HE'LL BREAK, FOR CERTAIN.

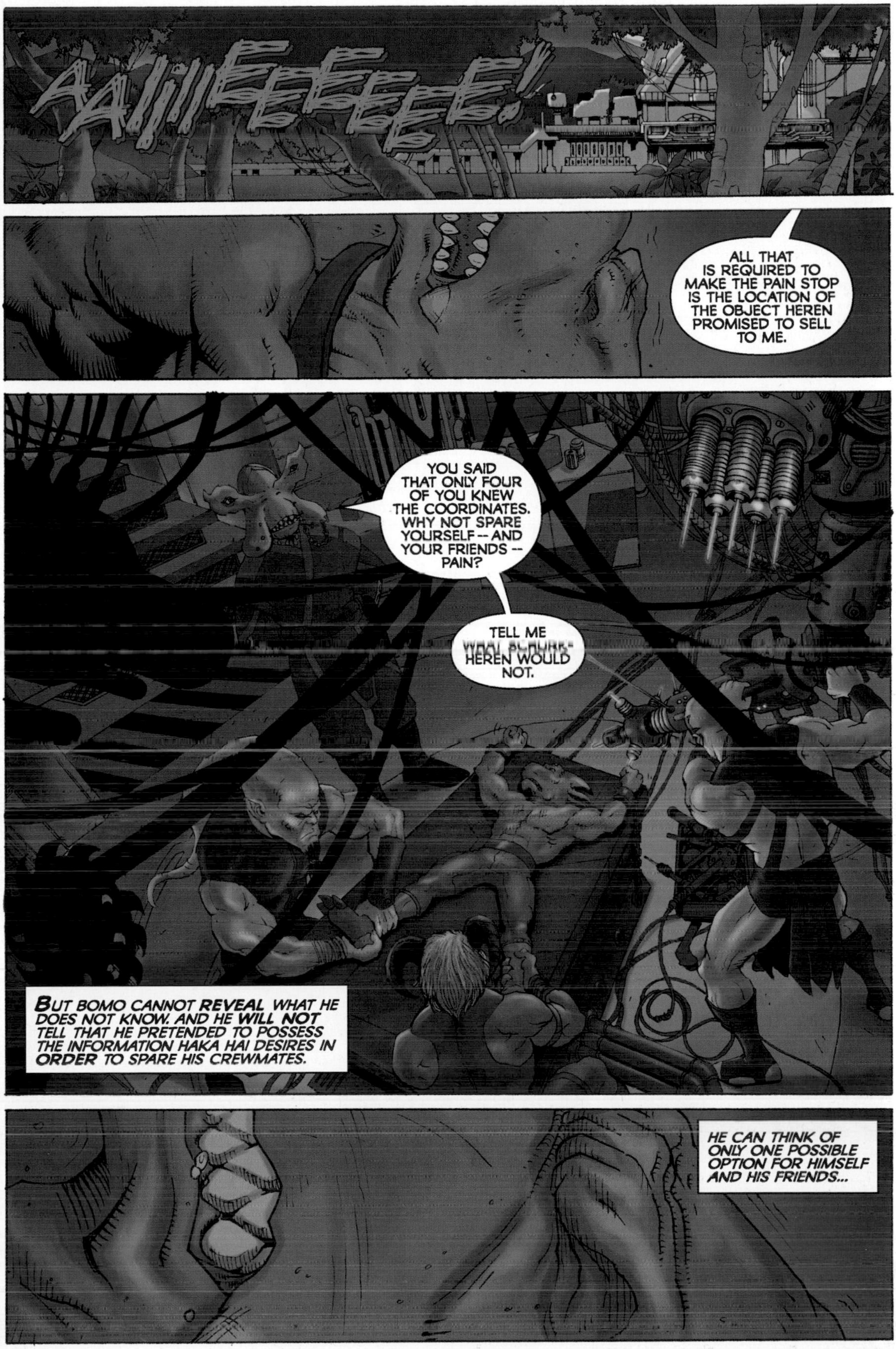
AAIIIEEEEEEE!
ALL THAT IS REQUIRED TO MAKE THE PAIN STOP IS THE LOCATION OF THE OBJECT HEREN PROMISED TO SELL TO ME.
YOU SAID THAT ONLY FOUR OF YOU KNEW THE COORDINATES. WHY NOT SPARE YOURSELF -- AND YOUR FRIENDS -- PAIN?
TELL ME WHAT SCHURK-HEREN WOULD NOT.
BUT BOMO CANNOT REVEAL WHAT HE DOES NOT KNOW. AND HE WILL NOT TELL THAT HE PRETENDED TO POSSESS THE INFORMATION HAKA HAI DESIRES IN ORDER TO SPARE HIS CREWMATES.
HE CAN THINK OF ONLY ONE POSSIBLE OPTION FOR HIMSELF AND HIS FRIENDS...

I'M NOT GETTING ANY ANSWERS.
BUT, BOSS, IF I CRANK IT UP ANY MORE IT MIGHT KILL HIM!
I'LL RISK IT.
WHATEVER YOU SAY...
ZZZAAAAAAK!
UH-OH...
IS HE DEAD?
NO, BUT HE'LL BE OUT FOR A WHILE.
VERY WELL--

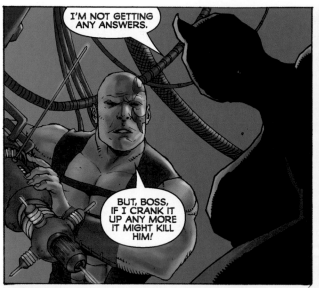

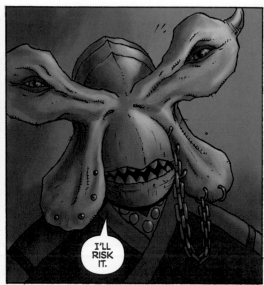

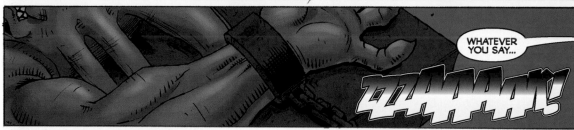

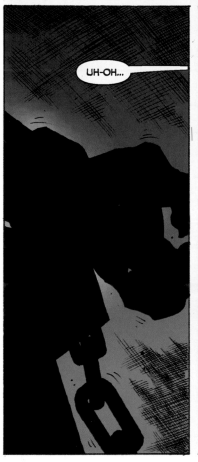

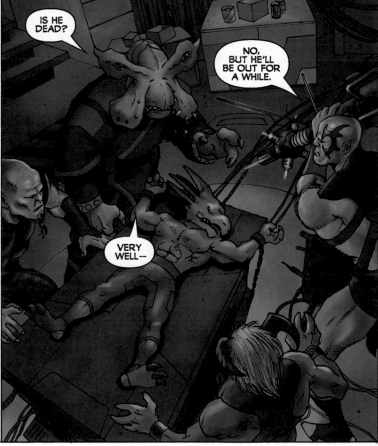

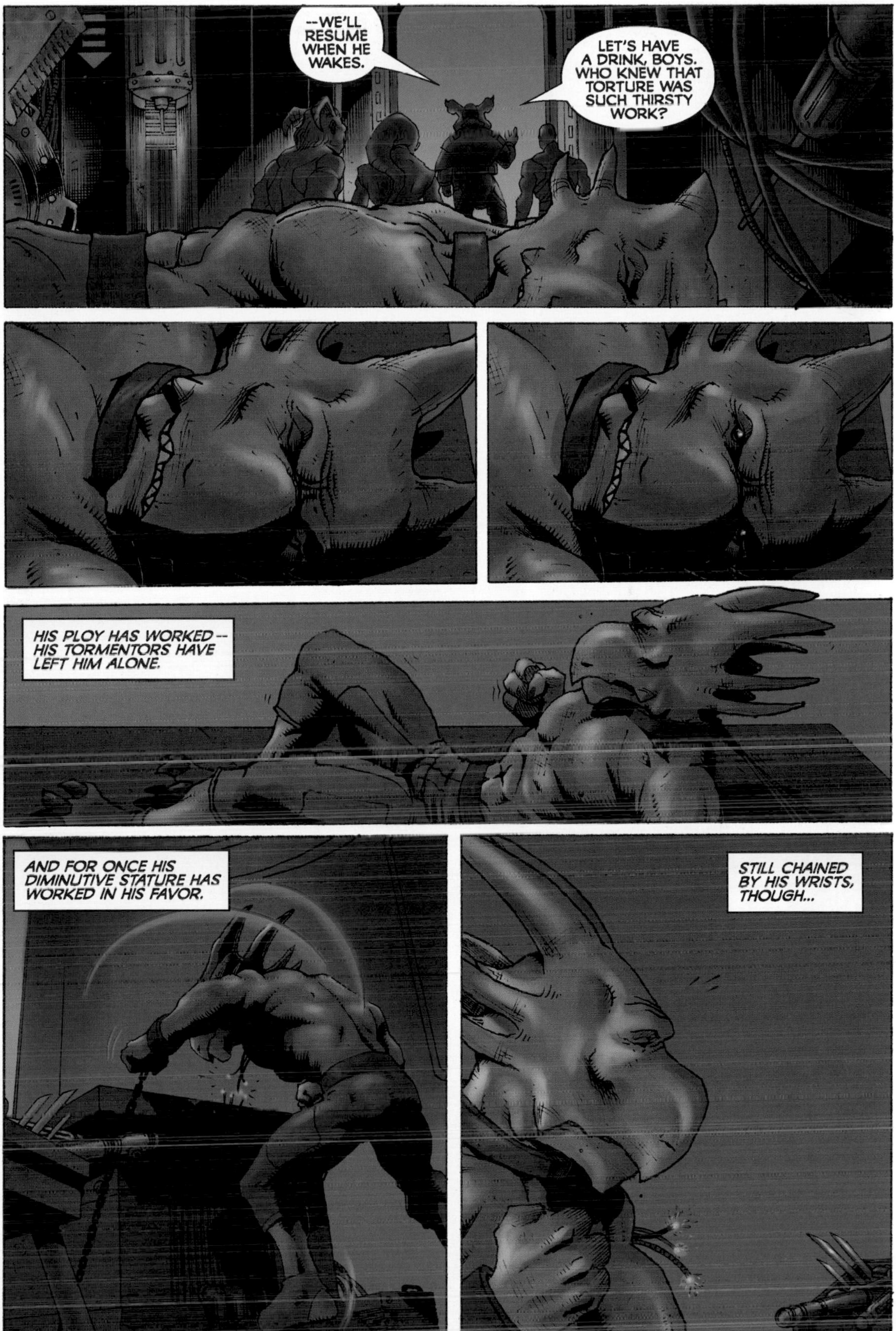
--WE'LL RESUME WHEN HE WAKES.
LET'S HAVE A DRINK, BOYS. WHO KNEW THAT TORTURE WAS SUCH THIRSTY WORK?
HIS PLOY HAS WORKED-- HIS TORMENTORS HAVE LEFT HIM ALONE.
AND FOR ONCE HIS DIMINUTIVE STATURE HAS WORKED IN HIS FAVOR.
STILL CHAINED BY HIS WRISTS, THOUGH...

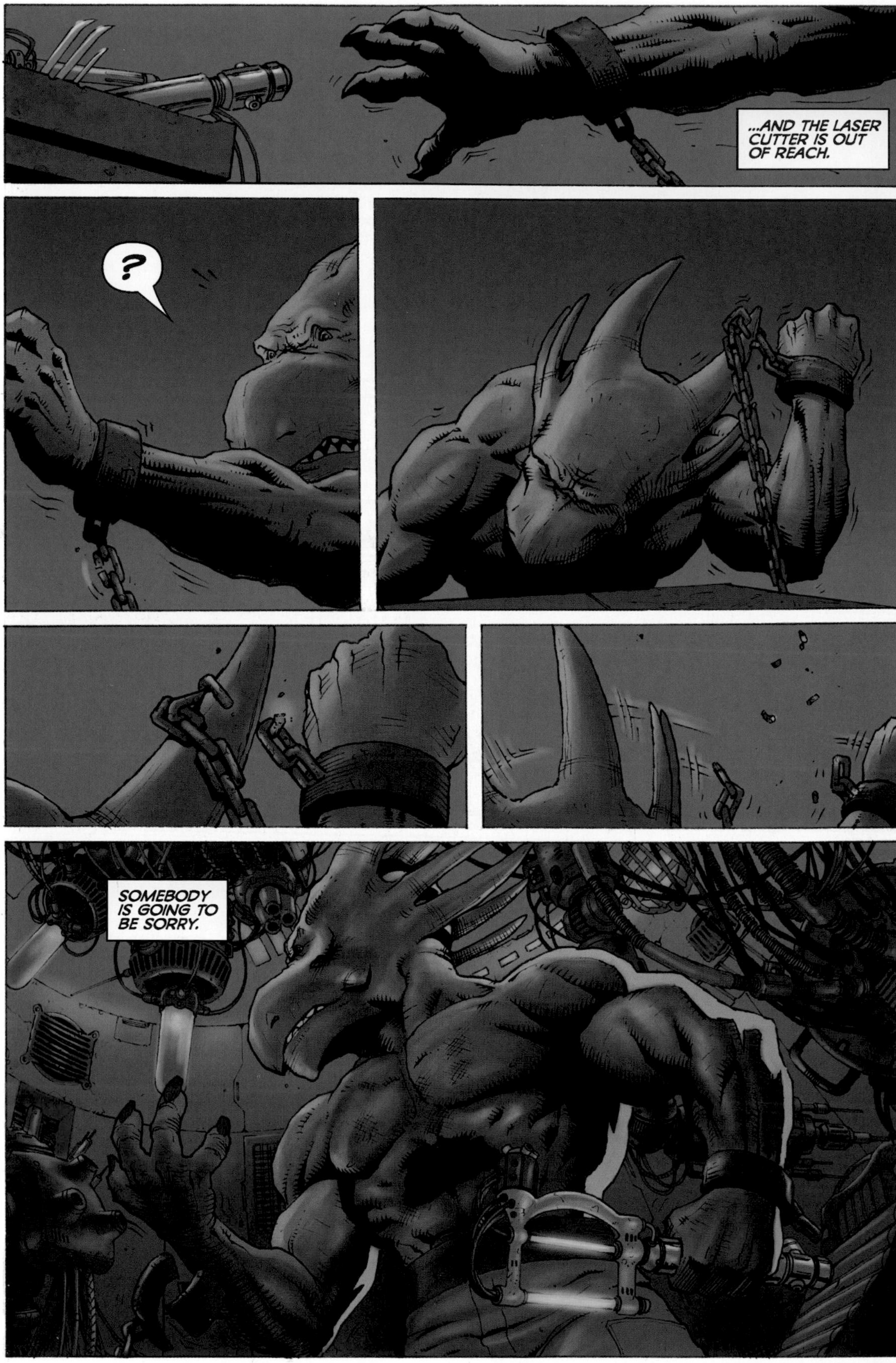
...AND THE LASER CUTTER IS OUT OF REACH.
?
SOMEBODY IS GOING TO BE SORRY.

PIRU! *CHASE PIRU,* COME IN!

THERE ARE ARMED BEINGS HEADED YOUR WAY! GET THE YOUNGLINGS INTO THE JUNGLE, AND --

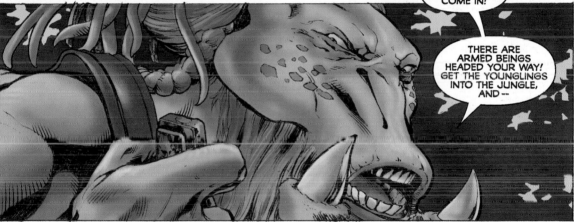

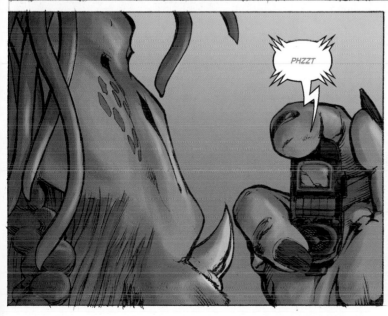

PHZZT

79

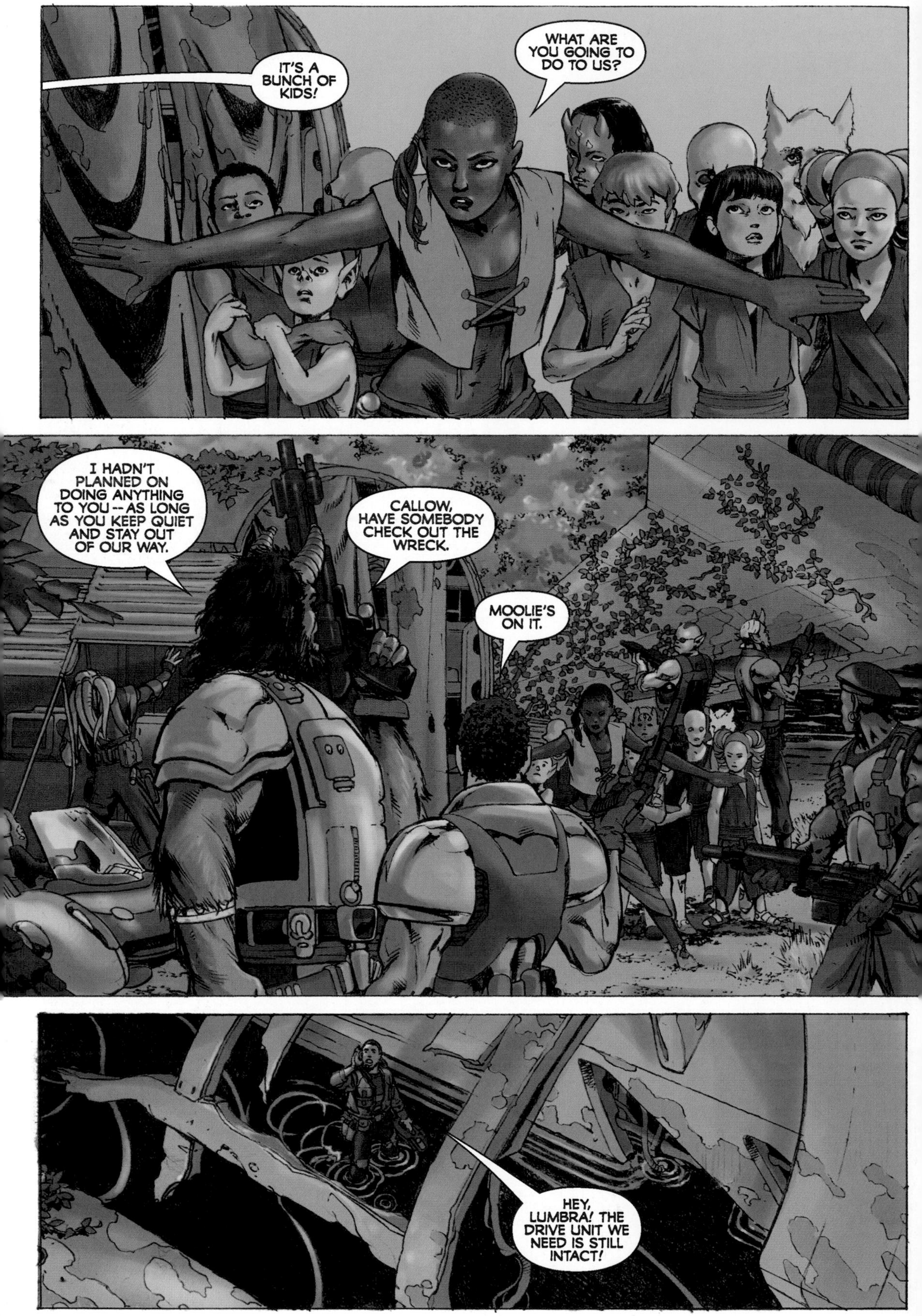
IT'S A BUNCH OF KIDS!
WHAT ARE YOU GOING TO DO TO US?
I HADN'T PLANNED ON DOING ANYTHING TO YOU -- AS LONG AS YOU KEEP QUIET AND STAY OUT OF OUR WAY.
CALLOW, HAVE SOMEBODY CHECK OUT THE WRECK.
MOOLIE'S ON IT.
HEY, LUMBRA! THE DRIVE UNIT WE NEED IS STILL INTACT!

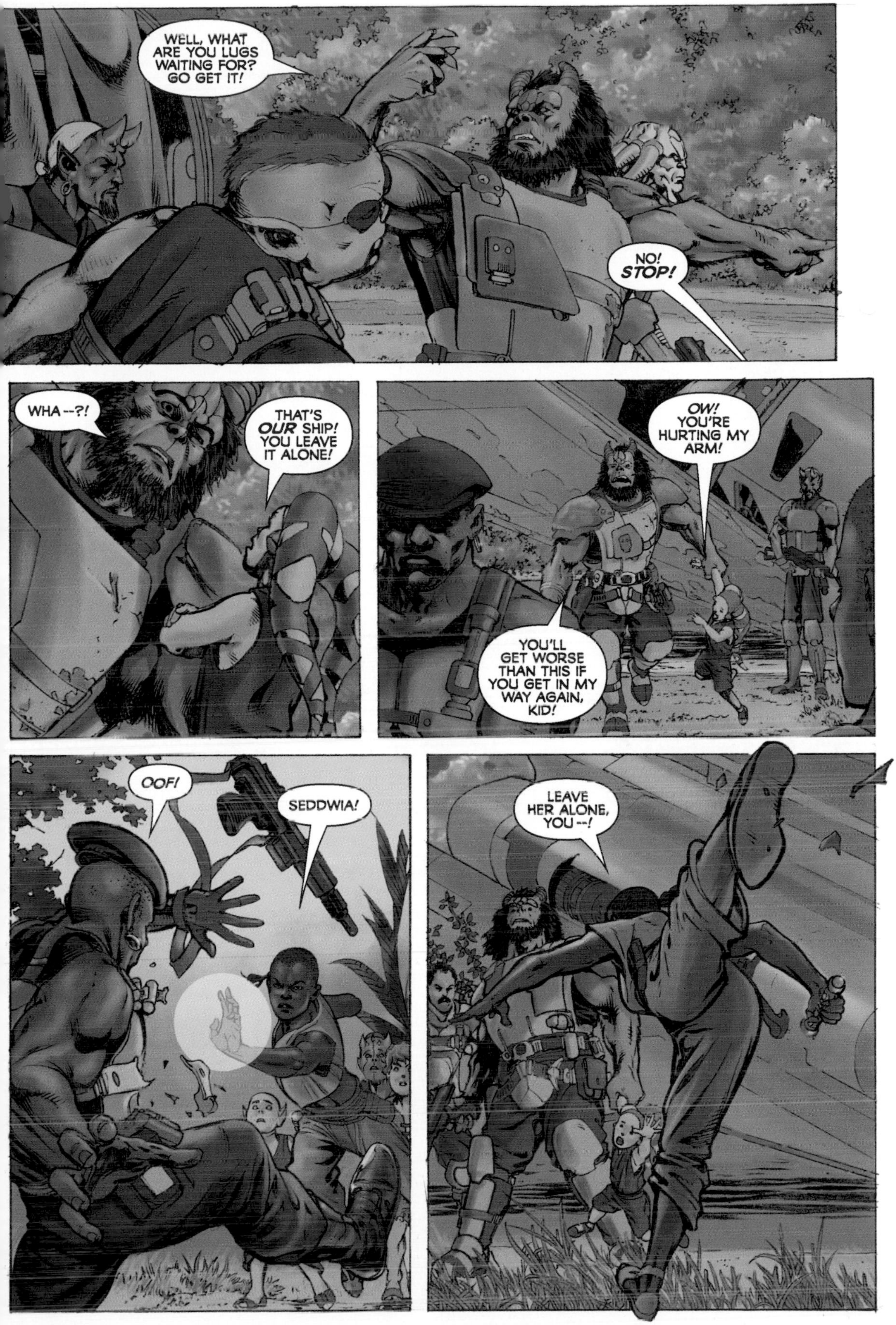
WELL, WHAT ARE YOU LUGS WAITING FOR? GO GET IT!
NO! STOP!
WHA--?!
THAT'S OUR SHIP! YOU LEAVE IT ALONE!
OW! YOU'RE HURTING MY ARM!
YOU'LL GET WORSE THAN THIS IF YOU GET IN MY WAY AGAIN, KID!
OOF!
SEDDWIA!
LEAVE HER ALONE, YOU --!

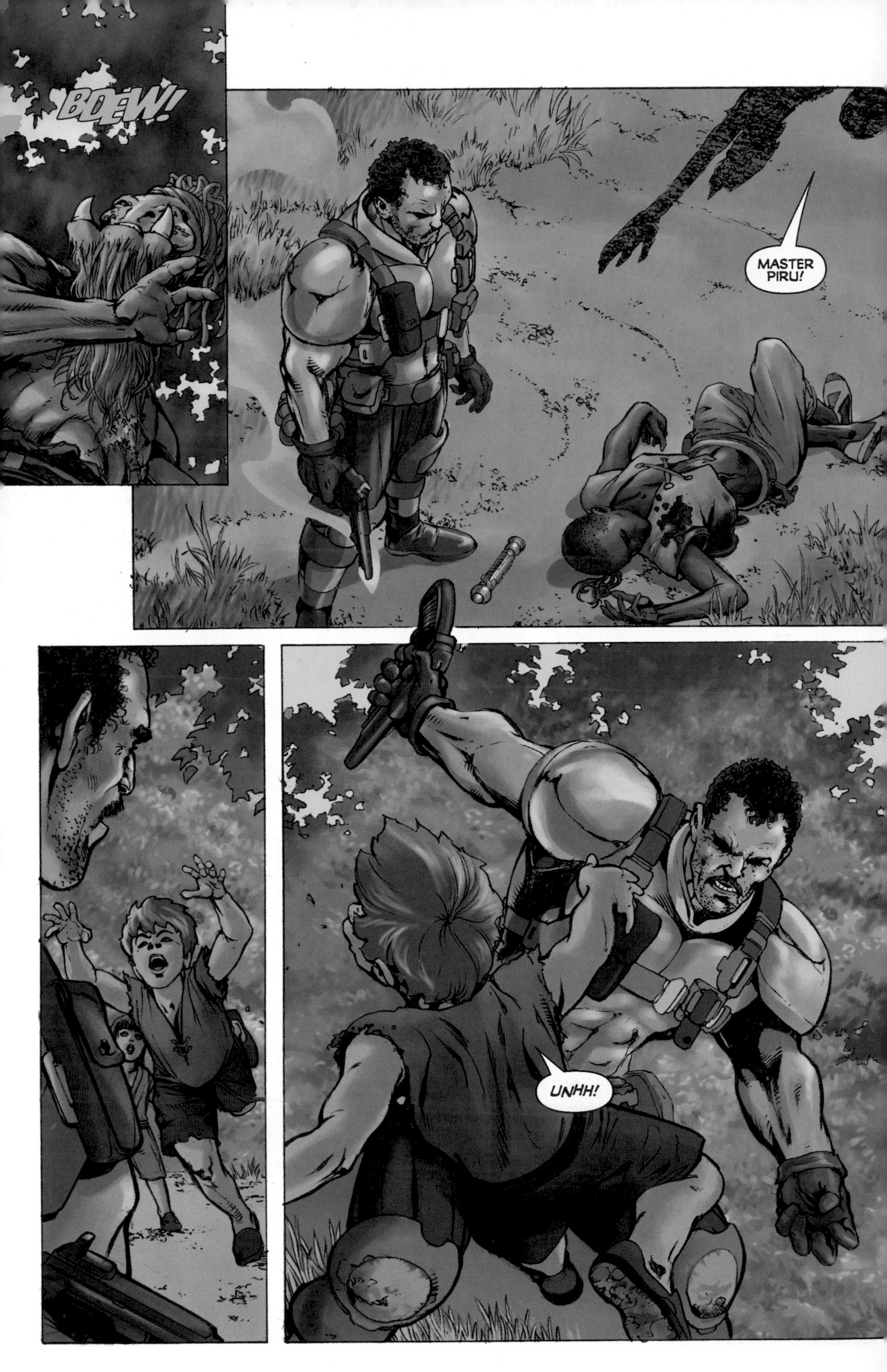
BDEW!
MASTER PIRU!
UNHH!

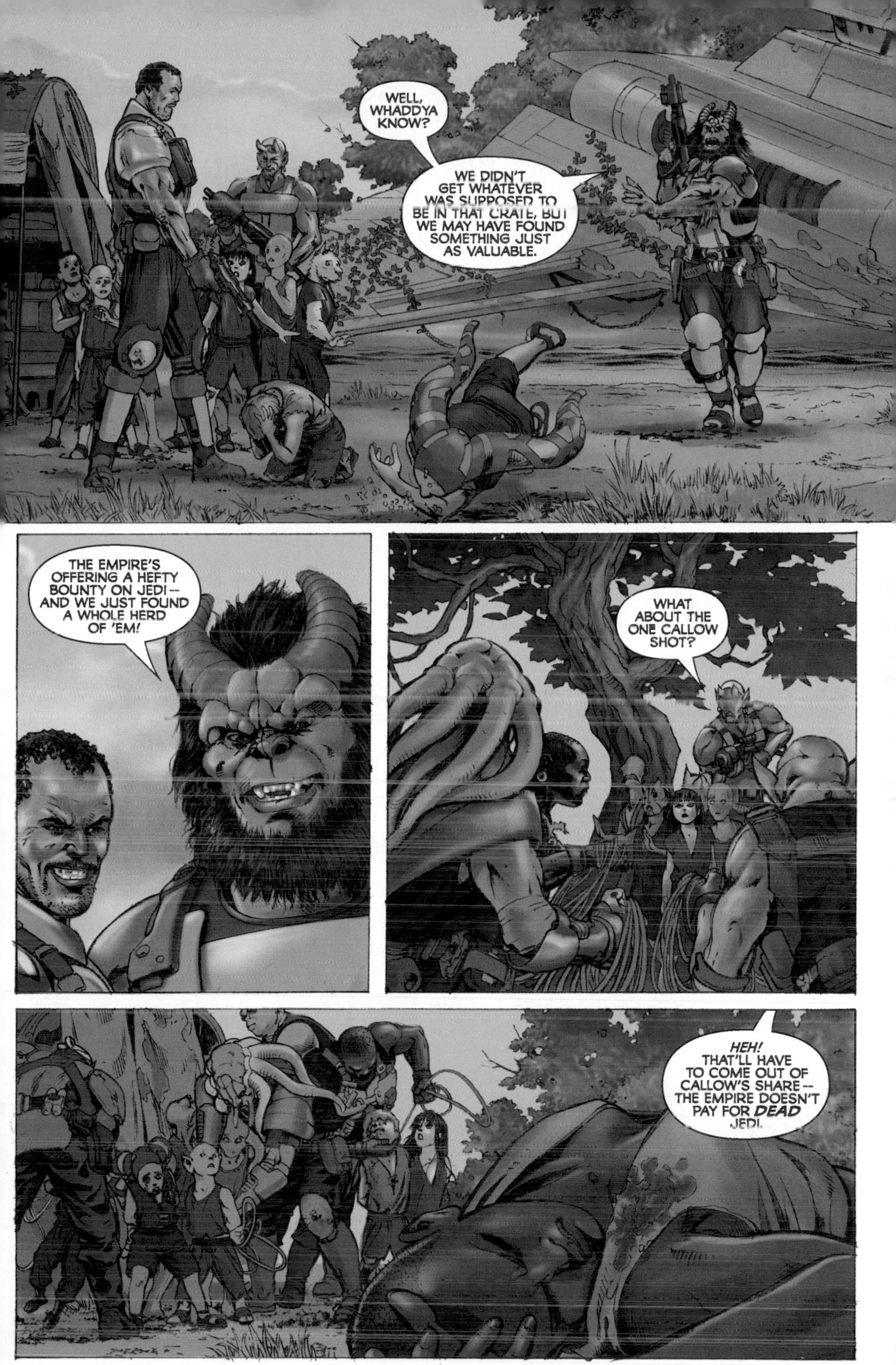
WELL, WHADDYA KNOW?
WE DIDN'T GET WHATEVER WAS SUPPOSED TO BE IN THAT CRATE, BUT WE MAY HAVE FOUND SOMETHING JUST AS VALUABLE.
THE EMPIRE'S OFFERING A HEFTY BOUNTY ON JEDI-- AND WE JUST FOUND A WHOLE HERD OF 'EM!
WHAT ABOUT THE ONE CALLOW SHOT?
HEH! THAT'LL HAVE TO COME OUT OF CALLOW'S SHARE-- THE EMPIRE DOESN'T PAY FOR DEAD JEDI.

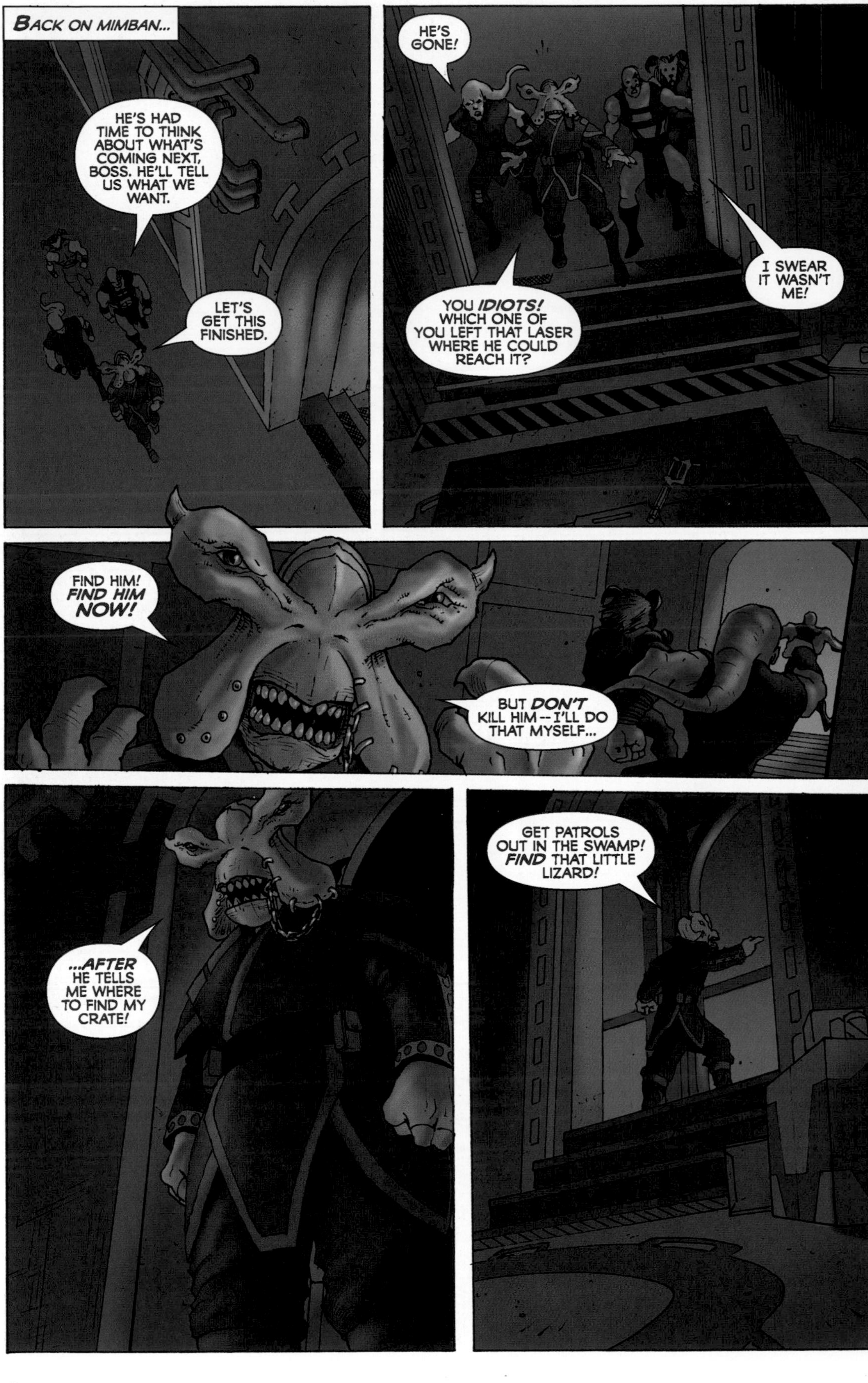
BACK ON MIMBAN...
HE'S HAD TIME TO THINK ABOUT WHAT'S COMING NEXT, BOSS. HE'LL TELL US WHAT WE WANT.
LET'S GET THIS FINISHED.
HE'S GONE!
YOU IDIOTS! WHICH ONE OF YOU LEFT THAT LASER WHERE HE COULD REACH IT?
I SWEAR IT WASN'T ME!
FIND HIM! FIND HIM NOW!
BUT DON'T KILL HIM -- I'LL DO THAT MYSELF...
...AFTER HE TELLS ME WHERE TO FIND MY CRATE!
GET PATROLS OUT IN THE SWAMP! FIND THAT LITTLE LIZARD!

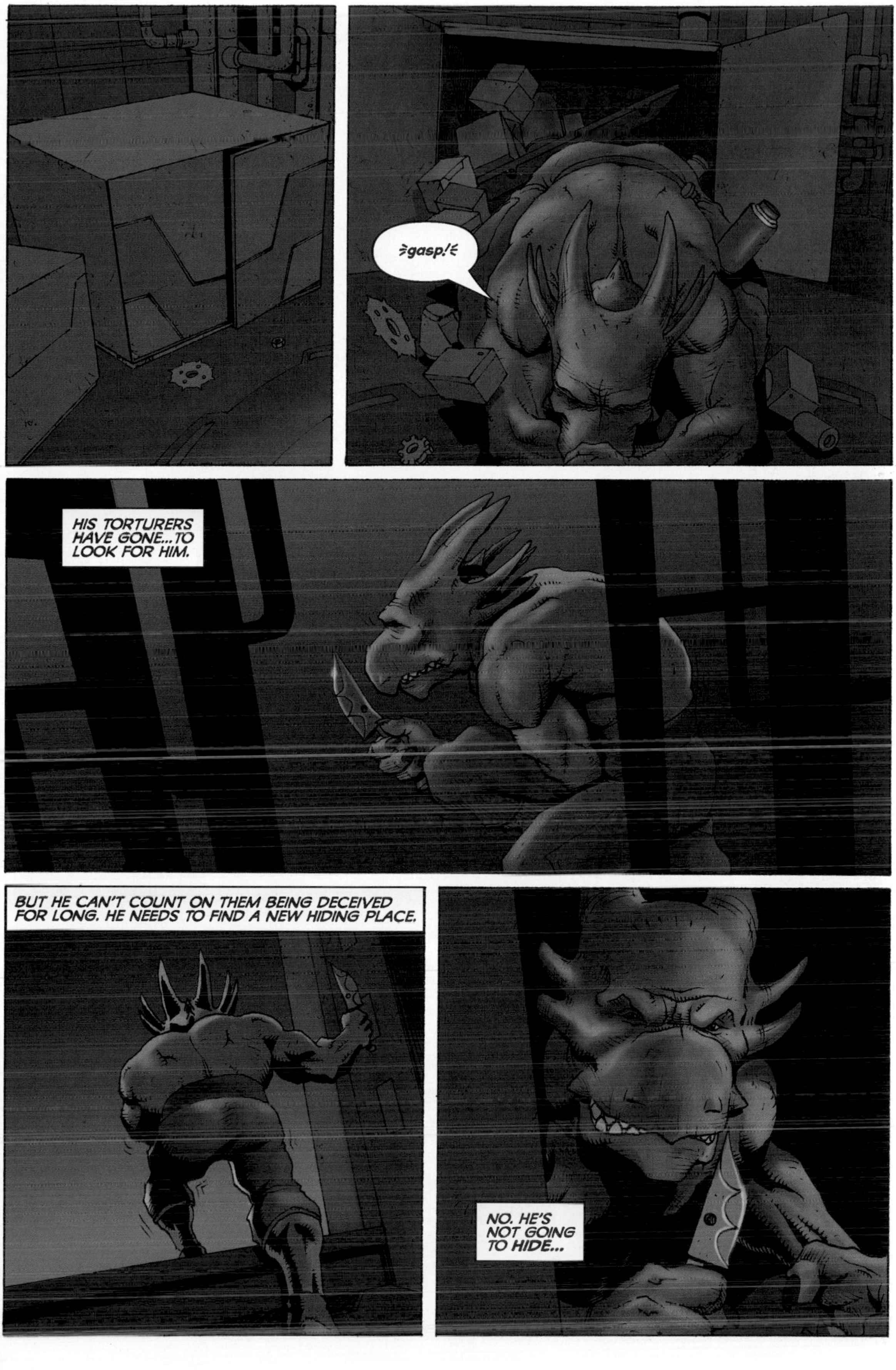
gasp!
HIS TORTURERS HAVE GONE...TO LOOK FOR HIM.
BUT HE CAN'T COUNT ON THEM BEING DECEIVED FOR LONG. HE NEEDS TO FIND A NEW HIDING PLACE.
NO. HE'S NOT GOING TO HIDE...

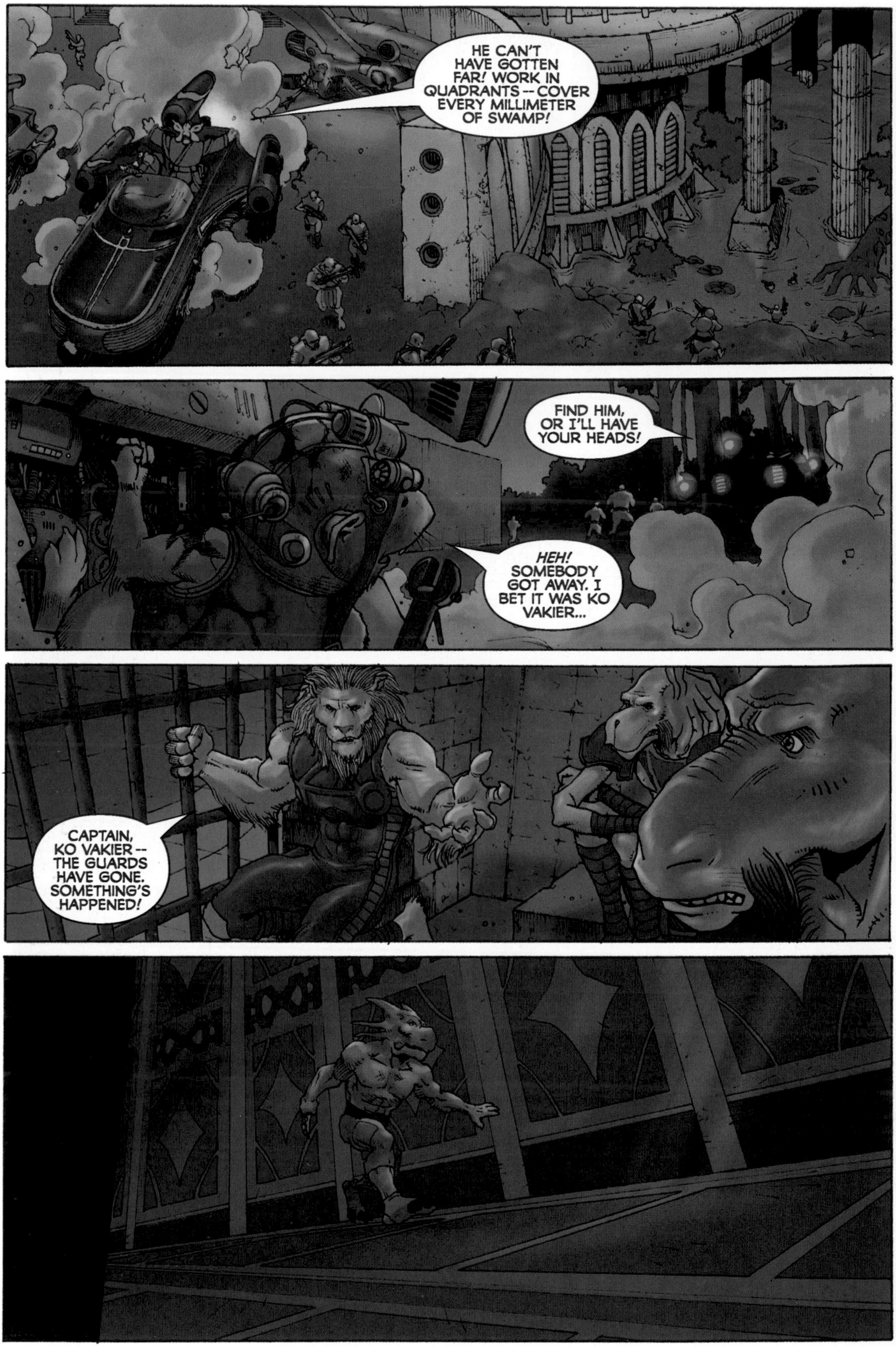
HE CAN'T HAVE GOTTEN FAR! WORK IN QUADRANTS -- COVER EVERY MILLIMETER OF SWAMP!
FIND HIM, OR I'LL HAVE YOUR HEADS!
HEH! SOMEBODY GOT AWAY. I BET IT WAS KO VAKIER...
CAPTAIN, KO VAKIER -- THE GUARDS HAVE GONE. SOMETHING'S HAPPENED!

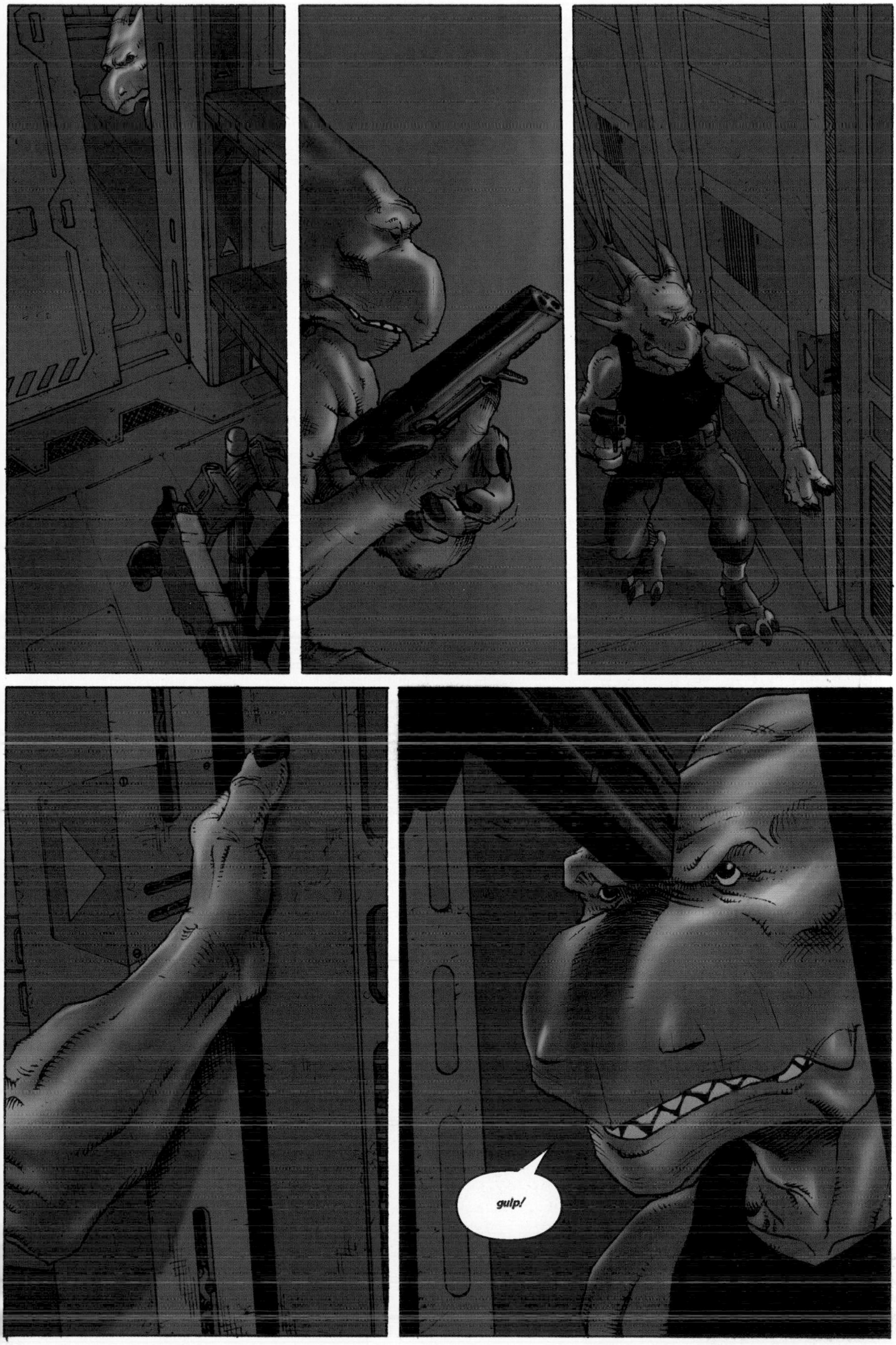
gulp!

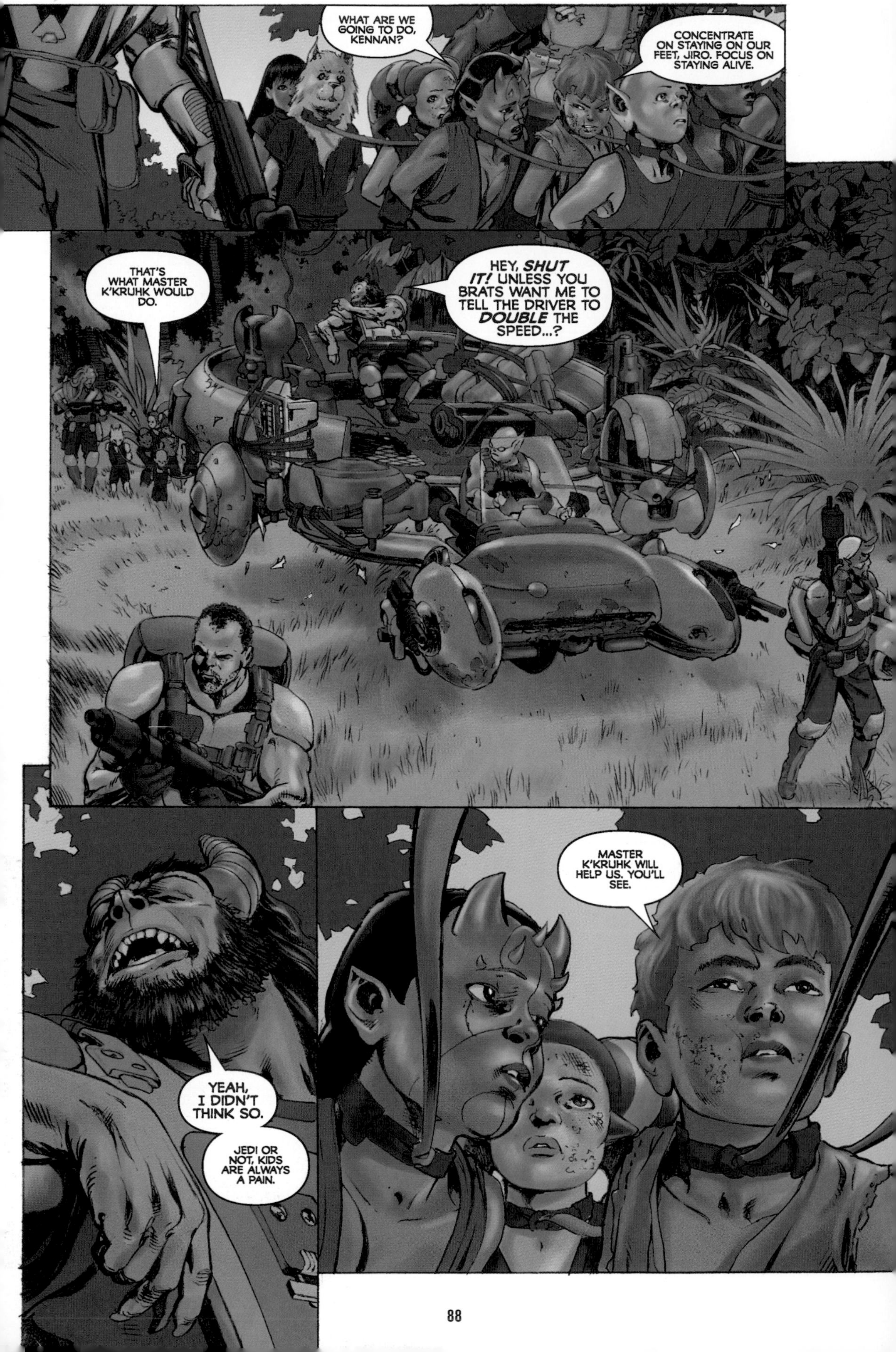
WHAT ARE WE GOING TO DO, KENNAN?
CONCENTRATE ON STAYING ON OUR FEET, JIRO. FOCUS ON STAYING ALIVE.
THAT'S WHAT MASTER K'KRUHK WOULD DO.
HEY, *SHUT IT!* UNLESS YOU BRATS WANT ME TO TELL THE DRIVER TO *DOUBLE* THE SPEED...?
YEAH, I DIDN'T THINK SO.
JEDI OR NOT, KIDS ARE ALWAYS A PAIN.
MASTER K'KRUHK WILL HELP US. YOU'LL SEE.

PIRU... CHASE PIRU!

AH. HOW DO YOU FEEL?

MASTER --! I WAS CERTAIN I WAS DEAD!

SO WAS WHOEVER SHOT YOU.

THEY TOOK THE YOUNGLINGS. THEY DISCOVERED WE WERE JEDI...

...WHEN I WAS LYING THERE, I HEARD ONE MAN SAY THAT THERE IS A BOUNTY ON JEDI.

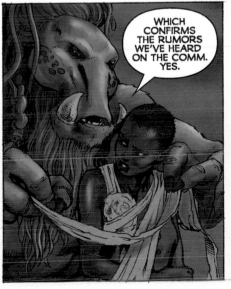

WHICH CONFIRMS THE RUMORS WE'VE HEARD ON THE COMM. YES.

CHASE, THOUGH I HAVE MORE OFTEN BEEN THE *RECIPIENT* OF THE HEALER'S ART THAN THE PRACTITIONER, I HAVE TENDED YOUR WOUND AS BEST I COULD.

IN A FEW DAYS YOU WILL BE ABLE TO USE YOUR ARM AGAIN...

...BUT WE HAVE ONLY HOURS IN WHICH TO ACT.

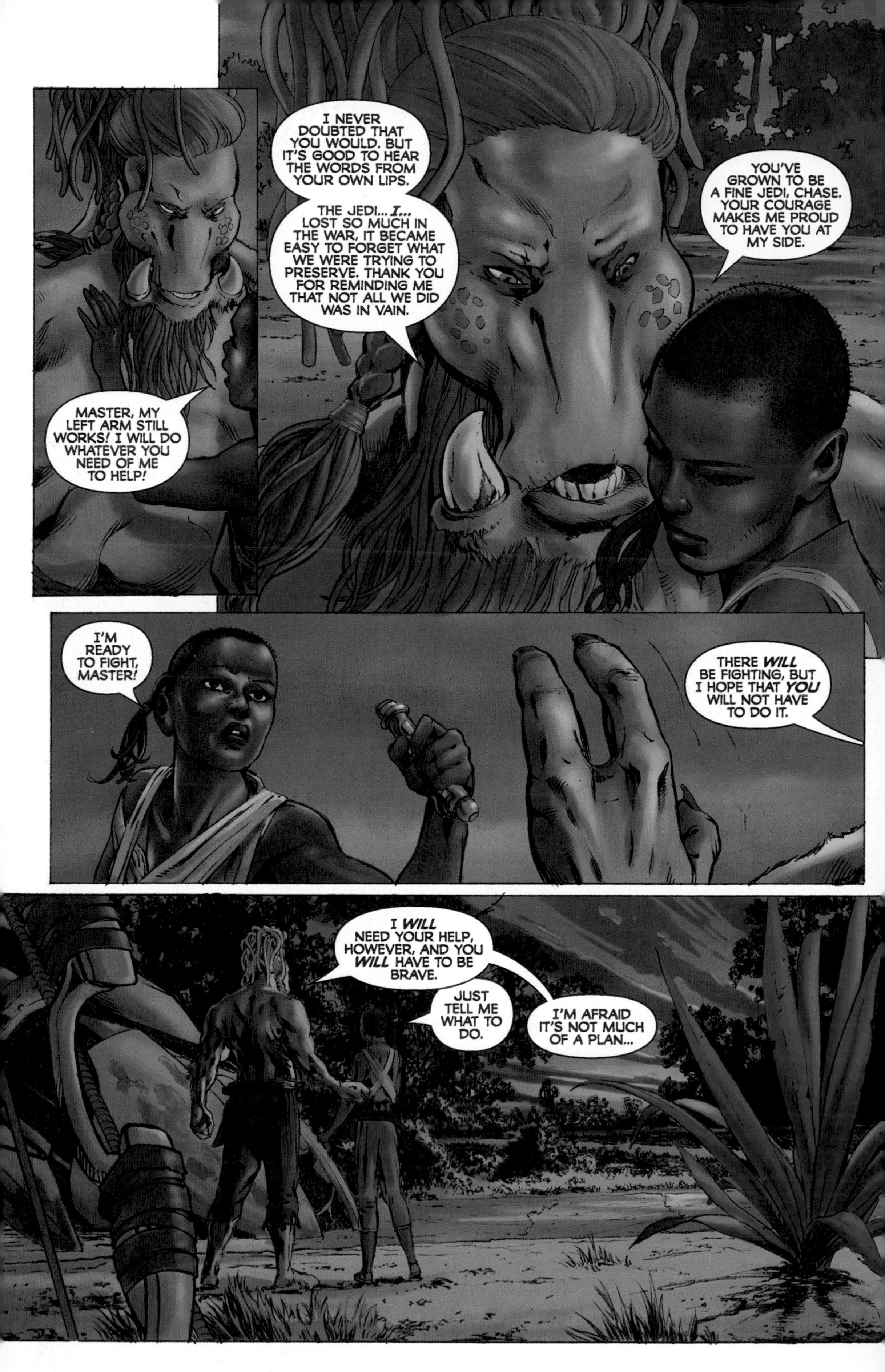
I NEVER DOUBTED THAT YOU WOULD. BUT IT'S GOOD TO HEAR THE WORDS FROM YOUR OWN LIPS.
THE JEDI... *I...* LOST SO MUCH IN THE WAR, IT BECAME EASY TO FORGET WHAT WE WERE TRYING TO PRESERVE. THANK YOU FOR REMINDING ME THAT NOT ALL WE DID WAS IN VAIN.
YOU'VE GROWN TO BE A FINE JEDI, CHASE. YOUR COURAGE MAKES ME PROUD TO HAVE YOU AT MY SIDE.
MASTER, MY LEFT ARM STILL WORKS*!* I WILL DO WHATEVER YOU NEED OF ME TO HELP*!*
I'M READY TO FIGHT, MASTER*!*
THERE *WILL* BE FIGHTING, BUT I HOPE THAT *YOU* WILL NOT HAVE TO DO IT.
I *WILL* NEED YOUR HELP, HOWEVER, AND YOU *WILL* HAVE TO BE BRAVE.
JUST TELL ME WHAT TO DO.
I'M AFRAID IT'S NOT MUCH OF A PLAN...

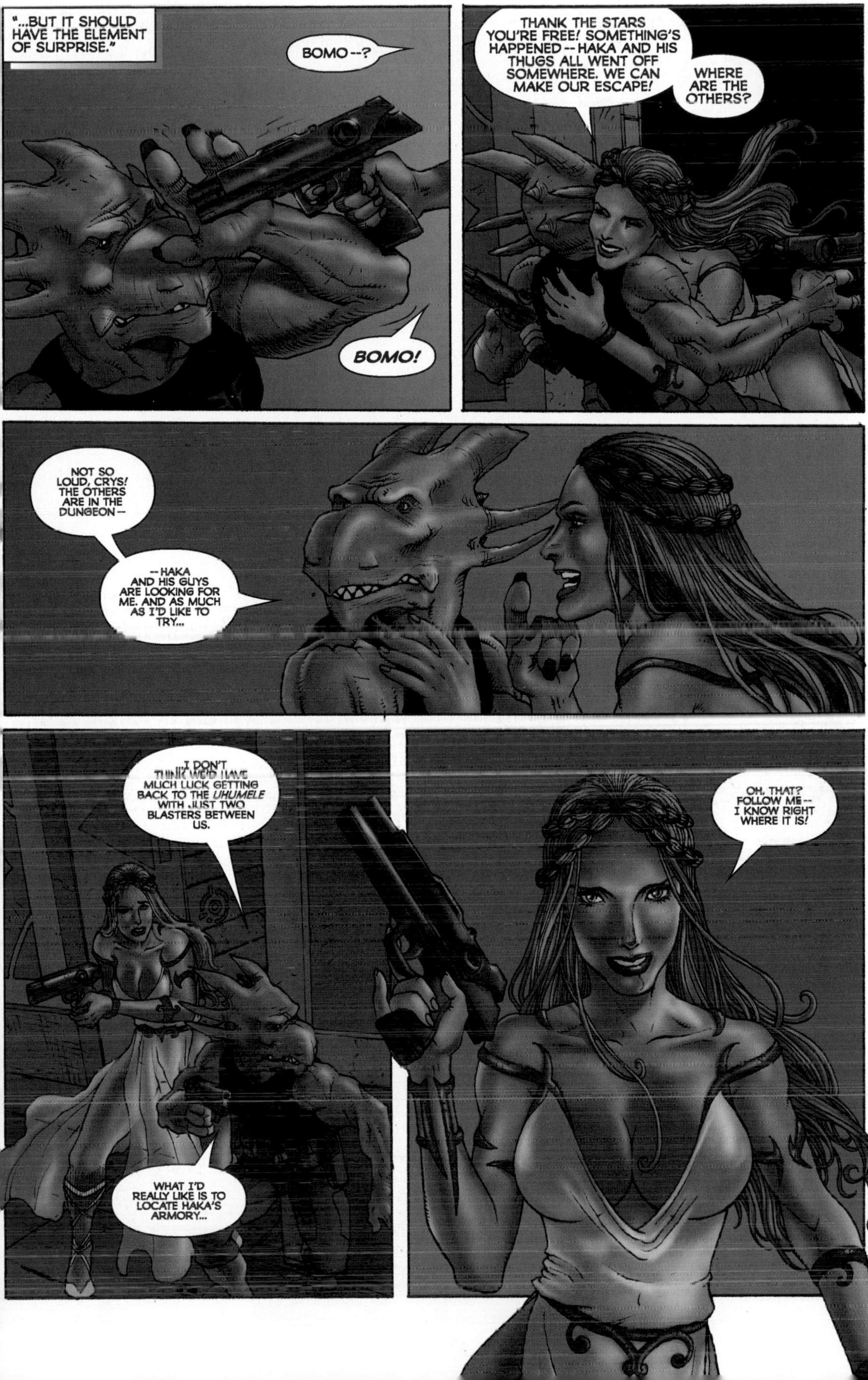
"...BUT IT SHOULD HAVE THE ELEMENT OF SURPRISE."
BOMO--?
BOMO!
THANK THE STARS YOU'RE FREE! SOMETHING'S HAPPENED--HAKA AND HIS THUGS ALL WENT OFF SOMEWHERE. WE CAN MAKE OUR ESCAPE!
WHERE ARE THE OTHERS?
NOT SO LOUD, CRYS! THE OTHERS ARE IN THE DUNGEON--
--HAKA AND HIS GUYS ARE LOOKING FOR ME. AND AS MUCH AS I'D LIKE TO TRY...
I DON'T THINK WE'D HAVE MUCH LUCK GETTING BACK TO THE *UHUMELE* WITH JUST TWO BLASTERS BETWEEN US.
WHAT I'D REALLY LIKE IS TO LOCATE HAKA'S ARMORY...
OH, THAT? FOLLOW ME-- I KNOW RIGHT WHERE IT IS!

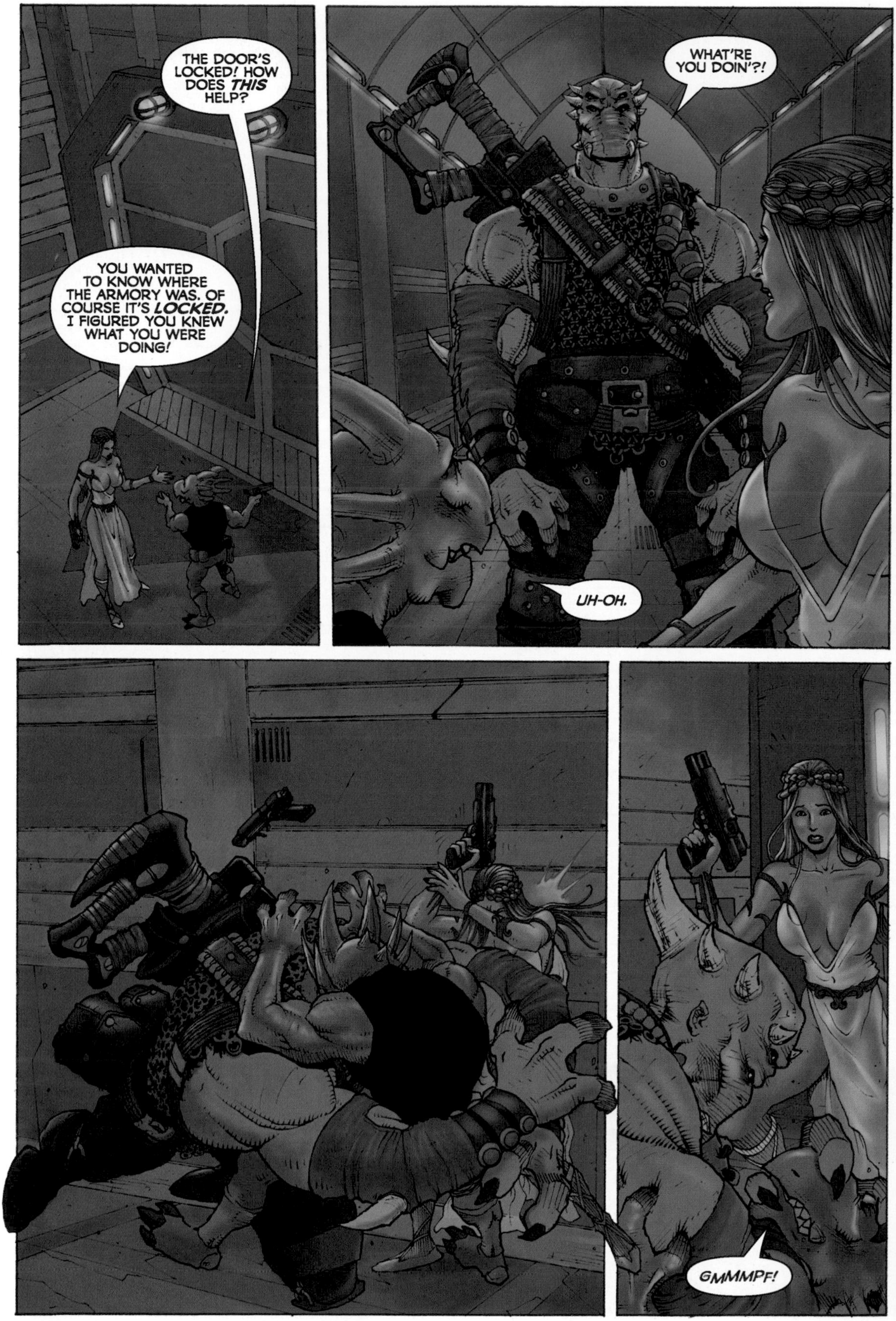
THE DOOR'S LOCKED! HOW DOES *THIS* HELP?
YOU WANTED TO KNOW WHERE THE ARMORY WAS. OF COURSE IT'S *LOCKED*. I FIGURED YOU KNEW WHAT YOU WERE DOING!
WHAT'RE YOU DOIN'?!
UH-OH.
GMMMPF!

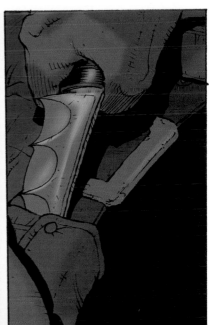

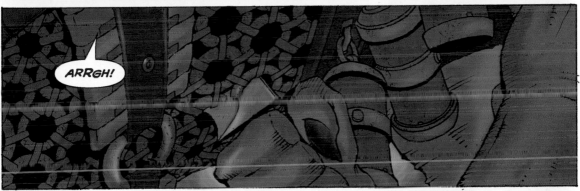

ARRGH!

SHOOT HIM, CRYS!

SHOOT!

BOOM!

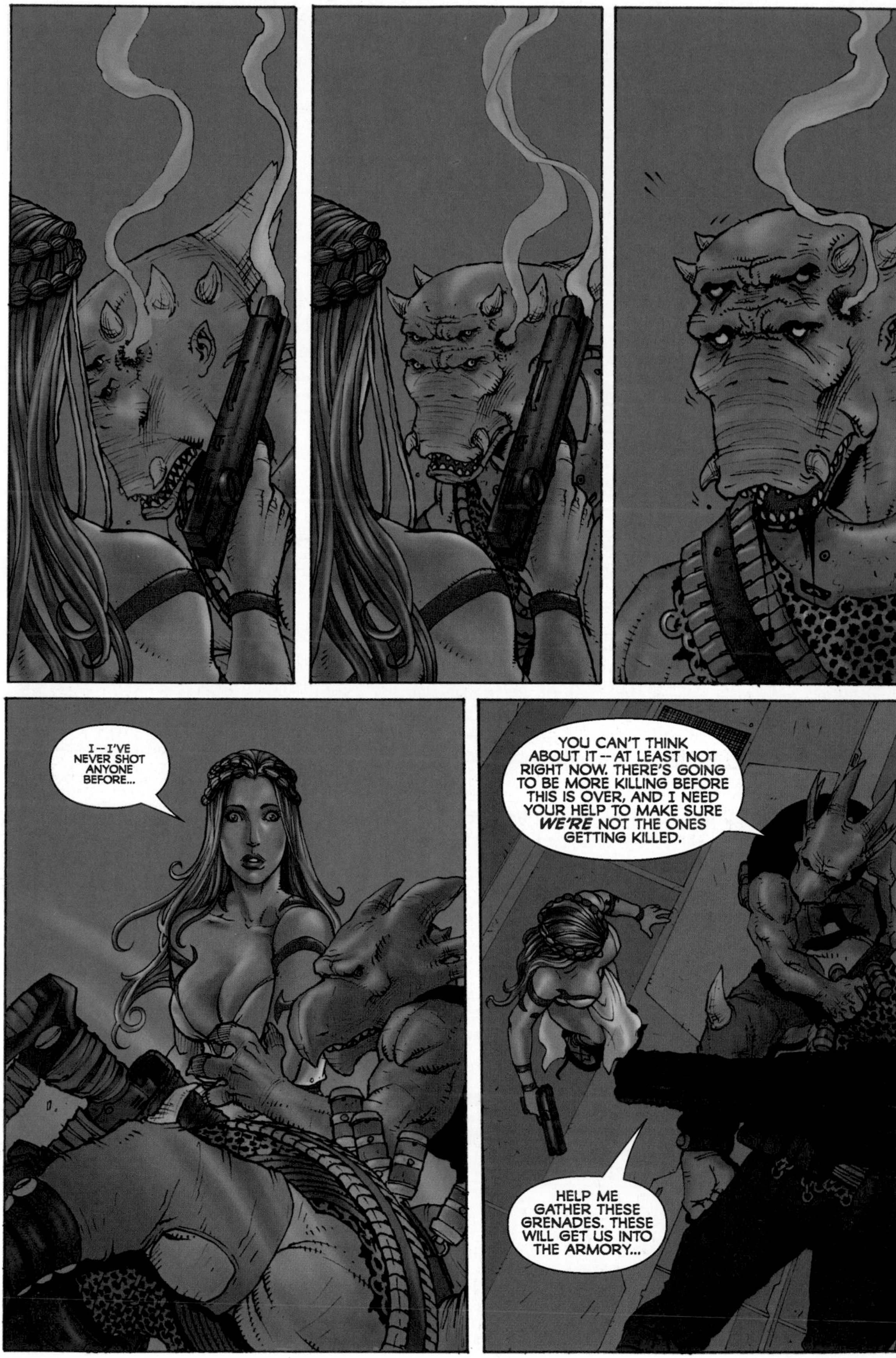
I--I'VE NEVER SHOT ANYONE BEFORE...
YOU CAN'T THINK ABOUT IT--AT LEAST NOT RIGHT NOW. THERE'S GOING TO BE MORE KILLING BEFORE THIS IS OVER, AND I NEED YOUR HELP TO MAKE SURE *WE'RE* NOT THE ONES GETTING KILLED.
HELP ME GATHER THESE GRENADES. THESE WILL GET US INTO THE ARMORY...

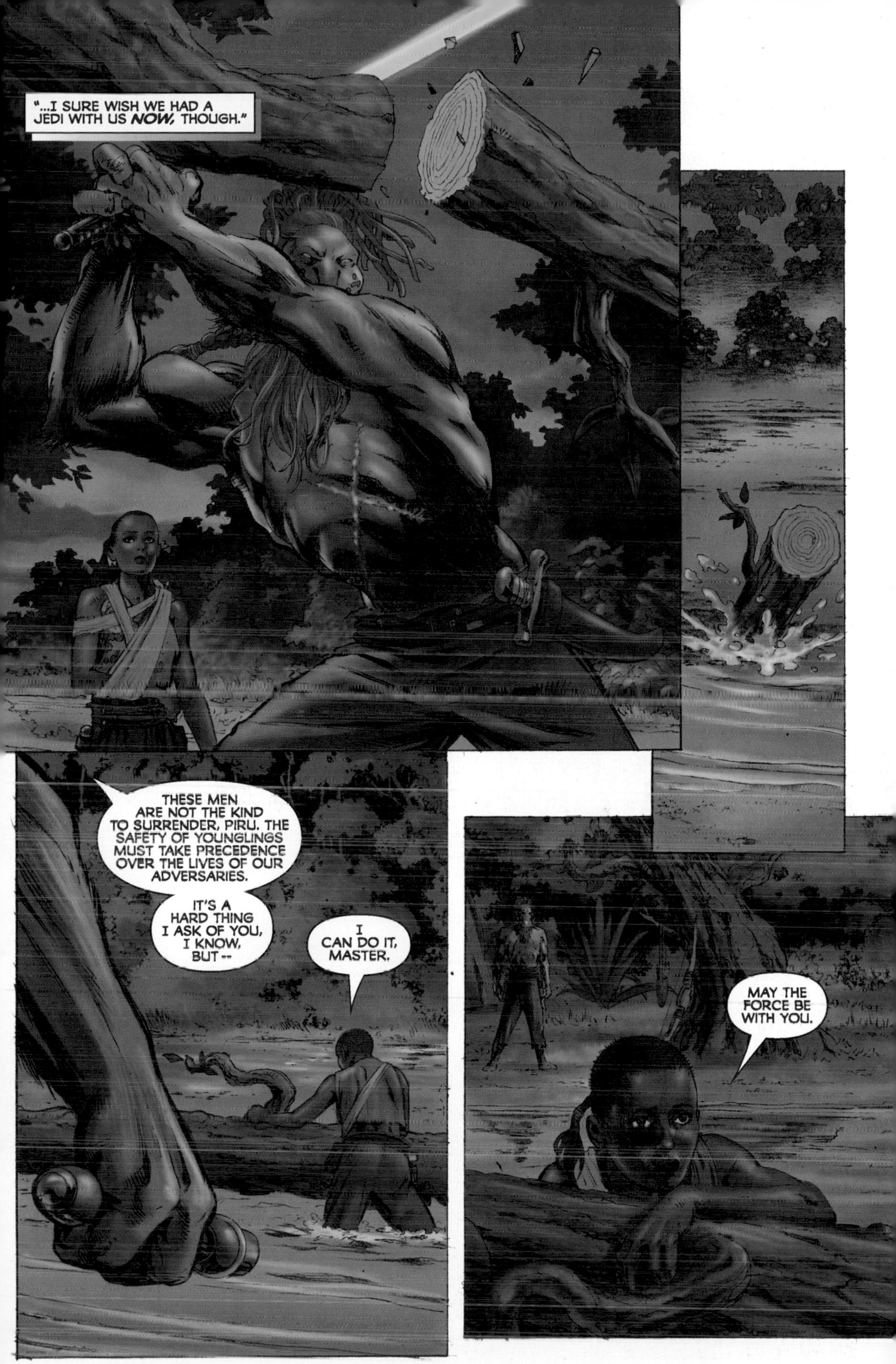
"...I SURE WISH WE HAD A JEDI WITH US *NOW,* THOUGH."
THESE MEN ARE NOT THE KIND TO SURRENDER, PIRU. THE SAFETY OF YOUNGLINGS MUST TAKE PRECEDENCE OVER THE LIVES OF OUR ADVERSARIES.
IT'S A HARD THING I ASK OF YOU, I KNOW, BUT --
I CAN DO IT, MASTER.
MAY THE FORCE BE WITH YOU.

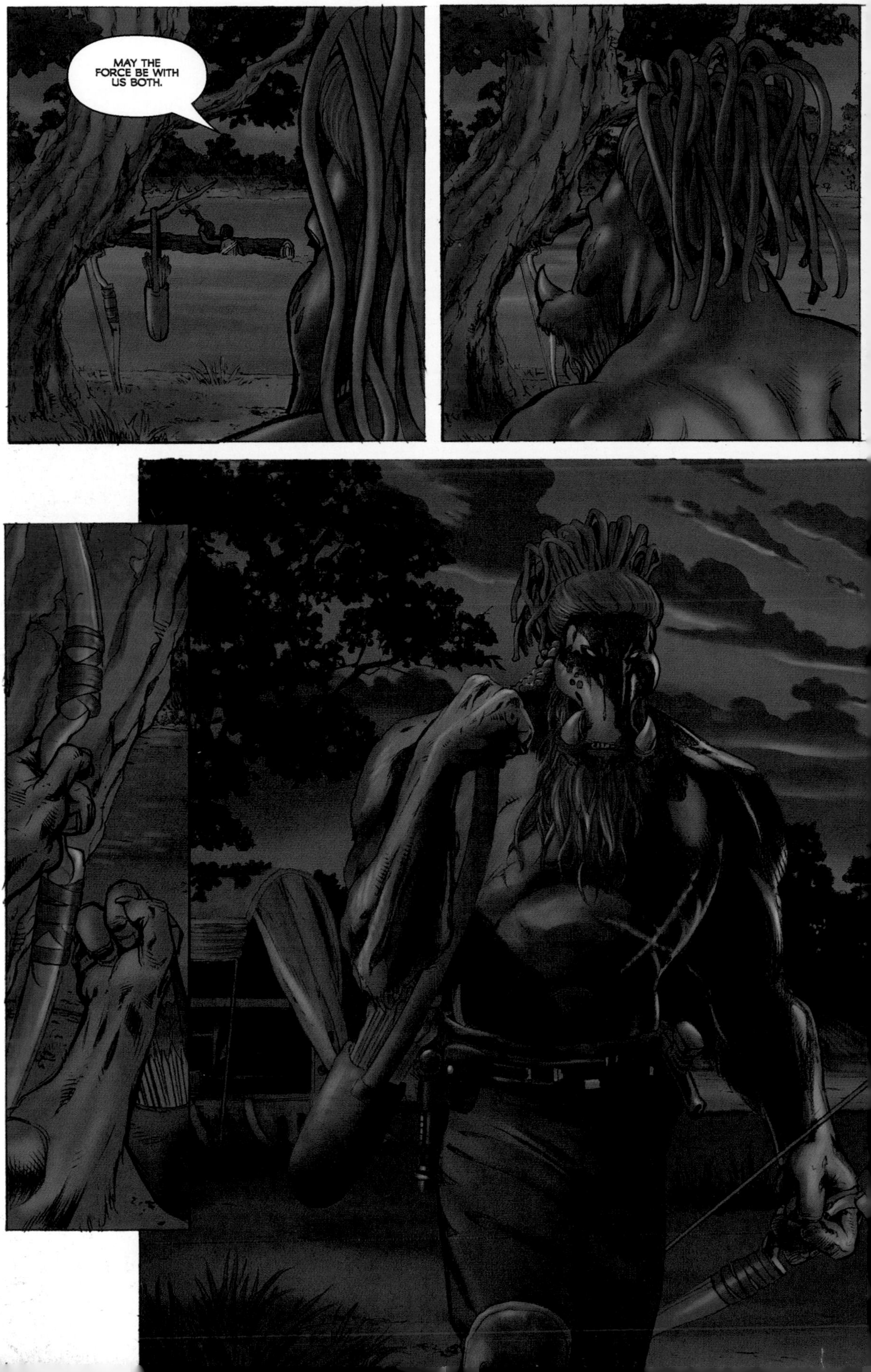
MAY THE FORCE BE WITH US BOTH.

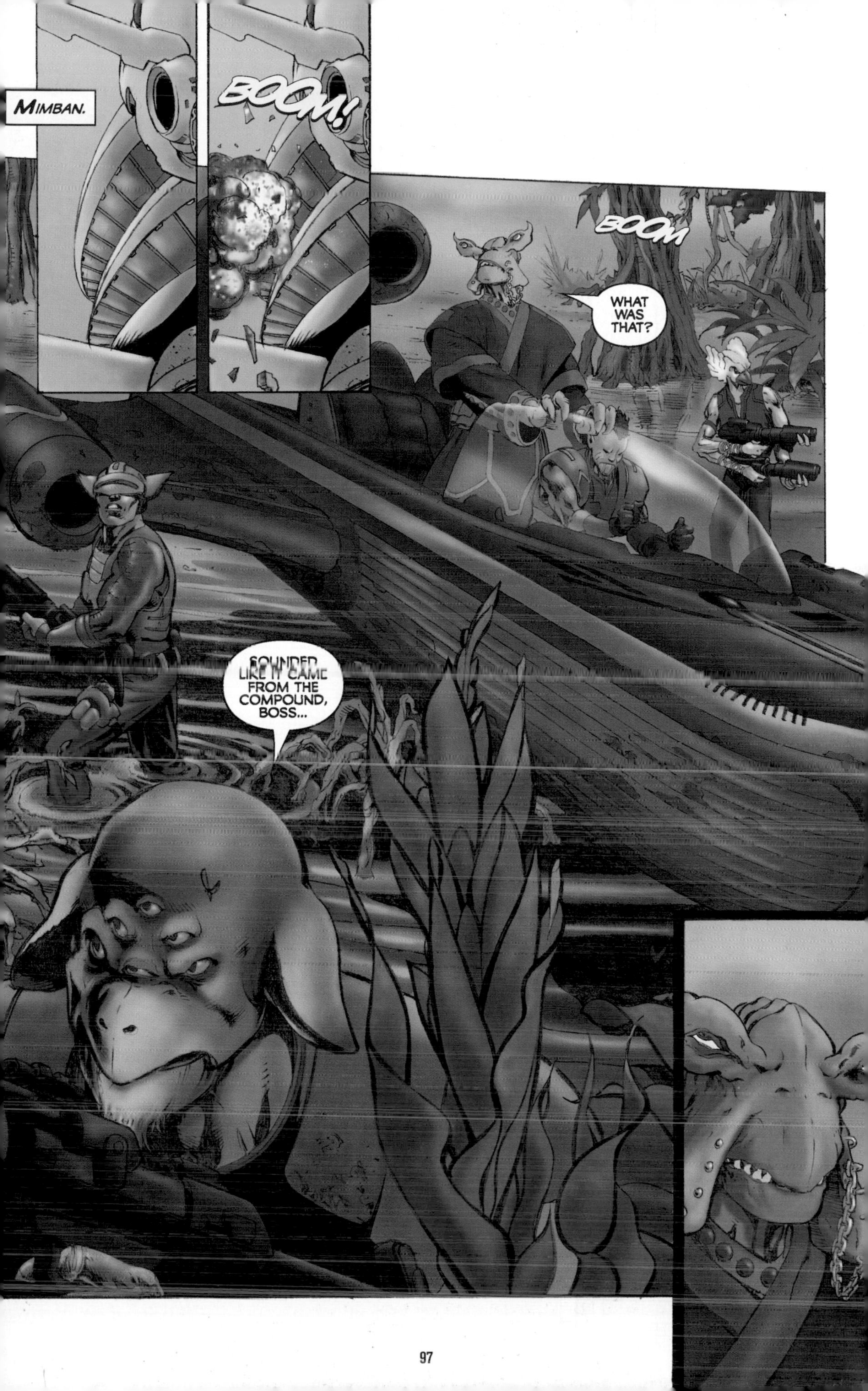
MIMBAN.
BOOM!
BOOM
WHAT WAS THAT?
SOUNDED LIKE IT CAME FROM THE COMPOUND, BOSS...

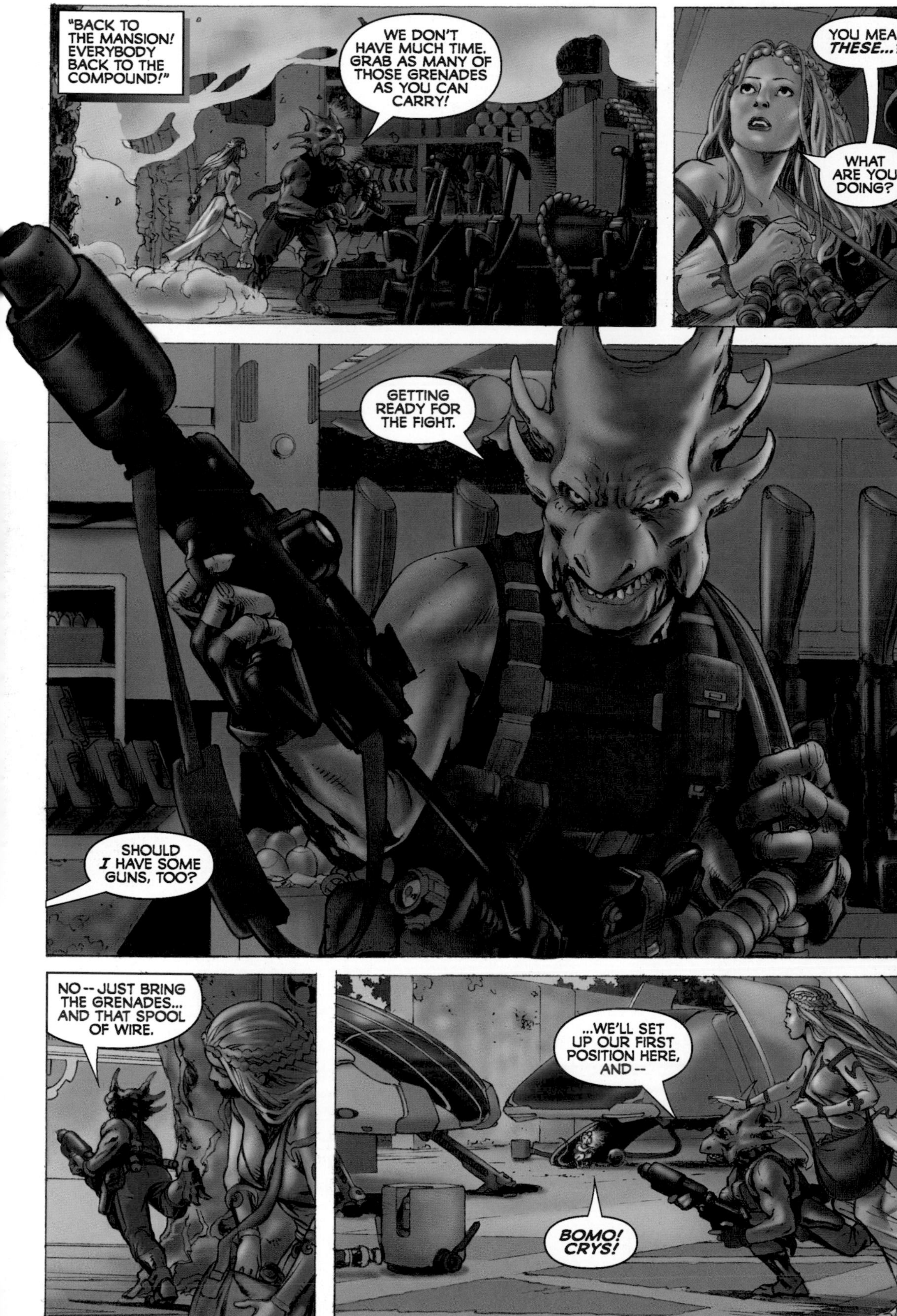
"BACK TO THE MANSION! EVERYBODY BACK TO THE COMPOUND!"
WE DON'T HAVE MUCH TIME. GRAB AS MANY OF THOSE GRENADES AS YOU CAN CARRY!
YOU MEAN THESE...?
WHAT ARE YOU DOING?
GETTING READY FOR THE FIGHT.
SHOULD I HAVE SOME GUNS, TOO?
NO -- JUST BRING THE GRENADES... AND THAT SPOOL OF WIRE.
...WE'LL SET UP OUR FIRST POSITION HERE, AND --
BOMO! CRYS!

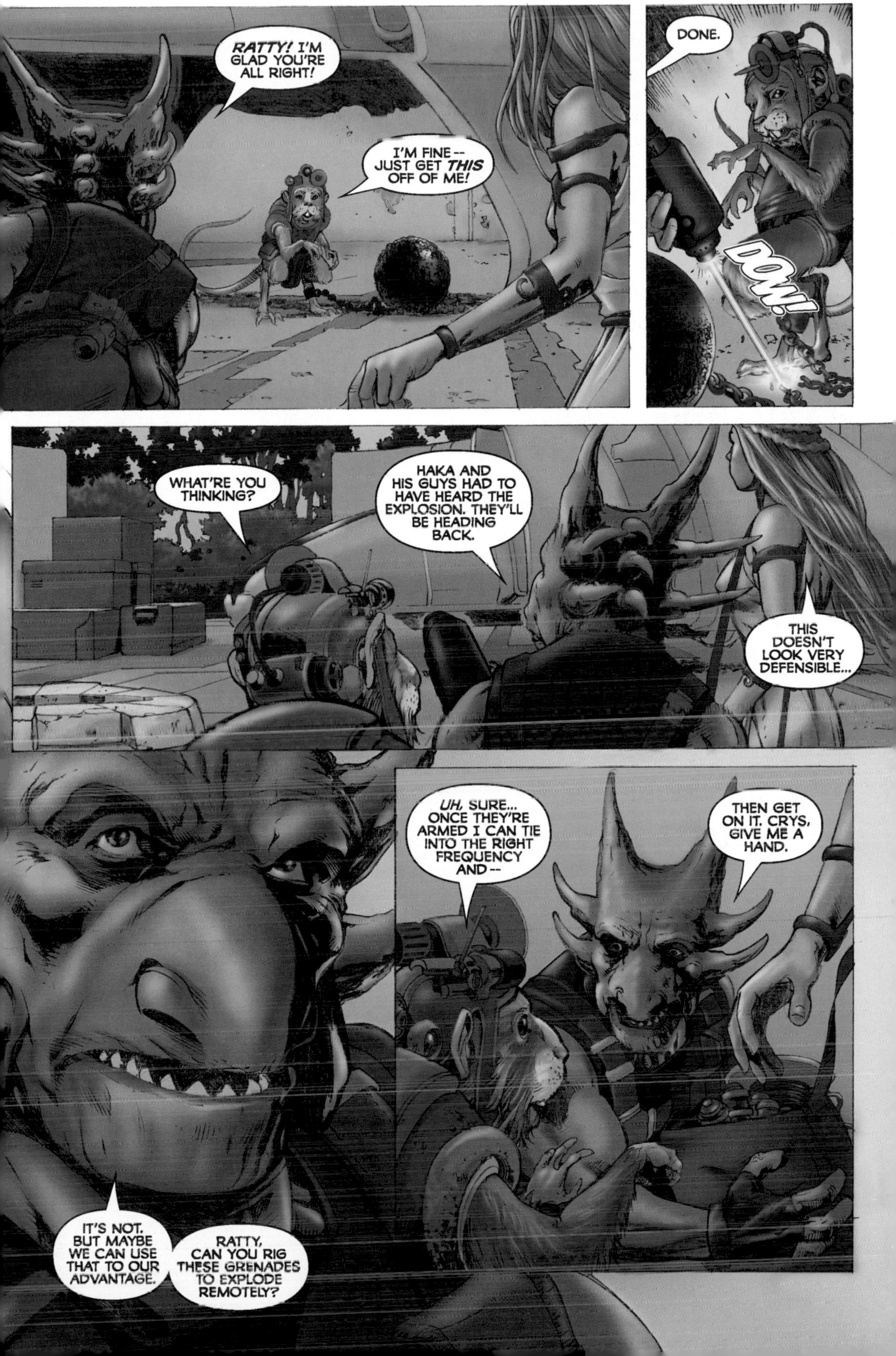
RATTY! I'M GLAD YOU'RE ALL RIGHT!
I'M FINE -- JUST GET THIS OFF OF ME!
DONE.
DOW!
WHAT'RE YOU THINKING?
HAKA AND HIS GUYS HAD TO HAVE HEARD THE EXPLOSION. THEY'LL BE HEADING BACK.
THIS DOESN'T LOOK VERY DEFENSIBLE...
IT'S NOT. BUT MAYBE WE CAN USE THAT TO OUR ADVANTAGE.
RATTY, CAN YOU RIG THESE GRENADES TO EXPLODE REMOTELY?
UH, SURE... ONCE THEY'RE ARMED I CAN TIE INTO THE RIGHT FREQUENCY AND --
THEN GET ON IT. CRYS, GIVE ME A HAND.

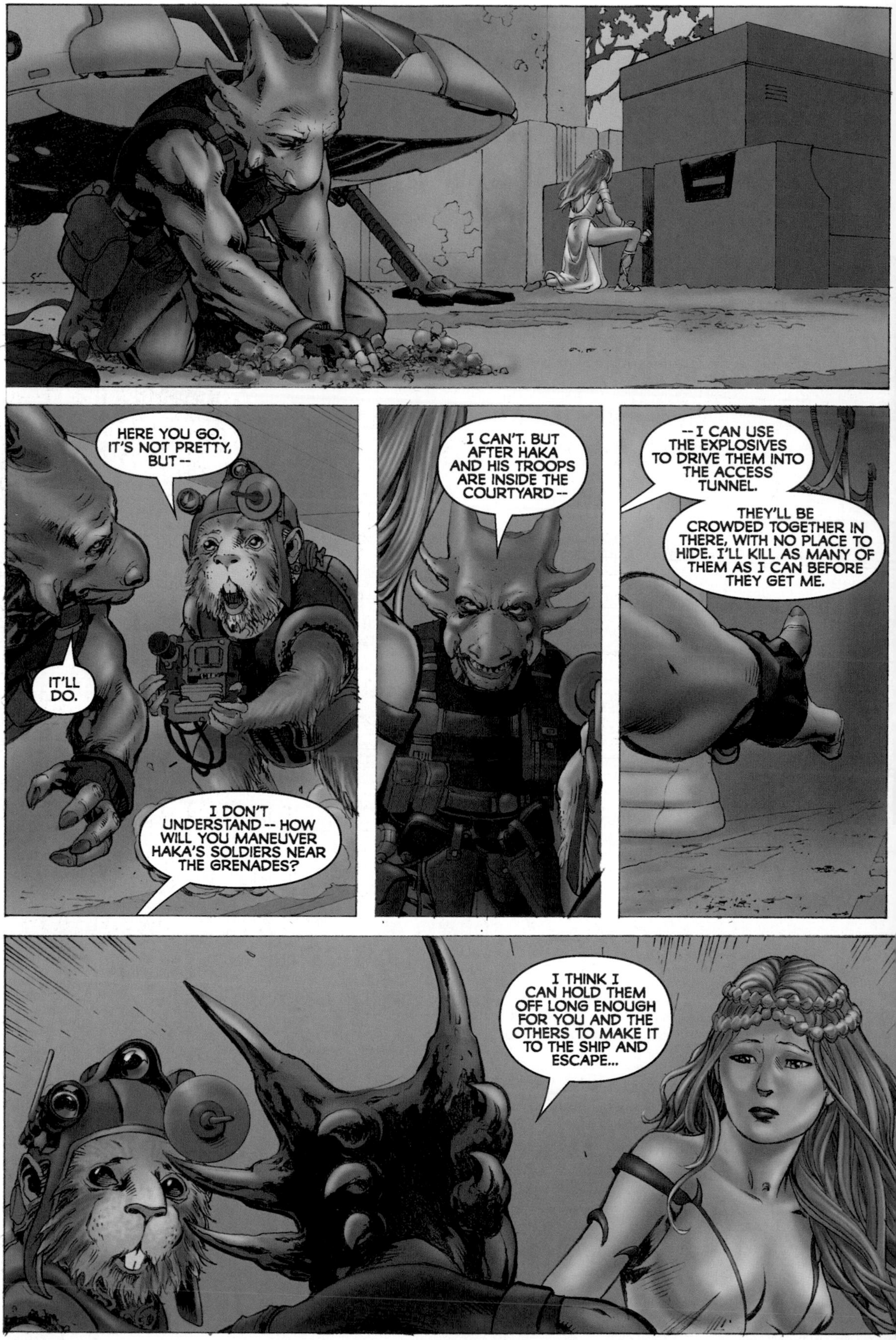
HERE YOU GO. IT'S NOT PRETTY, BUT --
IT'LL DO.
I DON'T UNDERSTAND -- HOW WILL YOU MANEUVER HAKA'S SOLDIERS NEAR THE GRENADES?
I CAN'T. BUT AFTER HAKA AND HIS TROOPS ARE INSIDE THE COURTYARD --
-- I CAN USE THE EXPLOSIVES TO DRIVE THEM INTO THE ACCESS TUNNEL.
THEY'LL BE CROWDED TOGETHER IN THERE, WITH NO PLACE TO HIDE. I'LL KILL AS MANY OF THEM AS I CAN BEFORE THEY GET ME.
I THINK I CAN HOLD THEM OFF LONG ENOUGH FOR YOU AND THE OTHERS TO MAKE IT TO THE SHIP AND ESCAPE...

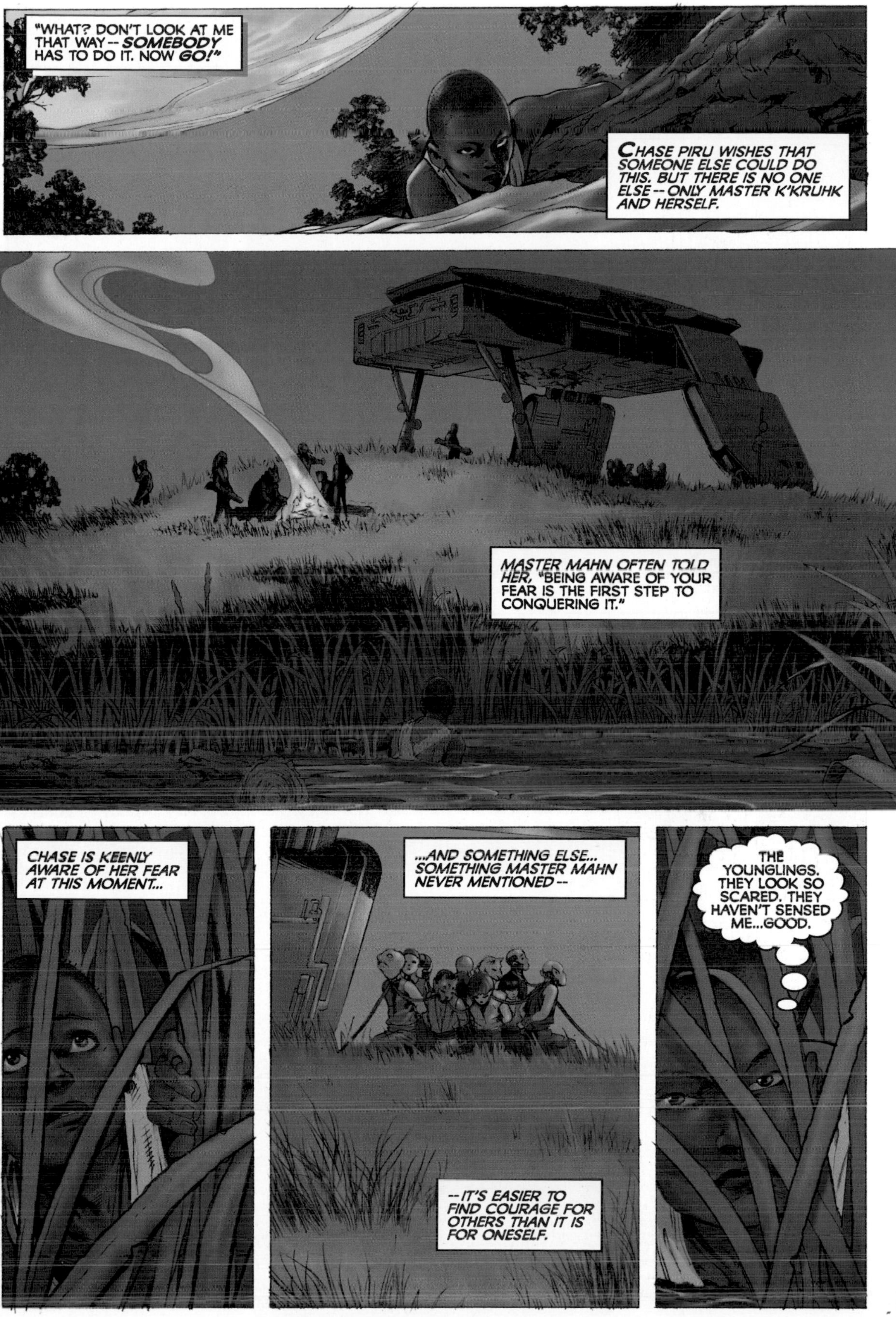
"WHAT? DON'T LOOK AT ME THAT WAY -- *SOMEBODY* HAS TO DO IT. NOW *GO!*"
CHASE PIRU WISHES THAT SOMEONE ELSE COULD DO THIS. BUT THERE IS NO ONE ELSE -- ONLY MASTER K'KRUHK AND HERSELF.
MASTER MAHN OFTEN TOLD HER, "BEING AWARE OF YOUR FEAR IS THE FIRST STEP TO CONQUERING IT."
CHASE IS KEENLY AWARE OF HER FEAR AT THIS MOMENT...
...AND SOMETHING ELSE... SOMETHING MASTER MAHN NEVER MENTIONED --
-- IT'S EASIER TO FIND COURAGE FOR OTHERS THAN IT IS FOR ONESELF.
THE YOUNGLINGS. THEY LOOK SO SCARED. THEY HAVEN'T SENSED ME...GOOD.

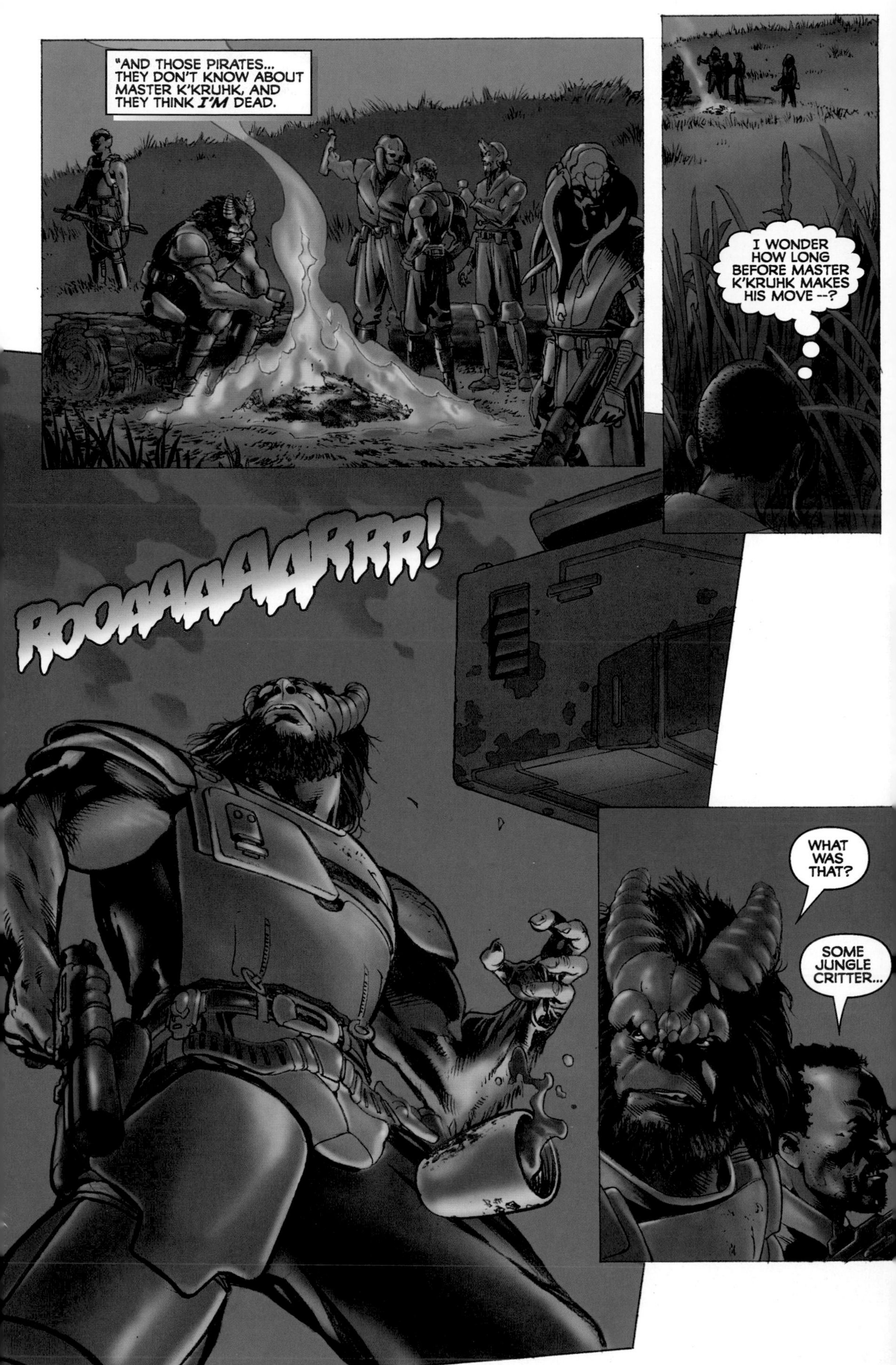
"AND THOSE PIRATES... THEY DON'T KNOW ABOUT MASTER K'KRUHK, AND THEY THINK *I'M* DEAD.
I WONDER HOW LONG BEFORE MASTER K'KRUHK MAKES HIS MOVE --?
ROOAAAAAARRRR!
WHAT WAS THAT?
SOME JUNGLE CRITTER...

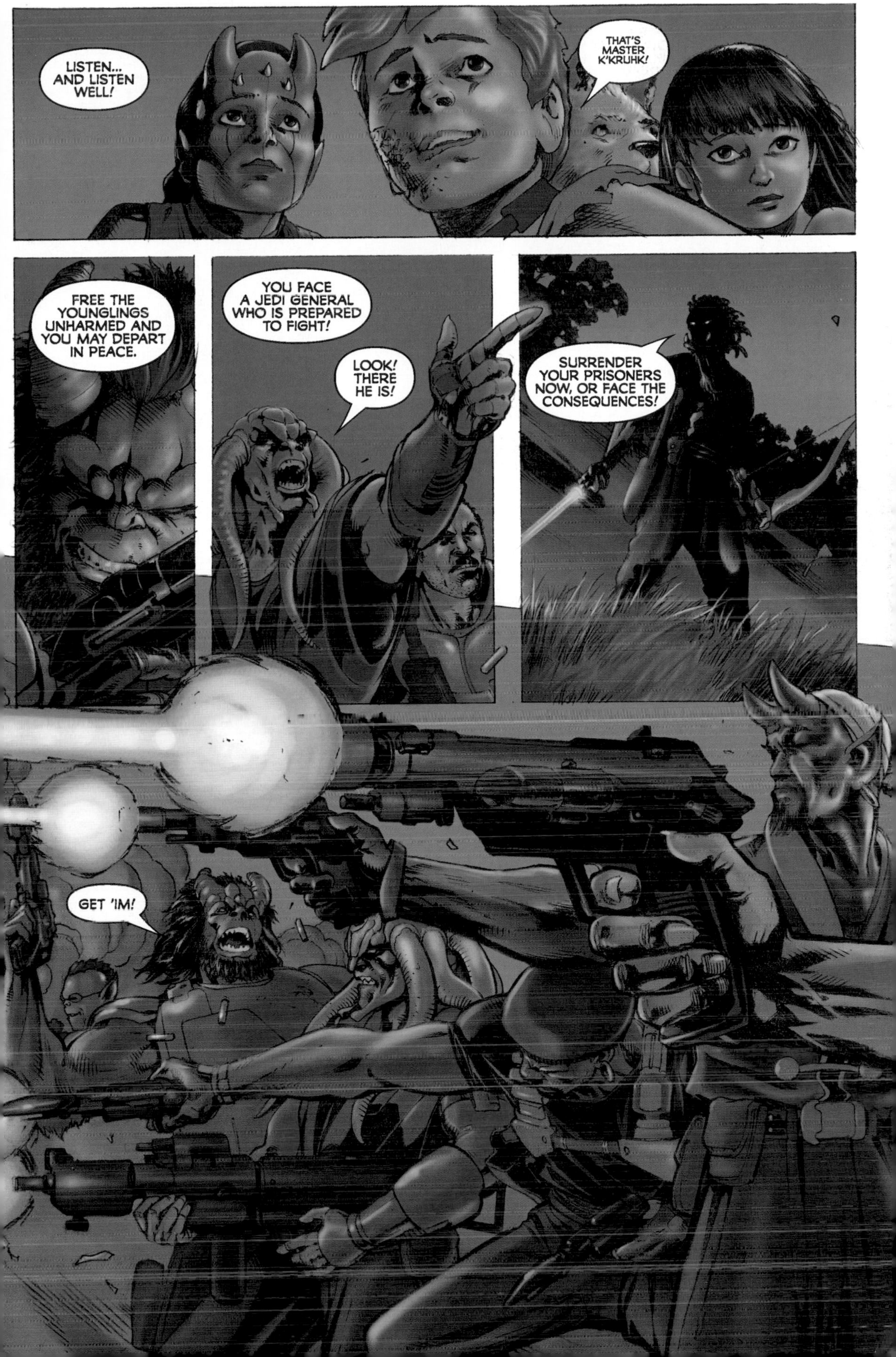
LISTEN... AND LISTEN WELL!
THAT'S MASTER K'KRUHK!
FREE THE YOUNGLINGS UNHARMED AND YOU MAY DEPART IN PEACE.
YOU FACE A JEDI GENERAL WHO IS PREPARED TO FIGHT!
LOOK! THERE HE IS!
SURRENDER YOUR PRISONERS NOW, OR FACE THE CONSEQUENCES!
GET 'IM!

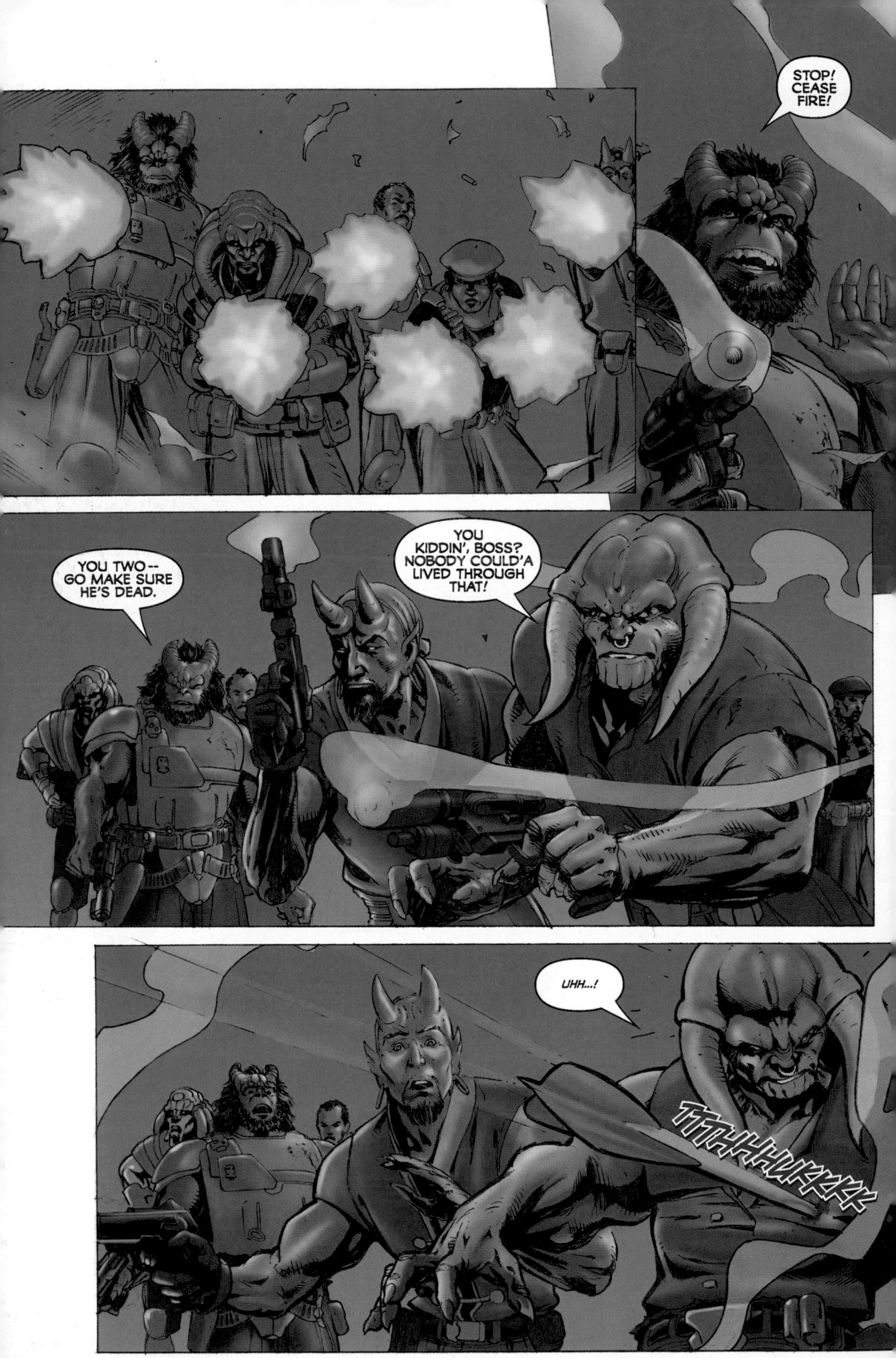
STOP! CEASE FIRE!
YOU TWO -- GO MAKE SURE HE'S DEAD.
YOU KIDDIN', BOSS? NOBODY COULD'A LIVED THROUGH THAT!
UHH...!
TTTHHUKKKK

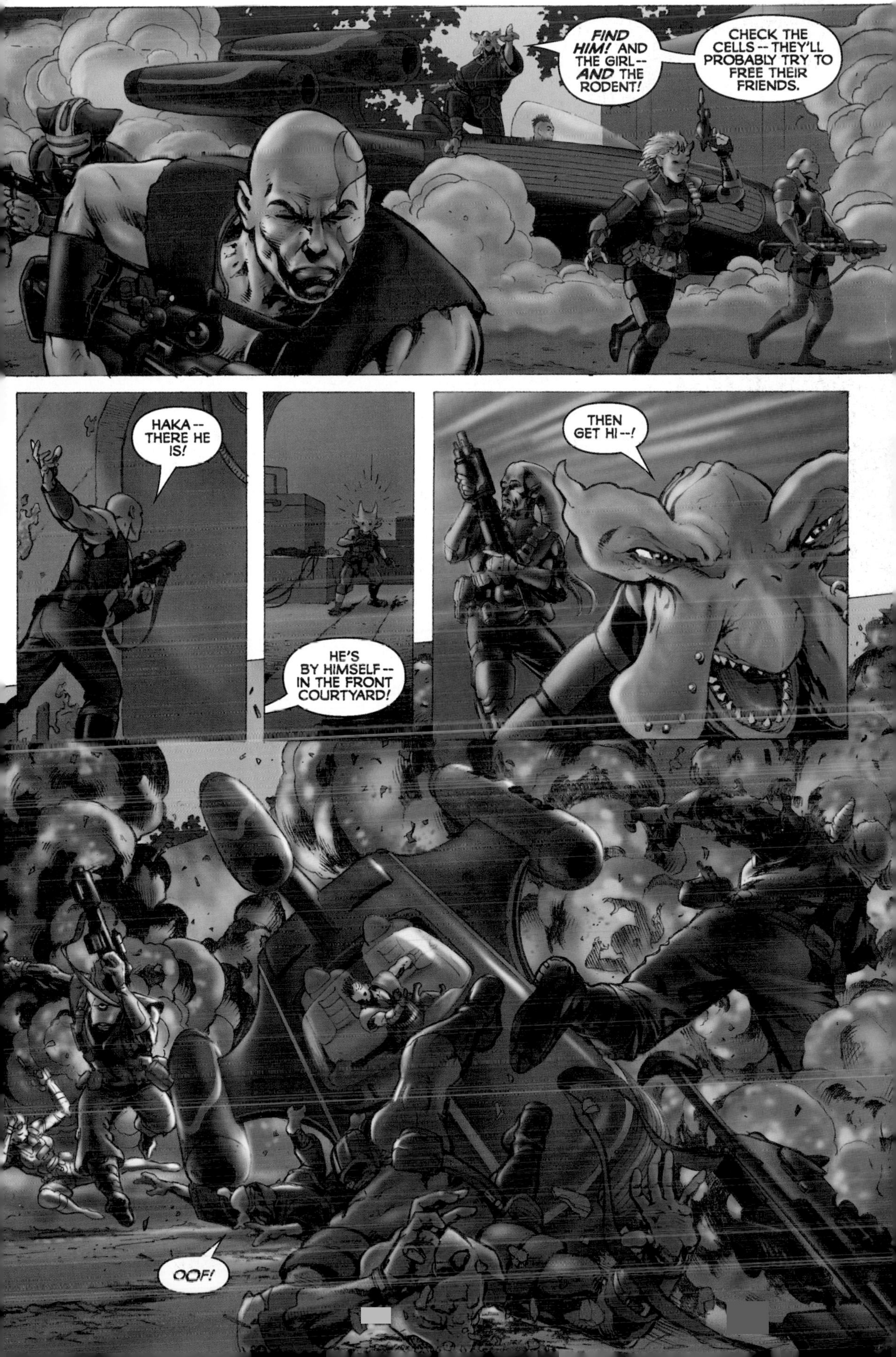
FIND HIM! AND THE GIRL-- AND THE RODENT!
CHECK THE CELLS -- THEY'LL PROBABLY TRY TO FREE THEIR FRIENDS.
HAKA -- THERE HE IS!
HE'S BY HIMSELF -- IN THE FRONT COURTYARD!
THEN GET HI --!
OOF!

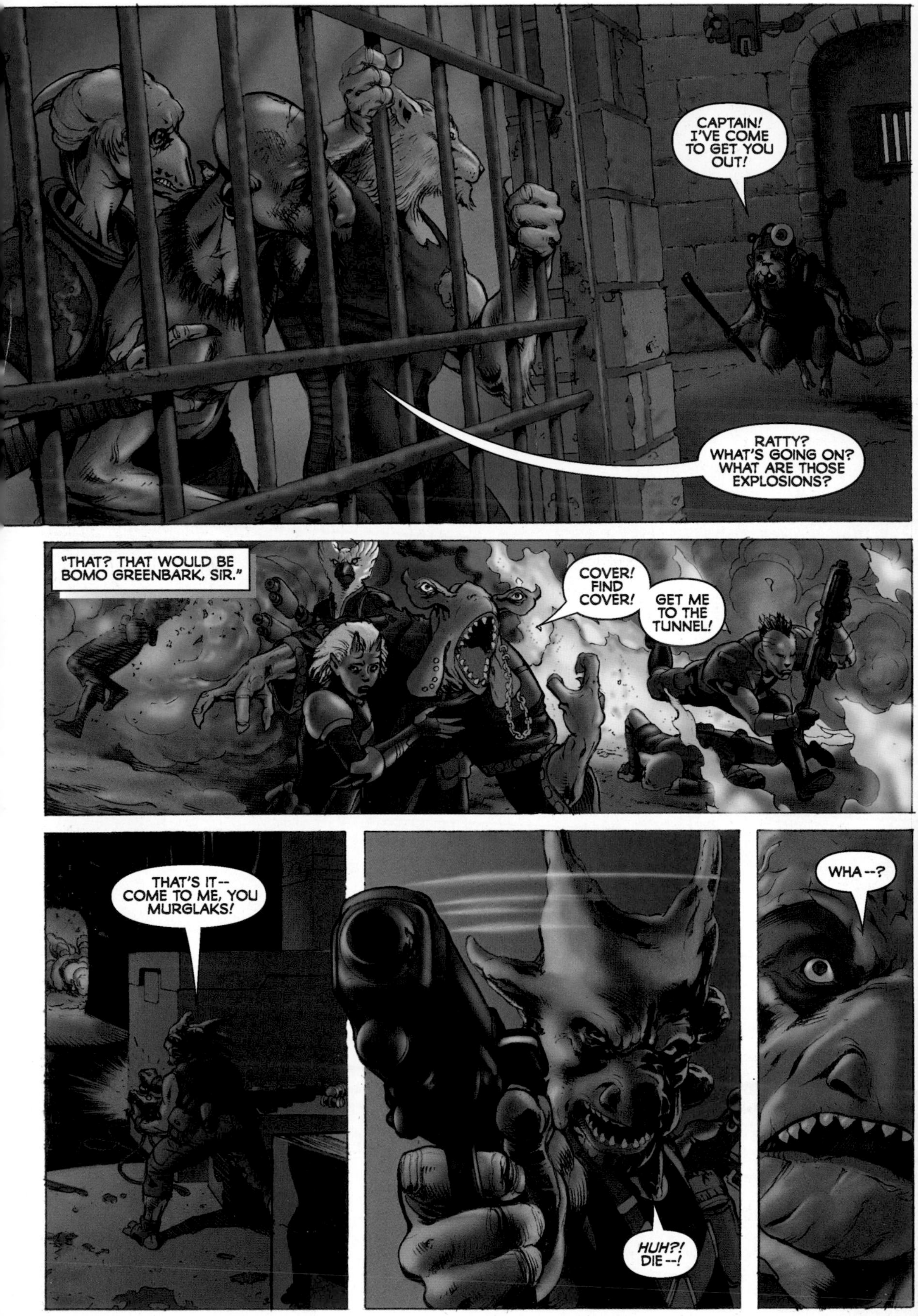
CAPTAIN! I'VE COME TO GET YOU OUT!
RATTY? WHAT'S GOING ON? WHAT ARE THOSE EXPLOSIONS?
"THAT? THAT WOULD BE BOMO GREENBARK, SIR."
COVER! FIND COVER!
GET ME TO THE TUNNEL!
THAT'S IT-- COME TO ME, YOU MURGLAKS!
HUH?! DIE--!
WHA--?

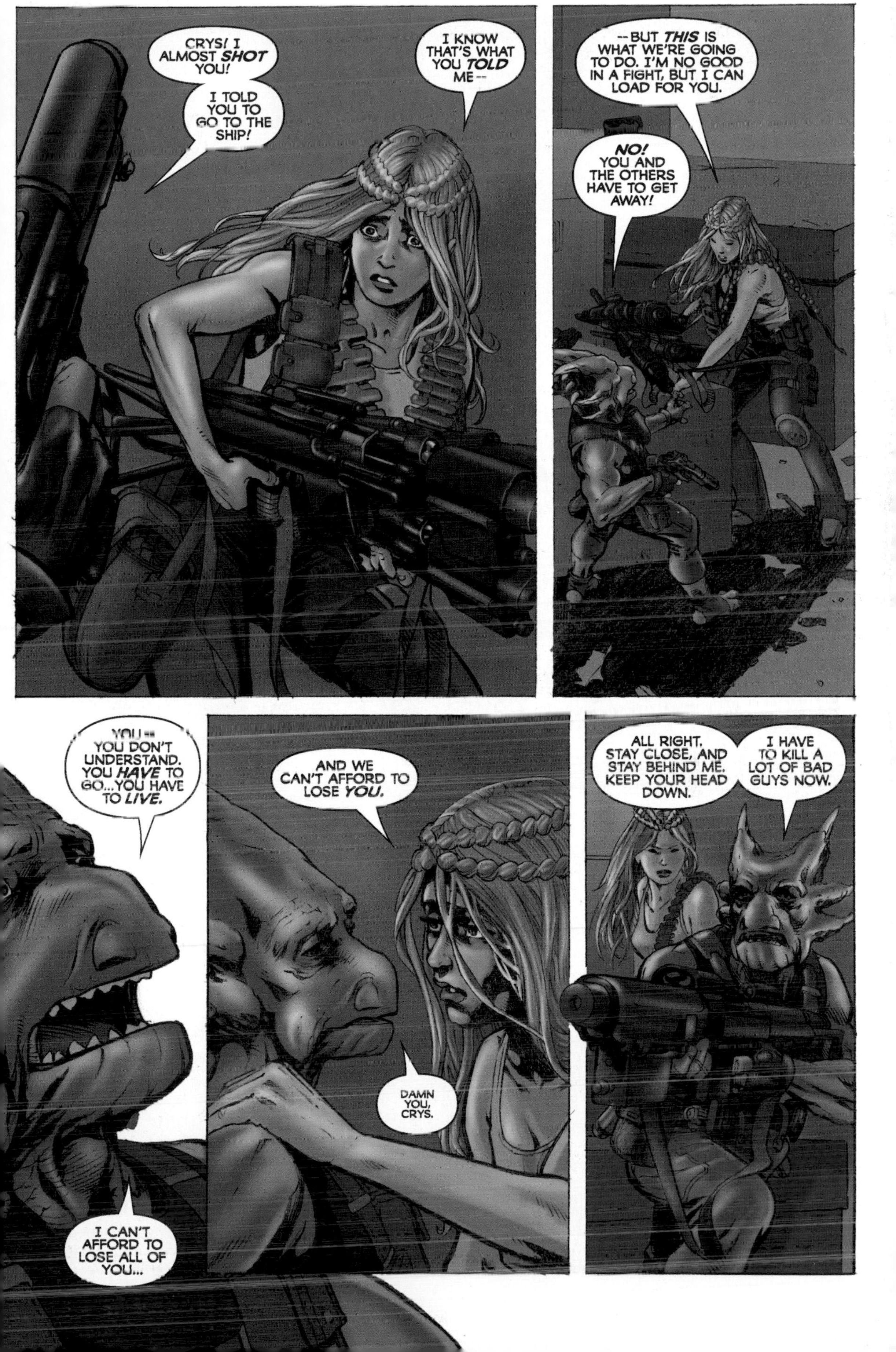
CRYS! I ALMOST SHOT YOU!
I TOLD YOU TO GO TO THE SHIP!
I KNOW THAT'S WHAT YOU TOLD ME--
--BUT THIS IS WHAT WE'RE GOING TO DO. I'M NO GOOD IN A FIGHT, BUT I CAN LOAD FOR YOU.
NO! YOU AND THE OTHERS HAVE TO GET AWAY!
YOU-- YOU DON'T UNDERSTAND. YOU HAVE TO GO...YOU HAVE TO LIVE.
I CAN'T AFFORD TO LOSE ALL OF YOU...
AND WE CAN'T AFFORD TO LOSE YOU.
DAMN YOU, CRYS.
ALL RIGHT. STAY CLOSE, AND STAY BEHIND ME. KEEP YOUR HEAD DOWN.
I HAVE TO KILL A LOT OF BAD GUYS NOW.

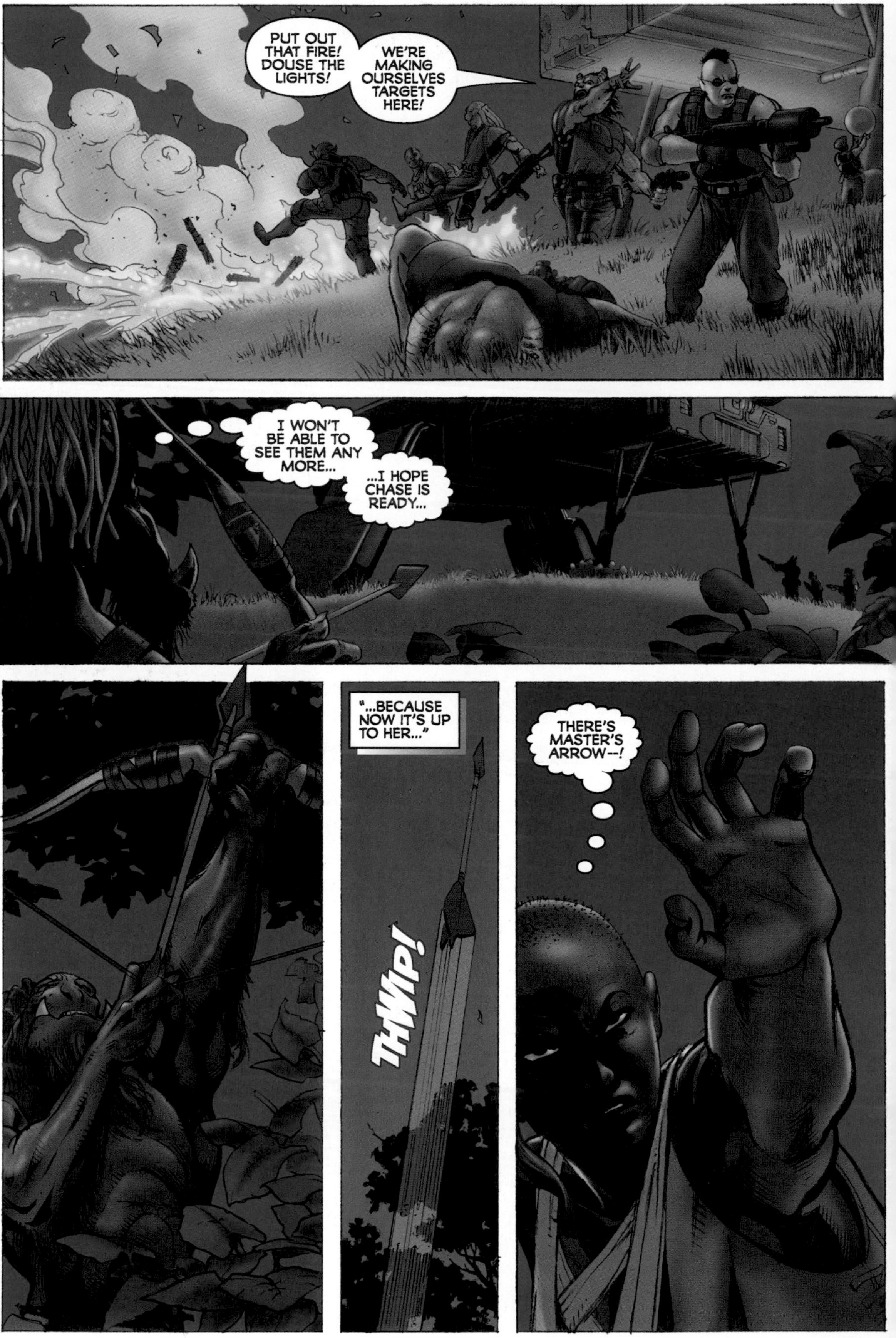
PUT OUT THAT FIRE! DOUSE THE LIGHTS!
WE'RE MAKING OURSELVES TARGETS HERE!
I WON'T BE ABLE TO SEE THEM ANY MORE...
...I HOPE CHASE IS READY...
"...BECAUSE NOW IT'S UP TO HER..."
THWIP!
THERE'S MASTER'S ARROW--!

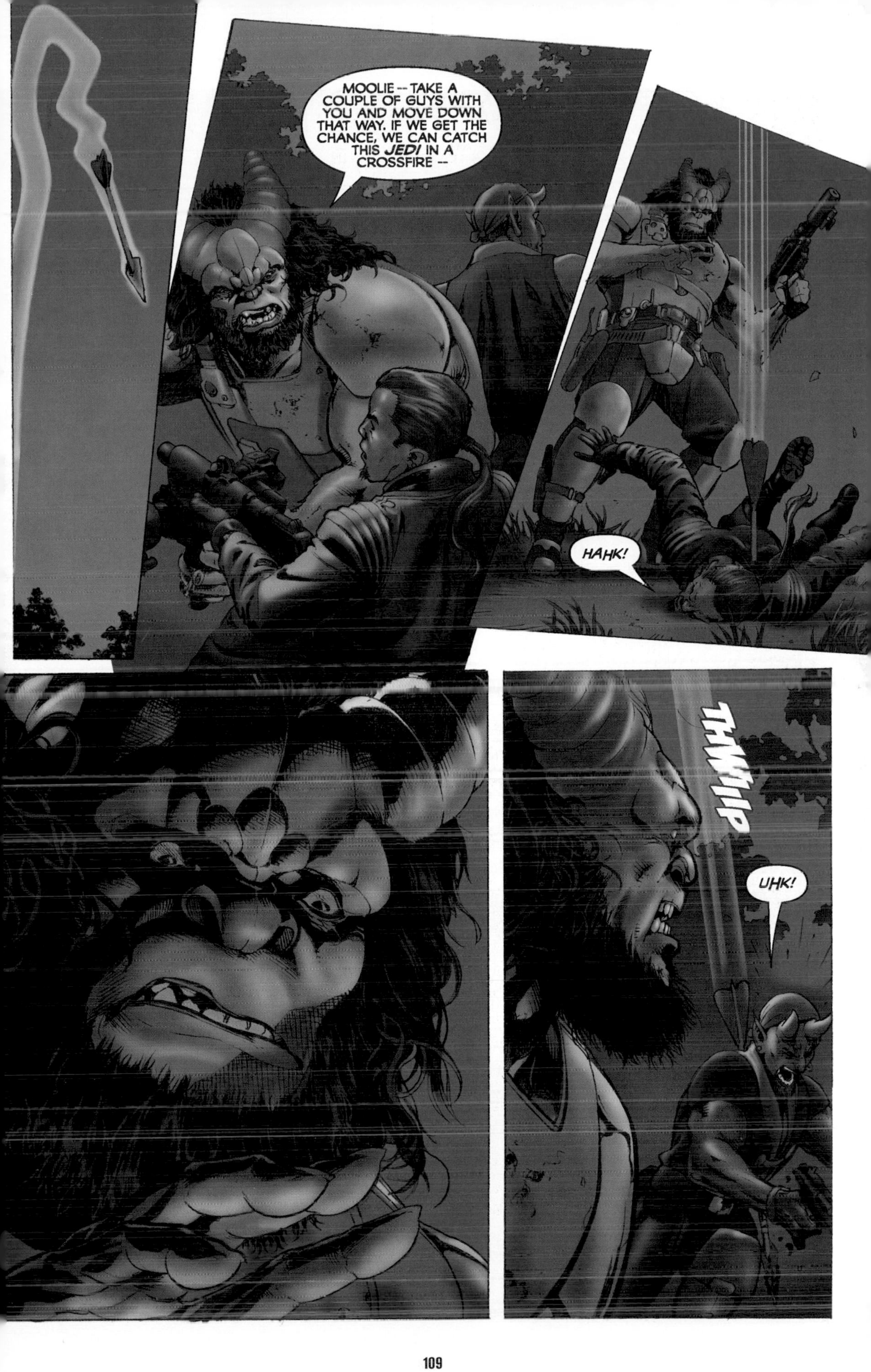
MOOLIE -- TAKE A COUPLE OF GUYS WITH YOU AND MOVE DOWN THAT WAY. IF WE GET THE CHANCE, WE CAN CATCH THIS *JEDI* IN A CROSSFIRE --
HAHK!
THWHIP
UHK!

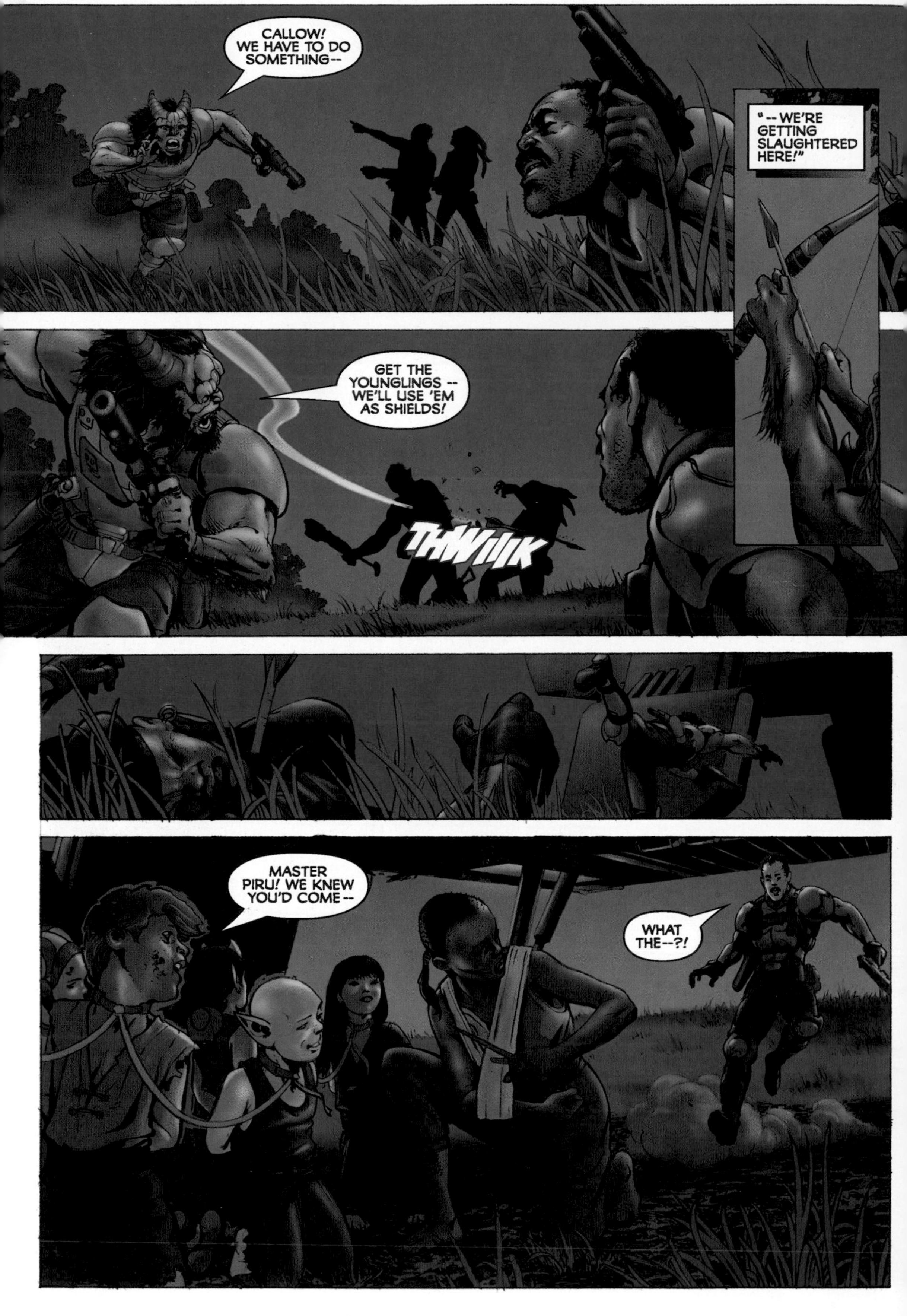

CALLOW! WE HAVE TO DO SOMETHING--
"--WE'RE GETTING SLAUGHTERED HERE!"
GET THE YOUNGLINGS -- WE'LL USE 'EM AS SHIELDS!
THWIIIK
MASTER PIRU! WE KNEW YOU'D COME--
WHAT THE--?!

DON!

DON!

BDOW!

DEW!

GET 'IM! WHAT'RE YOU WAITING FOR? HE'S JUST ONE GUY!

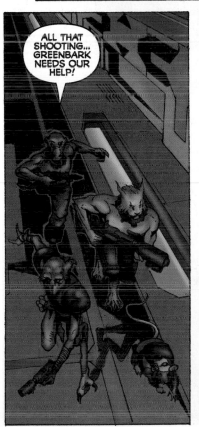

ALL THAT SHOOTING... GREENBARK NEEDS OUR HELP!

GIMME ANOTHER BLASTER! I HAVE THEM RIGHT WHERE I WANT THEM!

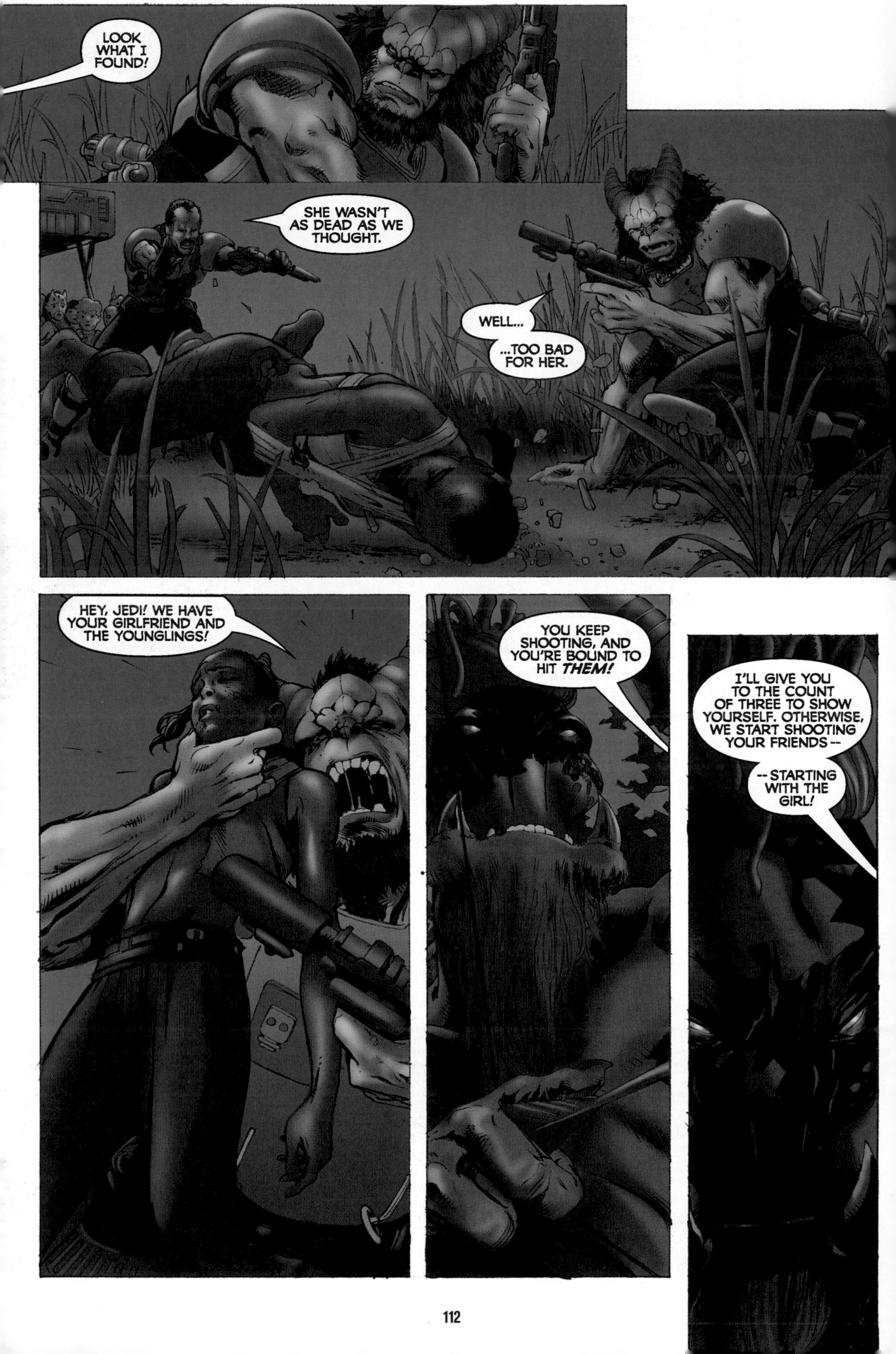
LOOK WHAT I FOUND!
SHE WASN'T AS DEAD AS WE THOUGHT.
WELL...
...TOO BAD FOR HER.
HEY, JEDI! WE HAVE YOUR GIRLFRIEND AND THE YOUNGLINGS!
YOU KEEP SHOOTING, AND YOU'RE BOUND TO HIT THEM!
I'LL GIVE YOU TO THE COUNT OF THREE TO SHOW YOURSELF. OTHERWISE, WE START SHOOTING YOUR FRIENDS --
-- STARTING WITH THE GIRL!

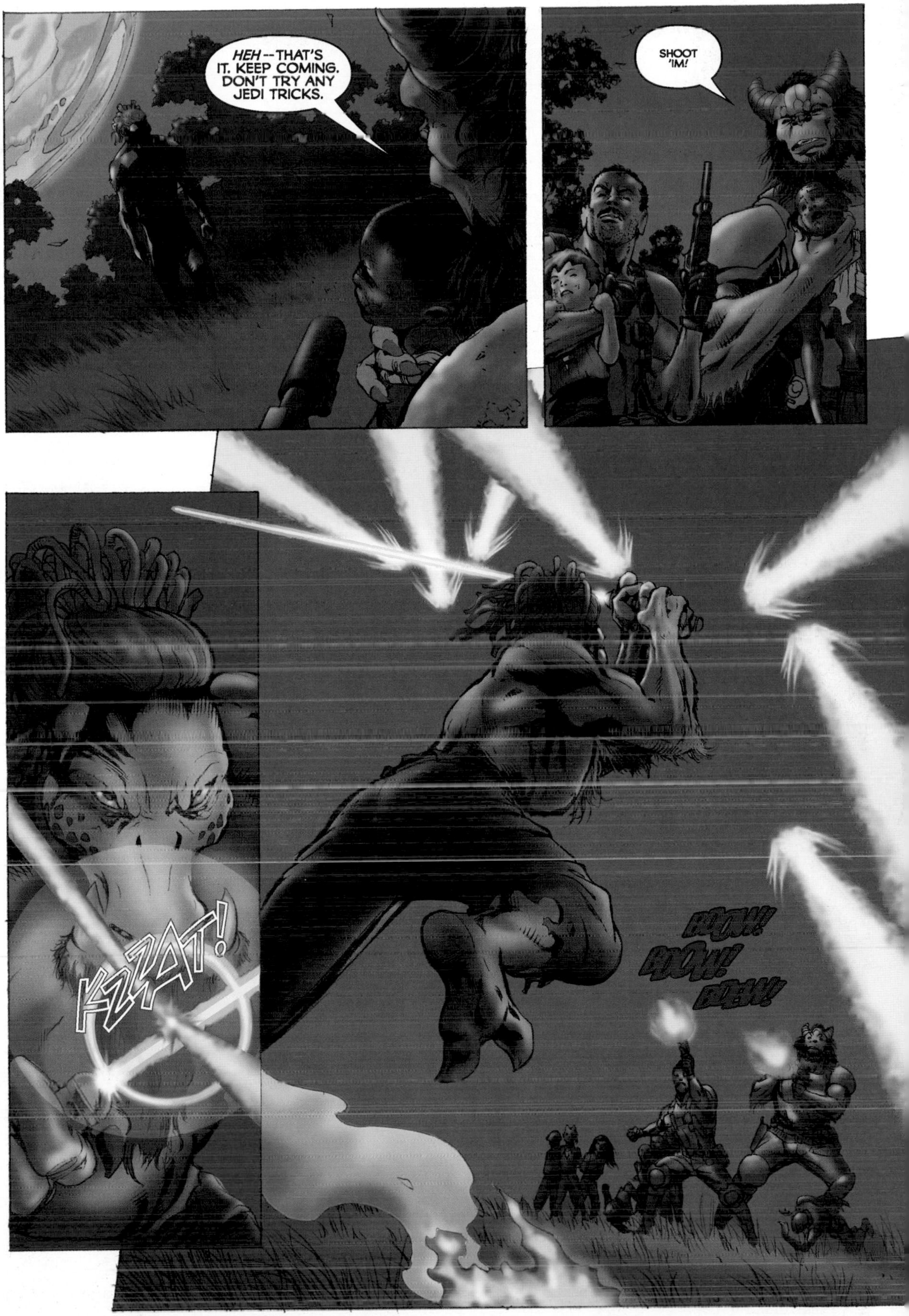
HEH--THAT'S IT. KEEP COMING. DON'T TRY ANY JEDI TRICKS.
SHOOT 'IM!
KZZAT!

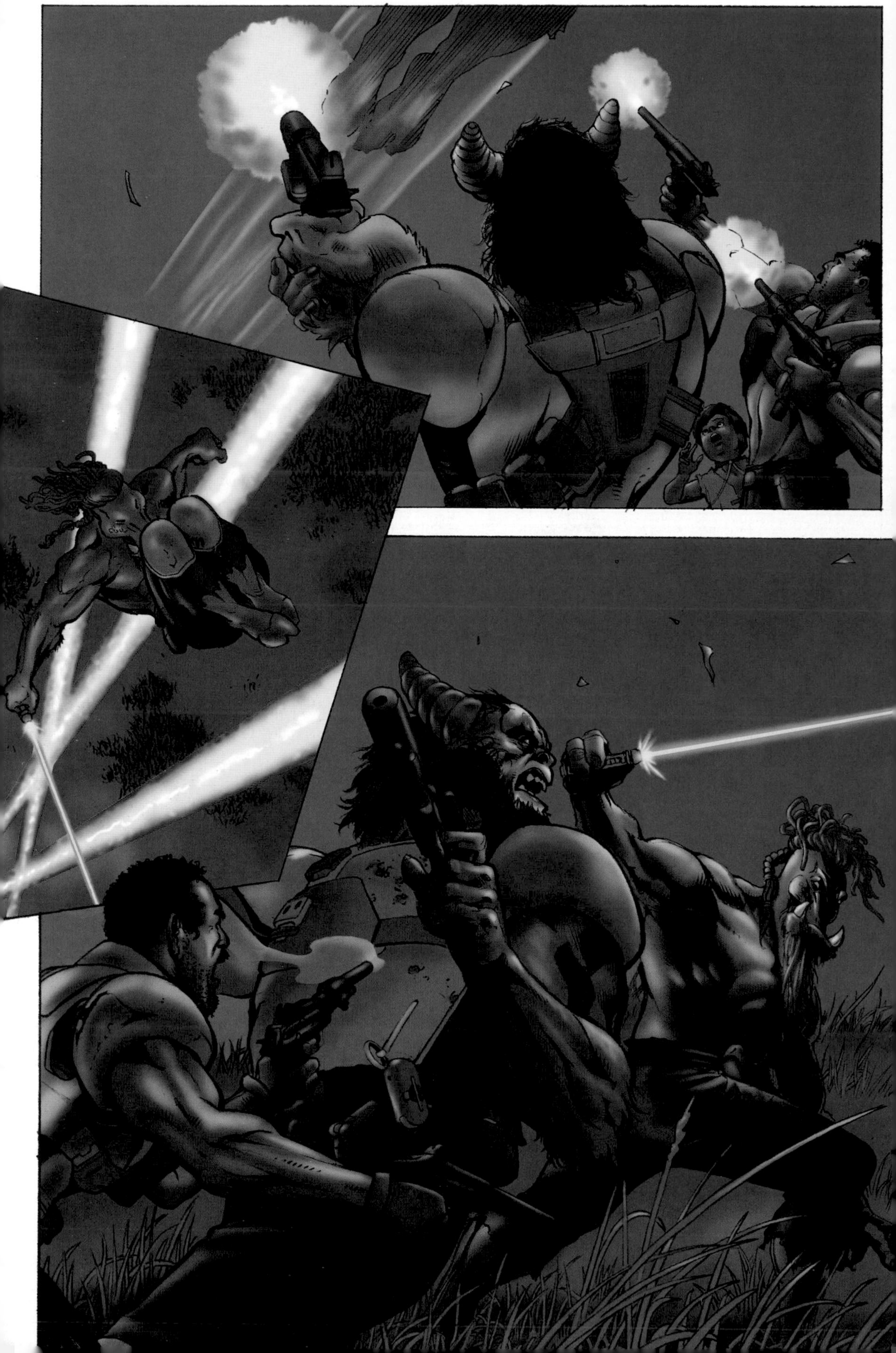

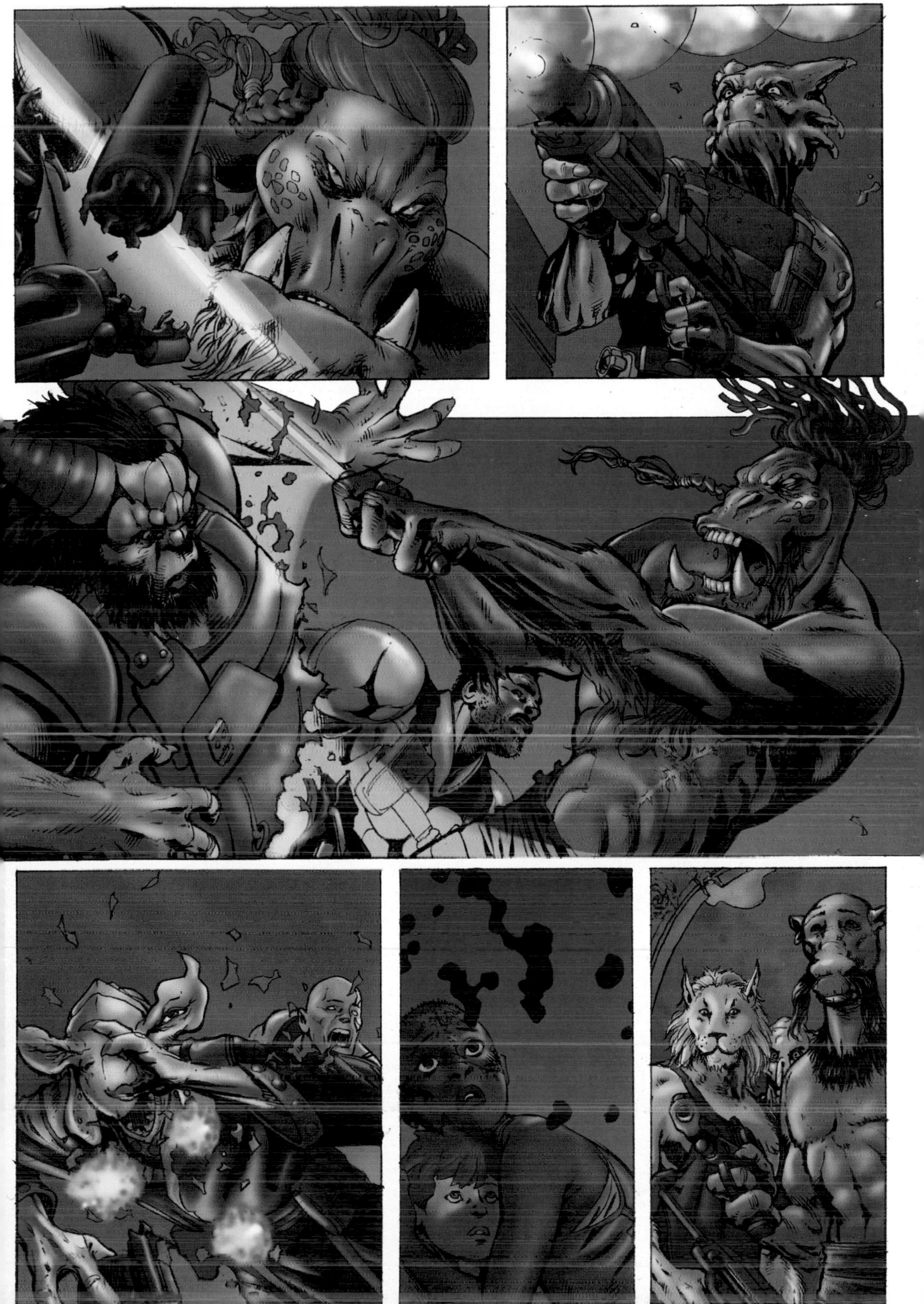

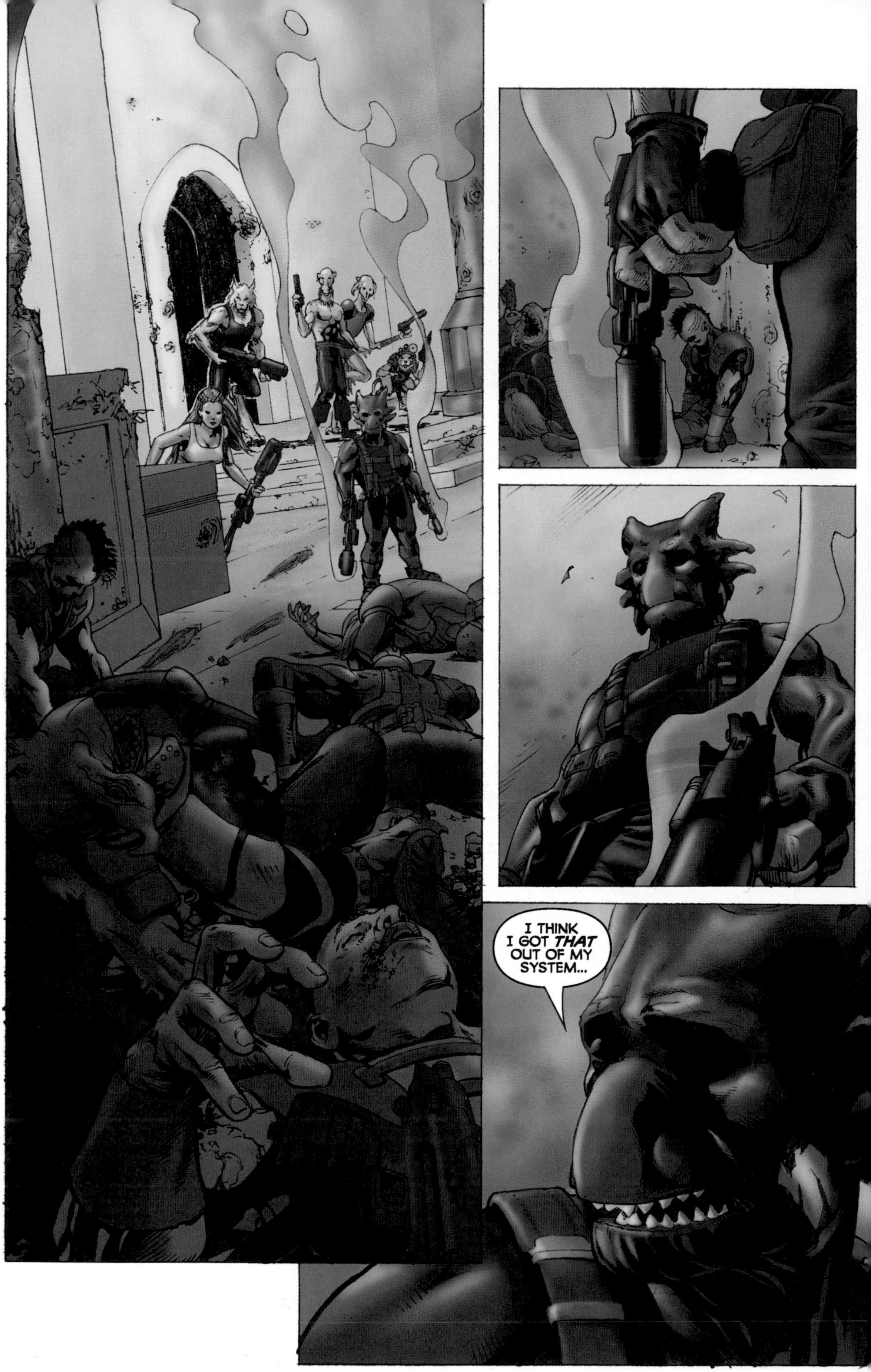
I THINK I GOT *THAT* OUT OF MY SYSTEM...

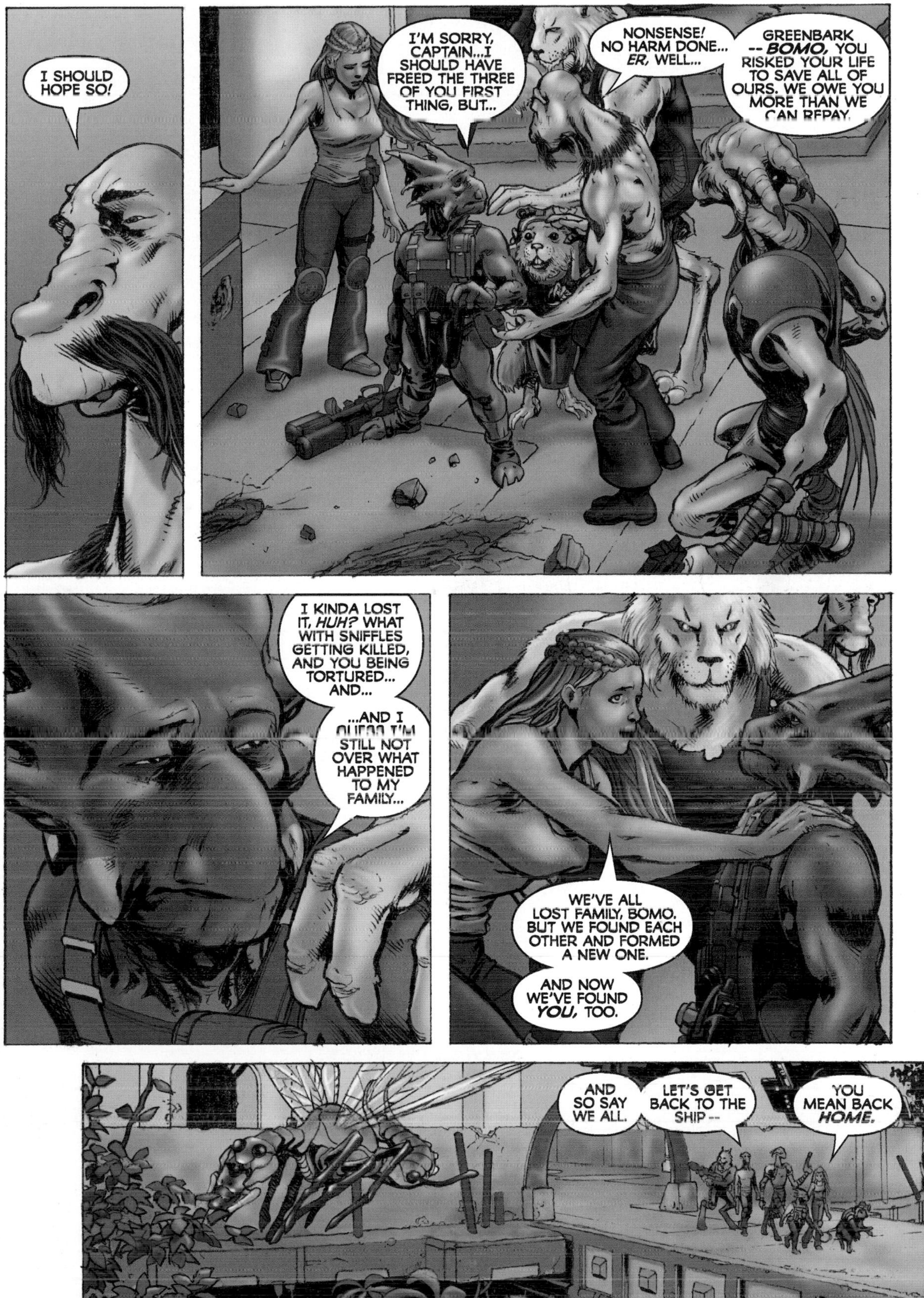
I SHOULD HOPE SO!
I'M SORRY, CAPTAIN...I SHOULD HAVE FREED THE THREE OF YOU FIRST THING, BUT...
NONSENSE! NO HARM DONE... ER, WELL...
GREENBARK -- BOMO, YOU RISKED YOUR LIFE TO SAVE ALL OF OURS. WE OWE YOU MORE THAN WE CAN REPAY.
I KINDA LOST IT, HUH? WHAT WITH SNIFFLES GETTING KILLED, AND YOU BEING TORTURED... AND...
...AND I GUESS I'M STILL NOT OVER WHAT HAPPENED TO MY FAMILY...
WE'VE ALL LOST FAMILY, BOMO. BUT WE FOUND EACH OTHER AND FORMED A NEW ONE.
AND NOW WE'VE FOUND YOU, TOO.
AND SO SAY WE ALL.
LET'S GET BACK TO THE SHIP --
YOU MEAN BACK HOME.

YOU UNDERSTAND WHY I DID WHAT I DID -- DON'T YOU, PIRU?

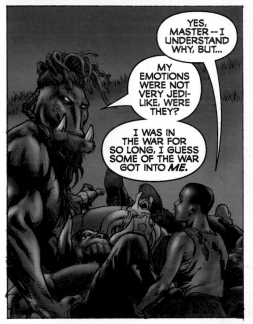

YES, MASTER -- I UNDERSTAND WHY, BUT...

MY EMOTIONS WERE NOT VERY JEDI-LIKE, WERE THEY?

I WAS IN THE WAR FOR SO LONG, I GUESS SOME OF THE WAR GOT INTO *ME.*

WHEN I SAW THAT YOU AND THE YOUNGLINGS WERE IN DANGER, SOMETHING INSIDE ME...

...I COULDN'T CONTROL IT...

MASTER, THOSE PIRATES -- THE MAN *CALLOW,* AND THE ONE CALLED *LUMBRA* -- BROUGHT ABOUT THEIR OWN DEATHS.

PERHAPS. BUT THEY DIDN'T DESERVE TO DIE *THAT WAY.* THAT WAS WRONG. *I* WAS WRONG.

IN TRYING TO *SAVE* SOMETHING I CARED ABOUT, I MAY HAVE *LOST* IT...FOREVER.

AFTER WE REPAIR THIS SHIP, WE'LL FIND SOMEWHERE SECURE FOR YOU AND THE YOUNGLINGS TO LIVE. I'LL CHECK IN ON YOU FROM TIME TO TIME, BUT I WON'T STAY.

I DON'T WANT TO BE A CONSTANT REMINDER TO THEM OF WHAT HAPPENED HERE. I CAN SEE THE FEAR IN THEIR EYES -- AND IN YOURS.

DO YOU THINK THEY'LL EVER GET OVER SEEING ME AS I WAS TONIGHT? WILL *YOU,* PIRU?

I DON'T KNOW, MASTER...

...I DON'T KNOW.

THE END

STAR WARS GRAPHIC NOVEL TIMELINE

Tales of the Jedi—5,000–3,986 BSW4
Knights of the Old Republic—3,964 BSW4
Jedi vs. Sith—1,000 BSW4
Jedi Council: Acts of War—33 BSW4
Prelude to Rebellion—33 BSW4
Darth Maul—33 BSW4
Episode I: The Phantom Menace—32 BSW4
Outlander—32 BSW4
Emissaries to Malastare—32 BSW4
Jango Fett: Open Seasons—32 BSW4
Twilight—31 BSW4
Bounty Hunters—31 BSW4
The Hunt for Aurra Sing—30 BSW4
Darkness—30 BSW4
The Stark Hyperspace War—30 BSW4
Rite of Passage—28 BSW4
Jango Fett—27 BSW4
Zam Wesell—27 BSW4
Honor and Duty—24 BSW4
Episode II: Attack of the Clones—22 BSW4
Clone Wars—22–19 BSW4
Clone Wars Adventures—22–19 BSW4
General Grievous—20 BSW4
Episode III: Revenge of the Sith—19 BSW4
Dark Times—19 BSW4
Droids—3 BSW4
Boba Fett: Enemy of the Empire—2 BSW4
Underworld—1 BSW4
Episode IV: A New Hope—SW4
Classic Star Wars—0–3 ASW4
A Long Time Ago . . .—0–4 ASW4
Empire—0 ASW4
Rebellion—0 ASW4
Vader's Quest—0 ASW4
Boba Fett: Man with a Mission—0 ASW4
Jabba the Hutt: The Art of the Deal—1 ASW4
Splinter of the Mind's Eye—1 ASW4
Episode V: The Empire Strikes Back—3 ASW4
Shadows of the Empire—3–5 ASW4
Episode VI: Return of the Jedi—4 ASW4
X-Wing Rogue Squadron—4–5 ASW4
Mara Jade: By the Emperor's Hand—4 ASW4
Heir to the Empire—9 ASW4
Dark Force Rising—9 ASW4
The Last Command—9 ASW4
Dark Empire—10 ASW4
Boba Fett: Death, Lies, and Treachery—11 ASW4
Crimson Empire—11 ASW4
Jedi Academy: Leviathan—13 ASW4
Union—20 ASW4
Chewbacca—25 ASW4
Legacy—130 ASW4

Old Republic Era
25,000 – 1000 years before
Star Wars: A New Hope

Rise of the Empire Era
1000 – 0 years before
Star Wars: A New Hope

Rebellion Era
0 – 5 years after
Star Wars: A New Hope

New Republic Era
5 – 25 years after
Star Wars: A New Hope

New Jedi Order Era
25+ years after
Star Wars: A New Hope

Legacy Era
130+ years after
Star Wars: A New Hope

Infinities
Does not apply to timeline

Sergio Aragonés Stomps Star Wars
Star Wars Tales
Star Wars Infinities
Tag and Bink
Star Wars Visionaries

BSW4 = before *Episode IV: A New Hope*. ASW4 = after *Episode IV: A New Hope*.

CLONE WARS ADVENTURES

Don't miss any of the action-packed adventures of your favorite STAR WARS® characters, available at comics shops and bookstores in a galaxy near you!

Volume 1
ISBN-10: 1-59307-243-0
ISBN-13: 978-1-59307-243-8

Volume 2
ISBN-10: 1-59307-271-6
ISBN-13: 978-1-59307-271-1

Volume 3
ISBN-10: 1-59307-307-0
ISBN-13: 978-1-59307-307-7

Volume 4
ISBN-10: 1-59307-402-6
ISBN-13: 978-1-59307-402-9

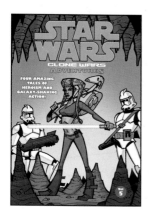

Volume 5
ISBN-10: 1-59307-483-2
ISBN-13: 978-1-59307-483-8

Volume 6
ISBN-10: 1-59307-567-7
ISBN-13: 978-1-59307-567-5

Volume 7
ISBN-10: 1-59307-678-9
ISBN-13: 978-1-59307-678-8

Volume 8
ISBN-10: 1-59307-680-0
ISBN-13: 978-1-59307-680-1
Coming in June!

$6.95 each!